THE
LISTS BOOK

THE LISTS BOOK

MITCHELL SYMONS

CHAMELEON

I dedicate this book, as always, to Penny and to our two sons, Jack and Charlie, and also to my sister, Jenny, who has been a source of support and comfort since before I could even count to ten.

First published in Great Britain in 1997 by Chameleon Books, an imprint of André Deutsch Ltd, 106 Great Russell Street, London WC1B 3LJ

André Deutsch is a subsidiary of VCI plc

Book design by Suzanne Perkins/Grafica

A catalogue record for this title is available from the British Library

ISBN 0 233 99111 5

Printed in Great Britain by WBC, Bridgend

TABLE OF CONTENTS

10 ACKNOWLEDGEMENTS

Wittingly or unwittingly, many people have given me a lot of help in putting together this book. The ten most helpful (witting) people – in no particular order – were:

1. Louise Dixon and all her colleagues at André Deutsch for making my work look far more impressive than it has any right to do

2. Tricia Martin for all her fabulous help in the years she worked for me – and in the years since

3. Russell Ash for lending a sympathetic and expert ear and for supplying a few of the lists. One or two with his permission

4. John Koski for the ideas and guidance he gave me when we wrote 'Journolists' for *You* magazine

5. Sue Carroll for taking me on at *Sunday* magazine and helping me to develop 'Populists'

6. Andy Simpson for his sympathetic editing of my lists at the *Daily Mail*

7. Richard Littlejohn for relieving the monotony of list-writing and for coming up with absolute gems at critical times

8. Alan Symons for being a mine of information

9. Simon Rose for his help on all things cinematic

10. Jeremy Beadle for his kind patronage. I can pay him no higher compliment than to say that he is 'The Governor'

Chapter 1

In the Beginning...

10 GOOD THINGS ABOUT BEING POOR

1. None of your family is going to be kidnapped

2. You can watch a telethon without feeling guilty

3. No chance of being poisoned by exotic food

4. You save time not having to agonise over which clothes to wear

5. You get to appear in earnest TV documentaries

6. You don't have to spend half your holiday waiting in airport lounges

7. No need to come up with excuses when the bank manager invites you out to lunch

8. You don't have to buy tickets from touts for the opera

9. You only have to buy one Sunday newspaper

10. You don't have to look for very small camels or very large needles to enter the Kingdom of Heaven

10 THINGS YOU ONLY DO IN A HOTEL

1. Eat a full English breakfast

2. Watch daytime TV

3. Open a Bible

4. Press your trousers

5. Have your shoes polished

6. Push single beds together

7. Use a shower cap

8. Drink miniature bottles of spirits

9. Smile at anyone before 9.00 in the morning

10. Eat two puddings

10 SIGNS THAT THE DIET'S OFF

1. You buy trousers with an elasticated waistband

2. You put the bathroom scales back on the carpet

3. You're spotted in Marks and Spencer's food hall

4. You dress in black

5. You stop talking about food all the time

6. If in doubt you buy clothes which are slightly too big

7. You skip meals

8. At the pub the smile is back on your face

9. The deep fat fryer comes out of the cupboard

10. You swap Japanese food for Chinese

10 THINGS BANKS SAY...AND WHAT THEY ACTUALLY MEAN

1. "Banking with all the latest technology"
   (It still takes a week to send a cheque book)

2. "We make it our policy to offer advice to small businesses" (Until, that is, they actually ask for it)

3. "There is no finer bank" (That's because we're all the same)

4. "We offer the best interest rates"
   (The highest for borrowers; the lowest for savers)

5. "We respond quickly to your needs"
   (Three months' bank charges the second you go overdrawn)

6. "We also have a lobby service"
   (We don't want queues in the street)

7. "All of our university branches have student advisers" (Who've been instructed to say 'You can't have an overdraft, man' instead of 'You can't have an overdraft, sir')

8. "We'd like you to think of the bank as your partner" (The sort of partner you take out for long, expensive lunches)

9. "We have thousands of cash dispensers all over the country" (Why only last week we heard of one which still had some cash left in it on a Sunday)

10. "We understand money" (That's why we charge you £25 for every letter we send you)

10 QUESTIONS FROM THE EXAM FOR 7 YEAR OLDS

1. Discuss the victimisation of Smiffy in *The Bash Street Kids*

2. Explain the appeal of Tekken 2

3. Calculate how much more efficient Postman Pat would be if the Royal Mail were to be privatised

4. Factor the number of times your mother has asked you to tidy your room by the number of times you've asked for a Play Station on the basis that "everyone's got one"

5. Design an alternative Channel Tunnel for *Blue Peter* using only a washing-up liquid bottle, some sticky-backed plastic and a pipe-cleaner

6. Consider the effect that the ban on corporal punishment has had on Dennis the Menace and Roger the Dodger

7. Rationalise the reason why Children's TV presenters persist in talking to children as though they were deaf or foreign (or indeed deaf *and* foreign)

8. Imagine a conversation between stranded, frustrated commuters and Thomas the Tank Engine. How would this be resolved without recourse to litigation or violence?

9. If Desperate Dan eats 10 cow pies and there is another BSE scare and he doesn't have private health care, how long will it be before he is admitted to an NHS hospital?

10. Contextualise Noddy's relationship with Big Ears in the light of non-heterosexist values

10 THINGS YOU ALWAYS FIND LURKING IN THE BACK OF THE WARDROBE

1. The buckle of a leather belt
2. An empty shoe box
3. Instructions for a vacuum cleaner
4. Unwashed sports socks
5. Satinette Atomic Rooster tour jacket
6. A broken tennis racket
7. A tie-dyed T-shirt
8. A torn school photograph
9. An acrylic tank top
10. A bright woollen poncho

10 THINGS THAT ONLY NEWLY-IN-LOVE COUPLES DO

1. Hold hands in public
2. Talk to each other in baby talk and address each other by pet names (usually extremely embarrassing ones)
3. Feed each other in restaurants
4. Break off from feeding each other in restaurants to kiss each other
5. Write to each other even when they're not apart
6. Buy children's cuddly toys for each other
7. Give the cuddly toys names and celebrate the cuddly toys' birthdays (every week in very bad cases)
8. Have more than one nickname for each other
9. Take ten times as long as any 'normal' couple to walk down the road because their arms are so entwined
10. Only stop telling each other how much they're in love to tell everyone else how much they're in love

10 GOOD THINGS ABOUT BEING BALD

1. You don't have to brush dandruff off your jacket
2. You don't have to put up with conversations which begin "So are you going on holiday this year?"
3. No need to call the plumber to clear a blocked pipe
4. You don't have to pick stray hairs off jumpers
5. You'll never be caught wearing a plastic shower cap
6. You've got a head start when it comes to auditioning for the local amateur dramatic society's production of *The King and I*
7. You'll never have to buy Grecian 2000
8. It doesn't matter if you forget to pack the hairbrush when you go on holiday
9. No one teases you for going thin on top
10. You don't even need to take one bottle into the shower

10 JOBS FOR OLDER PEOPLE

1. Bowls professional
2. Saga holiday rep
3. Undertaker's sales rep
4. Bouncer at the senior citizens' bring and buy sale
5. Companion to Joan Collins
6. Truss consultant
7. Confidant(e) for the Prince of Wales
8. Chairlift demonstrator
9. Roadie for a Val Doonican concert
10. Model for zip-up cardigans

10 FILMS FOR OLIVER REED

1. *The Booze Brothers*
2. *The Lost Week*
3. *Romancing The Stone's*
4. *One Threw Up Over The Chat Show Guest*
5. *Liver Let Die*
6. *The Best Beers Of Our Lives*
7. *Honey, I Drunk The Gins*
8. *Billy Budweiser*
9. *Close Encounters Of The Blurred Kind*
10. *For Whom The Bell's Tolls*

ARE YOU AN OLD GIT? 10 TELL-TALE SIGNS

1. You can't find any songs to hum any more
2. You can't tell boys and girls apart
3. You think that cars drive too fast
4. You don't like any of that foreign muck they serve up these days
5. You'd like to be shown a bit more respect by youngsters
6. You can remember really hot summers
7. You don't hold with all this real ale nonsense
8. You can't see why everyone doesn't read the *Sunday Express*
9. You know that Alan Shearer isn't fit to lace Dixie Dean's boots
10. You tell people that you can remember when you could go out for an evening and still get change out of a 10-bob note

10 QUESTIONS WHICH CAN RESULT IN A FIGHT

1. Are you sure that seat's taken?
2. Who do you think you're staring at?
3. You and whose army?
4. D'you reckon?
5. Who's rattled your cage, then?
6. Fancy yourself, do you?
7. Got a death wish?
8. Do you like hospital food?
9. Did you say what I think you said?
10. Outside?

10 THINGS WHICH SAY YOU'VE GOT IT

1. Giorgio Armani invites you to the preview of his autumn collection
2. You play backgammon for high stakes
3. You've outgrown your computer organiser
4. You're interviewed by *The Face*
5. You own a vintage Bentley
6. Everyone says your partner looks like a film star
7. You're invited to be in *Who's Who*
8. You spend your winter holidays in Aspen
9. You're tired of sushi
10. You enjoy reading Pasternak in the original Russian

10 THINGS WHICH SAY YOU HAVEN'T GOT IT

You have an account at Millets

You've just discovered *Trivial Pursuit*

You've only just bought a Filofax

Exchange and Mart spells your name wrong in an ad.

You're falling behind with the payments on your Yugo

Everyone says your partner looks like a *Coronation Street* star

You're not even on the local free newspaper round

You spend your winter holidays in Aston

You're impressed by nouvelle cuisine

You have trouble reading Harold Robbins in English

10 THINGS LOST IN SPACE

1. Bubble cars
2. The Jim Bowen joke
3. Packets of Spangles
4. Boadicea's chariot
5. Esso World Cup Collection coins
6. The Remains of the Tower of Babel
7. Rayon shirts
8. Lord Lucan
9. The missing millions from the *Mirror* Pension Fund
10. Any number of badly made Soviet spacecraft

THE 10 LONGEST DAYS

1. The day you spend looking after a friend's children
2. The day you come home from a holiday abroad
3. The day you move house
4. The day of your driving-test
5. The day you or your partner gives birth
6. The day your first child starts school
7. The day you start your jury service
8. The day you go to see your bank manager about your overdraft
9. The day *before* you go to the dentist's to have a filling
10. Christmas Day spent with your extended family

10 MORE THINGS FOR ARCHIMEDES TO DISCOVER IN THE BATH

1. The hot water always runs out just before you rinse your hair
2. The shower attachment never gives you the correct mix of hot and cold water
3. It is only when you actually sit down in the bath that you realise that the soap is in the basin
4. Nine times out of ten, if there are different types of conditioner by the bath, the one that you grab with your eyes full of shampoo will be the one least suitable for your hair
5. However carefully you place the bathmat, water always goes on the floor
6. Whichever radio station you selected before getting into the bath you'll wish you had selected another one before the bath is over
7. However clean you leave a bath, it is always dirty the next time you go to use it (even if you live on your own)
8. If the phone or doorbell is going to ring during your bath, it will happen precisely 30 seconds after you have fully submerged your body
9. Remembering to put your towel on the radiator increases the likelihood of getting shampoo in your eyes
10. Turning the taps on with your toes requires one and a half times as much effort as leaning forward to do it with your hands

THE 10 LAWS OF COMMITTEES

1. 'Any other business' takes longer than all the other items on the agenda put together
2. The dullest member of the committee will always do the most speaking
3. Any committee which cannot agree on the minutes of the last meeting is doomed to break up - in tears - within three months
4. The amount of time spent debating subjects is in inverse proportion to their importance
5. The less someone likes serving on committees, the more likely they'll be invited to join one
6. The secretary is always the hardest working person on any committee
7. The vice-chairman is always the laziest person on any committee
8. Whatever the purpose of a committee, if it has more than one meeting a month, the meetings become more important than its purpose
9. If you're friends with someone before you both serve on the same committee, you won't be afterwards
10. It needs all the committee members to make committee meetings enjoyable it only needs one committee member to make committee meetings hellish

10 PEOPLE WHO REALLY DESERVE HONOURS

1. Emma Thompson's acceptance speech writer
2. Jim Davidson's divorce lawyer
3. Chris Evans's accountant
4. Nick Hancock's agent
5. Ron Atkinson's jeweller
6. Oliver Reed's wine merchant
7. Liam Gallagher's press agent
8. Cher's plastic surgeon
9. Jo Brand's furniture upholsterer
10. The Duchess of York's travel agent

10 PEOPLE WHO REALLY DON'T DESERVE HONOURS

1. Bernard Manning's personal trainer
2. Zsa Zsa Gabor's marriage guidance counsellor
3. Paul Gascoigne's tailor
4. Chris Eubank's elocution teacher
5. Margaret Beckett's beautician
6. Paula Yates's image consultant
7. Lee Hurst's hairdresser
8. Cilla Black's couturier
9. Esther Rantzen's dentist
10. Kate Moss's chef

10 HOPES AGAINST EXPECTATION

1. Sending an entry into a *Reader's Digest* prize draw
2. Going to the latest Sylvester Stallone film
3. Buying the latest Jeffrey Archer novel
4. Voting for any party which promises greater freedom for the individual (or indeed just voting)
5. Staying for the second half of a heavy metal concert
6. Buying an item of clothing in the next size down to encourage you to diet
7. Tuning in to a TV chat show for some interesting conversation
8. Getting married for the second time
9. Looking for a parking meter in central London
10. Predicting the first three finishers in the Grand National

10 THINGS YOU'D NEVER DO SOBER

1. Heckle at a Karaoke evening
2. Sing at a Karaoke evening
3. Eat curry at midnight
4. Let your boss know precisely what you've always thought of him/her
5. Go bungee jumping
6. Tell perfect strangers that you love them ("Honest I do...")
7. Streak
8. Go to bed on a Club 18-30 holiday
9. Take part in a pram race
10. Get drunk

10 THINGS WHICH CAN'T BE EXPLAINED WITHOUT REFERENCE TO THE PARANORMAL

1. Why the Department of Transport festoons motorways with traffic cones but neglects to hire workmen

2. Why cream crackers split into three whenever you try to butter them

3. Why buses travel in threes

4. Why there's always a teaspoon left in the bowl when you've finished the washing-up

5. Why *Reader's Digest* is Britain's top-selling magazine when no one you know buys it

6. Why socks disappear

7. Why floorboards only creak at night

8. Why there are 365 days in the year when there are 52 weeks each consisting of seven days

9. Why you can't buy a tube of toothpaste without an extra 10% free

10. Why MPs believe that their pay needs to be increased dramatically to improve the calibre of applicants but nurses' pay doesn't

10 AREAS WHERE POLITICAL CORRECTNESS HAS YET TO STRIKE

1. In car advertisements ('just one lady owner')

2. On Page 3 of the *Sun*

3. In the SAS

4. In Bernard Manning's stage act

5. In Roy 'Chubby' Brown's stage act

6. In seaside postcards

7. In rugby changing-rooms

8. In striptease shows

9. In pantomime performances of *Snow White and the Seven Dwarfs*

10. In *Viz*

10 QUESTIONS OF ETIQUETTE POSED BY CALL WAITING

1. If you phone someone and get Call Waiting, is it more polite to hang up or stay on?

2. If you do hang up, are you obliged to let that person know later that it was you they heard on their Call Waiting?

3. Should the person who has the Call Waiting carry on with the first conversation?

4. If he/she does, should he/she ask the second caller to wait?

5. If he/she does ask the caller to wait and then keeps them waiting a long time, should he/she offer to pay for that caller's call?

6. If the person who has Call Waiting decides to get rid of the first caller, should the first caller ever bother to phone him/her ever again?

7. If they do, should they put the phone down immediately if they get Call Waiting?

8. If they wait, should they insist to the person who has the Call Waiting that, on the basis of historical precedent, they are obliged to take the second call?

9. If the person who has the Call Waiting doesn't agree, should the caller put the phone down and come round to give him/her a piece of his/her mind?

10. How long does it take to disconnect Call Waiting?

10 THINGS YOU ALWAYS FIND AT A CAR-BOOT SALE

1. A Polaroid camera (without film)
2. A chipped commemorative mug
3. Any number of new novelty pen and pencil sets bought in job lots as bankrupt stock
4. A 1983 *Beano* Annual
5. A torch (without batteries - and often without a bulb)
6. A Bobby Crush LP
7. Games for a Sinclair ZX 48 computer
8. A 1982 edition of *The Guinness Book Of Records*
9. A broken tea's-maid
10. Pre-recorded videos of totally obscure films

10 THINGS THAT MAKE YOU FEEL GROWN UP

1. Using a credit card
2. Allowing someone else to keep the Christmas cracker novelty
3. Being called Sir/Madam by a policeman
4. Meeting your child's teacher
5. Buying a classical LP
6. Waving away the sweet trolley in a restaurant
7. Not playing with your car's electric windows
8. The publican accepting your offer to have a drink with you
9. Flying on an aeroplane alone
10. Receiving junk mail

10 THINGS WHICH ALWAYS HAPPEN IN BOOKMAKERS' (WELL THEY ALWAYS HAPPEN TO ME)

1. If you take a price, the price goes out; if you don't take a price, the price goes in
2. They always take longer to pay you out than they did to take your money
3. Shouting "come on, my son" at the television set doesn't make your horse go any faster but it does upset people who have backed a different horse
4. If you pay the tax, your horse loses
5. Not paying the tax doesn't mean that your horse will win but on any occasion that you do happen to win, you'll wish that you'd paid the tax beforehand
6. After the race, there's always one person who insists on telling you how you should have known all along that the winning horse was going to win. This is wisdom after the event.
7. There is very rarely any wisdom *before* the event
8. If there is anyone else in the shop who is on the same horse as you it will always lose
9. The pens only work if you're not in a hurry
10. At the end of the day, everyone either claims that they won or that they "broke even"

10 THINGS THEY PUT IN FINANCIAL ADS...AND WHAT THEY REALLY MEAN

1. "We offer a complete financial service" (we'll try to flog you insurance as well as pensions)

2. "Do you have dependents?" (Give us their names and we can pester them too)

3. "Pay off all your old debts!" (and replace them with one huge new one)

4. "How would you like a free alarm clock?" (how would you like to make monthly payments for the rest of your natural)

5. "Your home is at risk if you don't keep up with mortgage repayments" (forget the sweet talk: we're watching you)

6. "Isn't your peace of mind worth something?" (it must be at least worth the cost of my holiday this year)

7. "Completely independent advice" (we don't mind what you buy - so long as you buy something)

8. "The value of investments can go down as well as up" (you're completely on your own now)

9. "You can talk to us in complete confidence" (hope you don't mind if we sell your name, address and financial profile to any company which wants to buy it)

10. "I used to be poor but now I own two homes and drive a brand new Mercedes" (...and it's all thanks to mugs like you!)

10 LISTS WE COULDN'T BRING YOU

1. 10 Faithful Politicians

2. 10 Programmes Not Presented By Nick Hancock

3. 10 People Who Talk Like Janet Street-Porter

4. 10 Great Modern British Tennis Players

5. 10 Things Worse Than A British Summer

6. 10 Witty One-Liners By Jim Bowen

7. 10 Fashionably Dressed BBC Weathermen

8. 10 Things On Which All The Members Of The Parliamentary Conservative Party Agree

9. 10 Foods Which Aren't Bad For You

10. 10 Famous Norwegians

10 SINGULAR PEOPLE

1. The Honest Estate Agent

2. The Articulate Footballer

3. The Reticent Insurance Salesman

4. The Kind Traffic-Warden

5. The Multi-Talented Supermodel

6. The Open-Minded Cabbie

7. The Zany Undertaker

8. The Interesting Accountant

9. The Feminist Lorry Driver

10. The Witty Children's TV Presenter

10 PATRON SAINTS

1. St. Michael - The patron saint of dinner parties

2. St. Moritz - The patron saint of après-ski

3. St. Albans - The patron saint of British Rail

4. St. Laurent - The patron saint of supermodels

5. St. Malo - The patron saint of seasickness

6. St. Clements - The patron saint of teetotallers

7. St. Leger - The patron saint of bookmakers

8. St. Ives - The patron saint of holidays

9. St. Ivel - The patron saint of corner grocery shops

10. St. Bernard - The patron saint of lamp-posts

10 PROVERBS FOR PESSIMISTS

1. One door closes - another one slams in your face

2. Every cloud has a black lining

3. Cast ne'er a clout till May, June, July and August be out - and then think twice about it

4. Worse things happen at sea if you're planning a cruise

5. He who pays the piper is obliged to listen to the awful racket he makes

6. All that glistens isn't even gold-plate

7. A bird in the hand isn't worth as much as the one in the bush

8. If the cap fits it'll make your hair greasy

9. Love will find a way to make you even more miserable than you were before

10. Many hands make... a right mess of things

10 THINGS THAT OTHER PEOPLE FIND FUNNY

1. 'Funny' birthday cards

2. TV programmes devoted to other people's home videos

3. Mr Bean

4. Practical jokes

5. *Peanuts*

6. Singing telegrams

7. 'Humorous' car stickers

8. Silent movies

9. Charlie Chaplin films

10. The last item on *News At Ten*

10 GOOD PIECES OF ADVICE

1. Never give your address to people you meet on holiday

2. Never buy a white car

3. Never turn up more than an hour in advance for a charter flight

4. Never agree to "to something a little different this time" at the hairdresser's

5. Never attempt to mend a TV set yourself

6. Never visit a fun-fair on a full stomach

7. Never ask a taxi driver for his opinion

8. Never buy clothes which are too small in the hope that you will lose weight

9. Never select *You've Lost That Loving Feeling* at a karaoke night

10. Never volunteer for anything

10 WAYS IN WHICH LIFE IS TOO SHORT

1. To queue for a bus on a Sunday

2. To bake your own bread

3. To wait in for a deliveryman

4. To drive to the coast on a Bank Holiday weekend

5. To learn shorthand

6. To read yet another in-depth profile of Emma Thompson

7. To applaud all the encores at the opera

8. To go to a timeshare presentation

9. To teach someone the rules of a board game

10. To peel a grape

10 EXAMPLES OF TIMESHARE SPEAK

1. "Congratulations, you have been chosen..."
   (That's right, we bought your name on a mailing list)

2. "Have you thought about a holiday investment?"
   (Who said anything about 'timeshare'?)

3. Come to our presentation and have a free drink on us"
   (This will be the most expensive glass of cooking sherry of your life)

4. "Of course, there is absolutely no commitment to buy"
   (Please note this only applies to Roger Cook and Esther Rantzen)

5. "Enjoy free holidays for the rest of your life"
   (Free except for the four-figure service charges)

6. "Buy now at this unbelievable price"
   (Even we're amazed at our nerve for charging so much)

7. "You have won either a car, a new home or a £100 voucher"
   (Well, which one do you think you're going to get?)

8. "Exclusive location"
   (Even the Spanish planning authorities didn't know it could be developed)

9. "Low season"
   (And what's wrong with the Peak District in January?)

10. "And why not tell your friends and family about it?"
    (If you don't, you can be sure we will)

10 THINGS NOT TO SAY TO A FRIEND WHO'S DIETING

1. "I'm so lucky, I can eat anything without putting on weight"

2. "A Banana Split can't be fattening: it's got fruit in it"

3. "Think of all the starving people in the world"

4. "I don't know why you bother, you always give up after a week"

5. "It's a shame to let this cheesecake go to waste"

6. "I'm having liposuction next week"

7. "You look so much better when you're nice and chubby"

8. "Go on, open that box of chocolates, you'll only eat one or two"

9. "Nine out of ten diets don't work, you know"

10. "I bet you could absolutely murder this bag of chips"

10 THINGS WHICH ARE A CONTRADICTION IN TERMS

1. Army Intelligence

2. Working Lunch

3. Self-regulation

4. BBC Enterprises

5. Safe Sex

6. Corporate Hospitality

7. Business Trip

8. Alcohol-free Lager

9. Friendly Fire

10. Operator Service

10 THINGS YOU WOULDN'T HAVE THOUGHT POSSIBLE AT THE END OF WORLD WAR II

1. Germany would be united again
2. We'd be paying our war widows less than the Germans are paying theirs
3. We would be apologising for Dresden
4. There would be talk of us having a common currency with the Germans
5. Servicewomen would be paid hundreds of thousands of pounds for getting pregnant
6. The Japanese would get away with not apologising to their victims and not paying adequate compensation
7. Germany and Italy would play in the World Cup finals but not England, Scotland, Northern Ireland or Wales
8. The USSR would no longer exist
9. People would deny the Holocaust
10. Neo-Nazis would be on the march again in Europe

10 THINGS SAID BY PRUDES

1. "I'm not a prude but…"
2. "I like a joke as much as the next person…"
3. "I was young myself once…"
4. "I don't mind when it's essential…"
5. "I'm not the sort of person who likes to complain…"
6. "I consider myself open-minded…"
7. "I've no wish to spoil anyone's enjoyment…"
8. "I think I'm pretty unshockable…"
9. "I don't mind people having a good time but…"
10. "I reckon I'm an average sort of person…"

10 THINGS IN WHICH WE BRITS STILL LEAD THE WORLD

1. Nostalgia
2. Hooliganism
3. Scandals
4. Tradition
5. Darts
6. Royal divorces
7. Pub crawling
8. Complaining about the weather
9. Pigeon fancying
10. Snobbery

10 EXAMPLES OF MURPHY'S LAW

1. Anything that can go wrong will go wrong
2. The first place to look for something is the last place you would expect to find it
3. When someone says, "it's not the money, it's the principle", nine times out of ten it's the money
4. Whenever you make a journey by bicycle, it's always more uphill than downhill
5. As soon as you mention something: a) if it's good, it goes away; b) if it's bad, it happens
6. You never find something until you replace it
7. When the train you are on is late, the bus to take you home from the station will be on time
8. If an experiment works, something has gone wrong
9. It always rains when you've just washed your car but washing your car to make it rain won't work
10. When you dial a wrong number, it is never engaged

THE 10 MOST ANNOYING THINGS PEOPLE SAY

1. "Who rattled your cage then?"
2. "Ask no questions and you'll be told no lies"
3. "Knock me down with a feather"
4. "How long's a piece of string?"
5. "It'll all come out in the wash"
6. "That's for me to know and you to find out"
7. "That won't get the baby a new dress"
8. "It's no skin off my nose"
9. "That's more than my job's worth"
10. "Shouting never solved anything"

10 EXAMPLES OF WHAT THE HOLIDAY BROCHURES SAY AND WHAT THEY ACTUALLY MEAN

1. "Only 15 minutes from the beach" (15 minutes by Tornado Jet)
2. "The hotel is brand new" (And the swimming-pool will be ready by 1999)
3. "The hotel is well-established" (The local health inspectors know the manager by name)
4. "This bustling town..." (Make sure your valuables are insured)
5. "...with its exciting nightlife" (The jails are full to bursting)
6. "You'll have so much fun you won't want to leave" (Which is just as well since the people who went last year are still waiting for the plane to take them home)
7. "Enjoy the local culture" (A pint of Guinness and a chorus of *Y Viva España*)
8. "For your peace of mind we have a representative who is always available" (Particularly if you're young and extremely good-looking)
9. "This resort is popular with all nationalities" (Don't even think of getting a seat by the pool)
10. "The island is totally unspoilt" (No point in asking for a doctor when you get food poisoning)

10 EXAMPLES OF THE LONGEST MINUTE

1. Waiting for a saucepan of water to come to the boil
2. The final minute of your driving test
3. Stuck in a tunnel on an underground train
4. Having a blood test
5. Queuing to use the loo
6. Standing outside a headteacher's study or a boss's office
7. The commercial break in a thriller on TV
8. The last minute of a walk home in the rain with a week's groceries
9. Giving birth
10. Watching someone giving birth

10 JOBS FOR ARNOLD SCHWARZENEGGER TO DO

1. Chief executive of a nationalised British Rail
2. Tesco's supermarket trolley supervisor
3. Inner-city Crime Prevention Officer
4. Manager of Brighton & Hove Albion FC
5. Head of Oftel
6. Presenter of *Question Time*
7. Bodyguard to the spice girls
8. Investigative reporter on *Watchdog*
9. Crew leader at McDonald's
10. Conservative Party Chief Whip

10 QUESTIONS TO WHICH THERE IS NO ANSWER: WHY IS IT THAT...

1. The clothes you like best in the sale are never in your size?
2. Wherever you park your car, it's always the only one in the road with all the bird muck on it?
3. You only bump into someone you really fancy when you've got a spot on your face?
4. "Bad" foods are more enjoyable than "good" ones?
5. You wait ages for a bus then two turn up at once?
6. Arms are too short to scratch the middle of the back?
7. Petrol station promotions expire just when you need one more token?
8. It always rains as soon as you wash your hair?
9. Cats always jump on to the lap of someone who hates cats - no matter how many cat lovers there are in the room?
10. As soon as you get into the bath the telephone goes?

10 PIECES OF NIGHTCLUB ENTERTAINER PATTER

1. "This is my favourite town"
   (I hope none of you heard me say the same thing in Swindon last night)

2. "I'd like to start off with a little number made famous by an old drinking pal of mine named Perry"
   (That's Mr Como to me)

3. "I don't like to talk about the work I do for the Variety Club"
   (Not much I don't)

4. "Did you see me on the telly the other night?"
   (It was on the Border TV local news and it was 18 months ago)

5. "I'd like you to put your hands together"
   (I wish I didn't have to ask for a round of applause)

6. "And now a song one or two of you might know"
   (That's right, it's *New York, New York*)

7. "Hey, you know Tarby and Brucie? Well, I've been playing a lot of golf recently"
   (But not with them)

8. "Mmm, that food looks good enough to eat"
   (I think I'll throw up if I see one more basket with scampi and chips in it)

9. "This song means a lot to me"
   (This was my only Top 75 hit)

10. "You've been a truly wonderful audience"
    (You've been an audience)

10 PROVERBS WHICH ARE CLEARLY NOT TRUE

1. You can't have your cake and eat it

2. Every cloud has a silver lining

3. You can't judge a book by its cover

4. Ask no questions and you will be told no lies

5. An apple a day keeps the doctor away

6. Barking dogs seldom bite

7. There is no accounting for taste

8. The race is not to the swift

9. It never rains but it pours

10. The best things in life are free

10 THINGS YOU BOUGHT IN THE JANUARY SALES AND NOW REGRET

1. A set of electronic scales
2. An exercise bicycle
3. A shop-soiled shirt which still looked awful after washing
4. An electric orange juice extractor
5. A mahogany-effect TV and video cabinet
6. A pair of shoes which were half-a-size too small
7. A wicker wine rack
8. A ten-volume guide to home car maintenance
9. A large bottle of bath oil which made your skin itchy
10. A set of miniature glass animals

10 THINGS WHICH CAN RESULT IN HEART FAILURE

1. Being told by the dentist that "this might be painful"

2. Finding a worm in an apple

3. Finding half a worm in an apple

4. A doctor's sudden intake of breath

5. Watching a penalty shoot-out on TV

6. Paying for an emergency plumbing job

7. Being stopped by the police on your way back from the pub

8. Being stopped by customs men on your way back from holiday

9. Having a microphone thrust into your hand on a karaoke evening

10. Watching a Quentin Tarantino movie on your own

STARTING WORK FOR THE FIRST TIME? 10 THINGS YOU MIGHT BE SENT TO FETCH

1. A tub of elbow grease

2. Some invisible nails

3. A pair of rubber scissors

4. Two dozen sky-hooks

5. A left-handed monkey-wrench

6. A glass hammer

7. A long weight

8. A horizontal ladder

9. A right-handed mug

10. A tin of striped paint

10 THINGS WE'LL ONE DAY LOOK BACK ON IN AMAZEMENT

1. MPs having more than one job

2. People keeping dogs in their home

3. Toll-free roads

4. The countries of Great Britain competing against each other in the World Cup rather than playing as one team

5. Having to pay for a TV licence

6. British beaches being polluted by raw sewage

7. People queuing in banks and post offices rather than doing all that sort of thing on the phone

8. Burglars being let off with a caution

9. Paying farmers money not to grow things

10. The police being routinely unarmed

10 ORGANS YOU WOULDN'T WANT TRANSPLANTED

1. Oliver Reed's liver

2. Princess Margaret's lungs

3. Saddam Hussein's heart

4. Paul Gascoigne's knee

5. Bruce Dickinson's ears

6. Victoria Gillick's womb

7. Janet Street-Porter's teeth

8. Sir Cyril Smith's hip

9. Warren Beatty's prostate

10. Melvyn Bragg's sinuses

ARE YOU A RIGHT B**TARD? 10 TELL-TALE SIGNS

1. You only use shampoo which *has* been tested on animals
2. You put bent coins in charity boxes in order to jam the slot
3. If you're in a car and you see a hitchhiker, you slow down - only to speed up again when they get within four feet
4. The only birthday you remember is your own
5. Your idea of a "joke" is to place a pile of leaves over some dog's mess on the pavement
6. You failed the interview to become a traffic warden because you were considered 'too sadistic'
7. You watch happy films back to front
8. On a bus, no matter how many people are standing, there's no way you'll move your bag off the seat
9. You cheat when you're playing cards for money...with children
10. If anyone asks you the way to the station, you send them in completely the wrong direction

10 OF THE WORST THINGS IN LIFE

1. The smell of the milk that you left in the fridge by mistake when you went on holiday
2. Getting a puncture on the motorway - at night and in the rain
3. Having to ask for loo-paper in a crowded pub
4. Putting on a wet bathing-costume
5. Filling out any form sent to you by the DSS
6. Being woken up by a wrong number at four in the morning when you have to be up at six
7. Discovering that the motorist you've just told to "get lost" is actually an off-duty policeman
8. Being stuck in a lift with a person who doesn't believe in wearing a deodorant
9. The sound of someone taking their first violin lesson
10. Watching Channel 4's *The Big Breakfast* from beginning to end

THE 10 WORST THINGS ABOUT ST VALENTINE'S DAY

1. Not getting any cards
2. Not even the one you sent to yourself
3. Getting a card and never finding out who sent it
4. Standing in line behind billing and cooing couples in McDonald's
5. Reading newspaper messages for people named "Fluffywinkle" and "Mrs Ploppywopps"
6. Feeling sick after guzzling a whole box of chocolates in one evening
7. Being forced to buy hideously sweet and horribly expensive cocktails at the pub
8. Being the only one of your mates not to have a date
9. Paying well over the odds for a bunch of flowers
10. The promises you made in the heat of the moment

ARE YOU A COUCH POTATO? 10 WAYS TO FIND OUT

1. You know the number of the local pizza delivery company off by heart
2. You think the contestants on *Telly Addicts* are really thick
3. You don't live in a county, you live in a TV region
4. You know the colour of Anna Ford's eyes but not your partner's
5. You can't remember the last time you wore shoes after 9pm
6. The only exercise you took last year was when you mislaid the remote control for an evening
7. You take all your holidays in England so you don't miss any of your favourite soaps
8. When you see a policeman walking down the street you have to stop yourself from asking him whether he knows Bob Cryer
9. It's a rare evening when you DON'T fall asleep in front of the telly
10. There's more money down the side of your armchair than there is in your pocket

10 NEW BADGES TO HELP THE BOY SCOUTS GET UP TO DATE

1. Skateboarding
2. Glueless Aeroplane Modelling
3. Safe Sex Awareness
4. Rapping
5. Toyboying
6. Theme Park Attendance
7. Alcohol-free Lager Brewing
8. Graffiti Art
9. Trainer-lacing
10. Microwave Cookery

10 SAYINGS THAT TEMPT FATE

1. "I haven't been to the dentist for years and I don't see the need for them"
2. "You don't need an electrician to do the rewiring"
3. "The French police just wear guns to look hard"
4. "I'm lucky, I never get sunburn"
5. "Now this is how you jump off a bus"
6. "I've smoked 40-a-day all my life and I've never had so much as a cough"
7. "This airline has a 100% safety record, you know"
8. "I've made my home absolutely burglar-proof"
9. "There's nothing wrong with a bit of mould on bread"
10. "Who needs zebra crossings?"

10 THINGS PEOPLE SAY WHICH ARE GUARANTEED NOT TO CHEER YOU UP

1. "There's many worse off than you"
2. "Every cloud has a silver lining"
3. "Pull yourself together"
4. "Cheer up, it may never happen"
5. "There are millions of people who'd like to have your problems"
6. "Worrying never solved anything"
7. "Your trouble is you don't know when you're well off"
8. "Worse things happen at sea"
9. "Why don't you look on the bright side?"
10. "You think *you've* got problems..."

10 THINGS WE KNOW ABOUT AMERICAN JUSTICE FROM THE MOVIES

1. Attorneys can only talk while they walk

2. Beautiful female defendants always fall in love with their attorneys

3. The better-looking a male defendant is, the more likely he is to be guilty

4. The better-looking a male juror is, the more likely he is to turn amateur detective to help the defence

5. The prosecuting attorney has to lean on the rail of the jury box to deliver his closing speech

6. The more untidily dressed and screwed up the defence attorney is, the more likely he is to win

7. The attorney who wins the most objections always loses the case

8. Witnesses who lie have to break down on the witness stand

9. The defence attorney always visits the judge at his home in the middle of the night

10. The most vital piece of evidence is only ever uncovered during the trial

10 EXCUSES FOR BREAKING THE DIET

1. Stretch trousers and baggy jumpers have just come back into fashion

2. Any chocolate bar which lists the calorific value on the packet must be good for you

3. You can't put on any weight if you eat food standing up

4. The orangey bit in a Jaffa Cake counts as fruit

5. You need to put on more weight before you can lose it all and become a Slimmer of The Year

6. Goodness knows how many calories you used up in running for the bus

7. Well it never did that Dawn French any harm, did it?

8. You had to finish off the kiddies' leftovers, didn't you?

9. That girl in the Flake ad isn't exactly what you'd call porky

10. There's always tomorrow

10 GREAT LIES

1. The cheque's in the post

2. You don't look a day over 30

3. I tried phoning you but you were constantly engaged

4. I'll still respect you in the morning

5. I could've sworn I had enough in my account

6. I've only had two glasses of wine, officer

7. Didn't you get my postcard?

8. Sorry, your serve was just out

9. This is my very first one-night stand

10. It's just what I've always wanted

10 THINGS WHICH HAPPEN EVERY BONFIRE NIGHT

1. The taper which comes with the box of fireworks doesn't light
2. There isn't a milk bottle for the rockets
3. The person who goes on most about the Firework Code is always the first to relight a firework that didn't go off
4. The firework you keep till the end turns out to be useless
5. The tomato soup boils over
6. The Catherine Wheel flies off the tree as soon as it starts spinning
7. The public fire display ends three minutes after you get there
8. The guy falls apart at the precise moment when he's too hot to be remade
9. Next door's display is always better than yours
10. Everyone agrees that it was a complete waste of money

10 THINGS ONLY AN OPTIMIST DOES

1. Takes a bottle of after-sun cream on a British holiday
2. Buys clothes in a smaller size in the hope that the diet'll work
3. Goes to watch the England cricket team (at home) without an umbrella
4. Gets married for the second time
5. Puts all the Grand National winnings on to a Derby outsider
6. Watches a TV soap in the expectation of seeing a storyline resolved
7. Buys a season ticket on the way to the job interview
8. Votes in a General Election
9. Sends off an entry to the *Which?* Prize Draw
10. Takes a car into the centre of London

10 THINGS WHICH ARE HARD TO BELIEVE

1. Eric Clapton and Phil Collins share the same tailor
2. Jerry Hall drinks Bovril
3. The M25 was built to relieve traffic congestion
4. The Prince of Wales preferred Camilla to Diana
5. The 200 dishes in the local Chinese restaurant are all fresh
6. Of St Winifred's School Choir, Joe Dolce Music Theatre and The Who, only The Who have never had a British No. 1
7. The Royal Family rely on Sir Jimmy Savile for advice
8. There are hosepipe bans in Yorkshire but not in the Costa del Sol
9. TV weathermen get a clothing allowance
10. Carol and Mark Thatcher are twins

10 THINGS YOU REGRET

1. Going for a curry after an evening at the pub

2. Making a sponsored bungee jump

3. Watching the late-night movie when you've got work the next day

4. Allowing your friend to store their belongings at your place when they go away for a year

5. Putting onions on a hot dog

6. Giving your telephone number when you send off for the double-glazing brochure

7. Sharing a boat with friends

8. Volunteering to look after a stall at the local fete

9. Taking the car to the seaside on a bank holiday

10. Pledging a month's salary to a telethon

10 PEOPLE YOU JUST HATE

1. People who can tell which way the wind is blowing just by sucking their fingers

2. People who can eat whatever they like without getting fat

3. People who can work out fuel consumption in terms of miles per litre

4. People who look immaculate whatever they're wearing and whatever they're doing

5. People whose kids are child prodigies

6. People who know the names of all of *The Magnificent Seven*

7. People who can eat spaghetti without getting in a mess

8. People who can whistle with their fingers in their mouths

9. People who passed their driving test first time

10. People who can immediately attract a waiter's attention

THE 10 LAWS OF GOING TO THE HAIRDRESSER'S

1. The salon will always have a punny name (like Cutting Times or Head Start)

2. The more the girl who washes your hair talks, the more likely she is to get water in your ear

3. The salon radio is always tuned (badly) to the local commercial radio station

4. When the hairdresser says: "we haven't seen you for ages" what they really mean is: "how dare you go anywhere else"

5. The mirror you're seated in front of is specially constructed to make your face look twice as fat as it actually is

6. However many hairdressers there are in the salon, it is always the person cutting your hair who goes off to answer the telephone

7. The first question you're asked is "are you going/have you been anywhere nice for your holidays?"

8. Whatever answer you give, the next three words you will hear are "oh that's nice"

9. There's no hairdressing bill so high that having conditioner can't double it

10. However much you tip, you always feel as though you didn't give enough

10 SIGNS THAT THE SCHOOL SUMMER HOLIDAYS HAVE STARTED

1. Mass outbreaks of graffiti

2. Shattered greenhouses

3. Your dustbin has been appropriated as a cricket wicket

4. Mothers are spotted ticking days off calenders

5. You keep slipping over Mars ice-cream wrappers

6. There isn't a single non-retractable aerial left standing in the road

7. You can't find a local cinema that isn't showing Disney films

8. Teachers stop moaning about their pay and conditions

9. You can't walk fifty yards without being knocked over by a skateboard

10. W.H. Smith's puts "Back to School" signs in their windows

10 SIGNS THAT THE SCHOOL SUMMER HOLIDAYS HAVE ENDED

1. There's a sharp increase in the number of bus drivers starting courses of Valium

2. The local cinema puts its Disney films back on the shelf

3. Mothers are spotted with smiles on their faces

4. Woolworth's lay off their security guards

5. Your children once again become friends with that ghastly child "Everybody Else" as in "Everybody Else wears jeans to school"

6. Public swimming pools are once again 100% water

7. You can walk twenty yards without being knocked over by a skateboard

8. Amusement arcades don't bother opening till four o'clock

9. Kids start writing their letters to Santa

10. Teachers go on strike

NEED TO GET AWAY FROM IT ALL? 10 PLACES WHERE NO ONE'LL FIND YOU

1. At an Andrew Ridgeley fan club meeting

2. In Newcastle United's defence

3. In Edwina Currie's smoking room

4. At a Bros reunion

5. In Bros

6. On the terraces at a Halifax Town home match

7. In a Lebanese tourist office

8. In Def Leppard's acoustic guitar section

9. In the House of Commons on a Friday afternoon

10. On a late-night Channel 4 discussion programme

10 PATHETIC EXCUSES FOR SPEEDING

1. "I'm counting cats eyes for a road traffic survey"

2. "I was being pursued by a double-glazing salesman"

3. "I was down to my last gallon of petrol"

4. "I was rushing to get to the police station to buy some tickets for the policeman's ball"

5. "I put Des O'Connor on the car stereo by mistake and I wanted to end it all"

6. "I'd run out of boiled sweets"

7. "I was trying to get home in time to watch *The Bill*"

8. "I thought my speedometer was registering kilometres per hour not miles per hour"

9. "I'm Damon Hill's brother-in-law"

10. "I needed to replace my furry dice"

10 GREAT SEXUAL LIES

1. "There's no one else but you"

2. "I want to wake up next to you in the morning"

3. "This is it"

4. "God, you're so beautiful"

5. "I won't tell a soul about this"

6. "My partner and I have an open relationship"

7. "I never knew it could be like this"

8. "You're the best"

9. "Sex is only a small part of a loving relationship"

10. "Thank God you phoned - I lost your telephone number"

Chapter 2

The Arts

10 BOOK TITLES AND WHERE THEY CAME FROM

1. *For Whom The Bell Tolls* (Ernest Hemingway) Taken from John Donne's *Devotions*

2. *Gone With The Wind* (Margaret Mitchell) Taken from Ernest Dowson's *Cynara*

3. *Now Voyager* (Olive Higgins Prouty) Taken from Walt Whitman's *Leaves of Grass*

4. *Paths of Glory* (Humphrey Cobb) Taken from Thomas Gray's *Elegy In A Country Churchyard*

5. *From Here To Eternity* (James Jones) Taken from Rudyard Kipling's *Gentlemen Rankers*

6. *Of Mice And Men* (John Steinbeck) Taken from Robert Burns's *To A Mouse*

7. *A Confederacy of Dunces* (John Kennedy Toole) Taken from Jonathan Swift's *Thoughts On Various Subjects*

8. *The Moon's A Balloon* (David Niven) Taken from e.e. cummings's *& N &*

9. *The Grapes of Wrath* (John Steinbeck) Taken from Julia Ward Howe's *The Battle Hymn of The American Republic*

10. *Tender Is The Night* (F. Scott Fitzgerald) Taken from John Keats's *Ode To A Nightingale*

10 BOOKS AND THEIR ORIGINAL TITLES

1. *Lady Chatterley's Lover* (D.H. Lawrence) *Tenderness*

2. *Treasure Island* (Robert Louis Stevenson) *The Sea-Cook*

3. *Jaws* (Peter Benchley) *The Summer of The Shark*

4. *War And Peace* (Leo Tolstoy) *All's Well That Ends Well*

5. *Moby Dick* (Herman Melville) *The Whale*

6. *The Man With The Golden Arm* (Nelson Algren) *Night Without Mercy*

7. *Of Mice And Men* (John Steinbeck) *Something That Happened*

8. *The Great Gatsby* (F. Scott Fitzgerald) *The High-bouncing Lover*

9. *Gone With The Wind* (Margaret Mitchell) *Ba! Ba! Black Sheep*

10. *Frankenstein* (Mary Shelley) *Prometheus Unchained*

10 PEOPLE WHO HAVE SERVED AS JUDGES FOR THE BOOKER PRIZE

1. Michael Foot (1988)
2. Benny Green (1979)
3. Lady Antonia Fraser (1970)
4. Robin Ray (1977)
5. Joan Bakewell (1981)
6. Trevor McDonald (1987)
7. Rabbi Julia Neuberger (1994)
8. Libby Purves (1983)
9. Ruth Rendell (1995)
10. Joanna Lumley (1985)

10 PEOPLE WHO WROTE CHILDREN'S BOOKS

1. Susannah York (*The Last Unicorn*)

2. Ian Fleming (*Chitty Chitty Bang Bang*)

3. David Byrne (*Stay Up Late*)

4. Roger McGough (*The Magic Fountain*)

5. Elizabeth Taylor (*Nibbles And Me*)

6. The Prince of Wales (*The Old Man of Lochnagar*)

7. Terry Jones (*Lady Cottington's Pressed Fairy Book*)

8. Colonel Muammar Gadaffi (*The Village, The Village, The Earth, The Earth...And The Suicide Of The Spaceman*)

9. Lenny Henry (*Charlie And The Big Chill*)

10. Nanette Newman (*Spider The Horrible Cat*)

10 THINGS A MARTIAN WOULD KNOW ABOUT ENGLAND FROM READING AGATHA CHRISTIE

1. Every house has at least three servants

2. Only ex-patriate Belgians live in town

3. Murder is the only crime

4. The police are incapable of solving murders

5. People only work as a hobby

6. People always attempt to change their wills just before they're murdered

7. All murderers commit at least two murders

8. People speak in italics - *especially when they're accused of murder!*

9. All secretaries (apart from Miss Lemon) are male

10. Butlers never commit murders - but doctors often do

10 NOVELS ORIGINALLY REJECTED BY PUBLISHERS

1. *Catch-22* (Joseph Heller)

2. *The Wind In The Willows* (Kenneth Grahame)

3. *A Time To Kill* (John Grisham)

4. *The Rainbow* (D.H. Lawrence)

5. *A River Runs Through It* (Norman MacLean)

6. *The War of The Worlds* (H.G. Wells)

7. *The Spy Who Came In From The Cold* (John Le Carré)

8. *Animal Farm* (George Orwell)

9. *Tess of The D'Urbervilles* (Thomas Hardy)

10. *Lord of The Flies* (William Golding)

10 NOVELISTS MORE FAMOUS FOR OTHER THINGS

1. Naomi Campbell (*Swan*)

2. Benito Mussolini (*The Cardinal's Mistress*)

3. Julie Andrews (*The Last of The Really Great Whangdoodles*)

4. Martina Navratilova (*Total Zone*)

5. Jilly Johnson (*Double Exposure*)

6. Sir Winston Churchill (*Savrola*)

7. Carly Simon (*Amy The Dancing Bear*)

8. Tony Curtis (*Kid Andrew Cody And Julie Sparrow*)

9. George Kennedy (*Murder On Location*)

10. Whoopi Goldberg (*Alice*)

10 BOOKS WHICH WERE BANNED

1. *The Adventures of Tom Sawyer* (Mark Twain) Banned by several London libraries (in politically correct Labour-controlled boroughs) in the mid-1980s on account of the book's 'racism' and 'sexism'.

2. *Black Beauty* (Anna Sewell) Banned by the African country, Namibia, in the 1970s because the Government took offence at the 'racist' title.

3. *The Scarlet Pimpernel* (Baroness Orczy) was banned by the Nazis - not because of its language or its theme (though Leslie Howard starred in an anti-Nazi film entitled *(Pimpernel Smith)* - but because Baroness Orczy was Jewish. Other authors banned by the Nazis for the same reason included Erich Maria Remarque, Thomas Mann, Sigmund Freud and Marcel Proust. Authors banned by the Nazis because of their political sentiments included Ernest Hemingway, Upton Sinclair and Jack London.

4. *Catcher In The Rye* (J.D. Salinger) Banned in Boron, California, in 1989 because of the word 'goddamn'. It was also banned in another U.S. State because of the words 'Hell' and 'For Chrissake'. This is probably the most famous work of fiction never to have been turned into a feature film.

5. *Noddy* (Enid Blyton) Banned by several British libraries in the 1960s - along with other Enid Blyton books - because they weren't thought to be 'good' for children.

6. *The Grapes of Wrath* (John Steinbeck) Banned from schools in Iowa, U.S.A. in 1980, after a parent complained that the classic novel - by the Nobel Prize-winner - was 'vulgar and obscene'. Steinbeck's other famous novel, *Of Mice And Men*, has also been banned in other U.S. States for similar reasons.

7. *The Joy of Sex* (Alex Comfort) Banned in Ireland from its publication until 1989 on account of the book's uninhibited approach to sex and relationships. The Irish have done more than their share of banning: all of Steinbeck's and Zola's novels were banned in Ireland in 1953 for being 'subversive' and/or 'immoral'. Other books banned by the Irish include: *Brave New World* (Aldous Huxley), *Elmer Gantry* (Sinclair Lewis) and *The Sun Also Rises* (Ernest Hemingway).

8. *Billy Bunter* books (Frank Richards) Banned from British libraries in the 1970s in case it led children to tease overweight schoolmates. In more recent years, other politically correct institutions have banned the books because of the black character, Hurree Ramset Jam Singh, known to all his pals as 'Inky'.

9. *On The Origin of Species* (Charles Darwin) Banned in several U.S. States (especially in the Christian Fundamentalist South) through the years - but particularly before World War II - on account of the fact that Darwin didn't accept the Bible's account of Creation. Incredibly, Desmond Morris's *The Naked Ape* has been banned from one or two U.S. libraries on the same basis. Darwin's book was also banned by the USSR because it was 'Immoral'.

10. *My Friend Flicka* (Mary O'Hara) Banned from schoolchildren's reading lists in Clay County, Florida, in 1990 because the book contains the word 'bitch' to describe 'a female dog'. It's decisions like that which put satirists out of business...

10 THINGS GUILTY AGATHA CHRISTIE CHARACTERS DO AND 10 THINGS INNOCENT AGATHA CHRISTIE CHARACTERS DO

GUILTY	INNOCENT
1. Behave perfectly normally	Act extremely suspiciously
2. Co-operate fully with the police	Display hostility towards the police
3. Call Poirot "M. Poirot" and ask him to solve the murder for them	Dismiss Poirot as "a damned foreign mountebank"
4. Have foreign blood	Have defiant eyes
5. Cough and declare that "life won't get back to normal until the murderer is caught"	Toss their heads back and exclaim that they "want to start living!"
6. Lose their tempers at the end of the book	Lose their tempers at the start of the book
7. Take Miss Marple seriously	Dismiss Miss Marple as "an old pussy"
8. Have secret pasts	Have secret presents
9. Curse Poirot when they're discovered	Thank Poirot for sorting out everything
10. Talk in italics when *they're found out!*	Talk about marrying the person they've always loved

10 CHARACTERS – ALL MEMBERS OF BERTIE WOOSTER'S CIRCLE – INVENTED BY P.G. WODEHOUSE

1. Barmy Fotheringay-Phipps
2. Stilton Cheesewright
3. Pongo Twistleton-Twistleton
4. Gussie Fink-Nottle
5. Biscuit Biskerton
6. Stiffy Stiffham
7. Catsmeat Potter-Pirbright
8. Dogface Rainsby
9. Oofy Prosser
10. Freddie Fitch-Fitch

10 FICTIONAL CHARACTERS AND THEIR FIRST NAMES

1. Inspector (Endeavour) Morse
2. (Rupert) Rigsby (*Rising Damp*)
3. Mr (Quincy) Magoo
4. Inspector (Jules) Maigret
5. (John) Rambo
6. Captain (George) Mainwaring (*Dad's Army*)
7. (Wilfred) Ivanhoe
8. (Hugh) Bulldog Drummond
9. (James) Shelley (*Shelley*)
10. Little Lord (Cedric) Fauntleroy

10 PUBLISHED DIARISTS

1. Evelyn Waugh
2. Tony Benn
3. Anthony Sher
4. Roger Moore
5. Andy Warhol
6. Richard Crossman
7. Will Carling
8. Barbara Castle
9. Sir Peter Hall
10. Vaslav Nijinsky

10 NOVELISTS WHO APPEARED IN FILMS

1. Saul Bellow: *Zelig*
2. Damon Runyon: *The Great White Way*
3. Sir Arthur Conan Doyle: *The $5,000,000 Counterfeiting Plot*
4. Jean-Paul Sartre: *La Vie Commence Demain*
5. Mickey Spillane: *Ring of Fear*
6. Mark Twain: *A Curious Dream*
7. William Burroughs: *It Don't Pay to be an Honest Citizen*
8. G.K. Chesterton: *Rosy Rapture - The Pride of the Beauty Chorus*
9. Graham Greene: *Day for Night*
10. Norman Mailer: *King Lear*

10 CELEBRITY COOKBOOKS

1. Len Deighton: *The ABC of French Food*
2. Jane Asher: *Jane Asher's Quick Party Cakes*
3. Lindsay Wagner: *The High Road To Health: A Vegetarian Cookbook*
4. Floella Benjamin: *Caribbean Cookery*
5. George Baker: *A Cook For All Seasons*
6. Tessie O'Shea: *The Slimmer's Cookbook*
7. Linda McCartney: *Home Cooking*
8. Nanette Newman: *Summer Cookpot*
9. Pearl Bailey: *Pearl's Kitchen*
10. The Earl Of Bradford: *The Eccentric Cookbook*

10 NOMS DE PLUME AND THE PEOPLE THEY CONCEAL

1. Saki (Hector Munro)
2. Lewis Carroll (Charles Lutwidge Dodgson)
3. John Le Carré (David Cornwell)
4. George Sand (Amandine Dupin)
5. Molière (Jean-Baptiste Poquelin)
6. Mark Twain (Samuel Langhorne Clemens)
7. Sapper (Cyril McNeile)
8. George Orwell (Eric Blair)
9. Voltaire (François Marie Arouet)
10. James Herriot (James Alfred Wright)

10 DOGS IN LITERATURE

1. Nana: *Peter Pan* by J.M. Barrie
2. Toto: *The Wizard of Oz* by Frank Baum
3. Timmy: *The Famous Five* books by Enid Blyton
4. Edison: *Chitty Chitty Bang Bang* by Ian Fleming
5. Montmorency: *Three Men In A Boat* by Jerome K. Jerome
6. Bullseye: *Oliver Twist* by Charles Dickens
7. Jip: *Dr Dolittle* by Hugh Lofting
8. Argos: *The Odyssey* by Homer
9. Jock: *Jock of the Bushveld* by Sir Percy Fitzpatrick
10. Pongo: *One Hundred and One Dalmatians* by Dodie Smith

10 DICKENS CHARACTERS

1. Barnet Skettles (*Dombey And Son*)
2. Chevy Slyme (*Martin Chuzzlewit*)
3. Dick Swiveller (*The Old Curiosity Shop*)
4. Conkey Chickweed (*Oliver Twist*)
5. Sophy Wackles (*The Old Curiosity Shop*)
6. Minnie Meagles (*Little Dorrit*)
7. Canon Crisparkle (*The Mystery of Edwin Drood*)
8. Peepy Jellyby (*Bleak House*)
9. Nicodemus Boffin (*Our Mutual Friend*)
10. Count Smorltork (*The Pickwick Papers*)

THE 10 MOST TAUGHT SHAKESPEARE PLAYS IN BRITISH SCHOOLS

1. *Macbeth*
2. *Romeo And Juliet*
3. *The Merchant of Venice*
4. *King Lear*
5. *A Midsummer Night's Dream*
6. *Antony And Cleopatra*
7. *Twelfth Night*
8. *Julius Caesar*
9. *The Tempest*
10. *Hamlet*

10 PEOPLE WHO HAVE HAD THEIR PAINTINGS EXHIBITED

1. Tony Curtis
2. Joni Mitchell
3. Desmond Morris
4. Prince Charles
5. Anthony Quinn
6. Bryan Ferry
7. Ronnie Wood
8. Sylvester Stallone
9. Miles Davis
10. Sir Noel Coward

10 SHAKESPEARE PLAYS WHICH HAVE YET TO BE TURNED INTO MOVIES (as opposed to 'filmed plays')

1. *Titus Andronicus*
2. *The Two Gentlemen of Verona*
3. *The Merry Wives of Windsor*
4. *Pericles*
5. *Cymbeline*
6. *Love's Labours Lost*
7. *Troilus And Cressida*
8. *Timon of Athens*
9. *The Winter's Tale*
10. *King John*

10 FILMS BASED ON SHAKESPEARE PLAYS

FILM	PLAY
1. *West Side Story*	*Romeo and Juliet*
2. *Rosencrantz and Guildenstern Are Dead*	*Hamlet*
3. *Joe Macbeth*	*Macbeth*
4. *The Boys From Syracuse*	*The Comedy of Errors*
5. *A Double Life*	*Othello*
6. *Carry On Cleo*	*Antony and Cleopatra*
7. *The Dresser*	*King Lear*
8. *Kiss Me Kate*	*The Taming of the Shrew*
9. *An Honourable Murder*	*Julius Caesar*
10. *Forbidden Planet*	*The Tempest*

10 FICTITIOUS PLACES

1. Erinsborough (*Neighbours*)
2. Walmington-On-Sea (*Dad's Army*)
3. Holby (*Casualty*)
4. Fulchester (*Viz*)
5. Llareggub (*Under Milk Wood*)
6. Nutwood (*Rupert Bear*)
7. Gotham City (*Batman*)
8. Newtown (*Z Cars*)
9. Melchester (*Roy of The Rovers*)
10. St Mary Mead (*The Murder At The Vicarage* and all the Agatha Christie films and novels featuring Jane Marple)

10 PEOPLE WHO HAVE HAD SHOWS WRITTEN ABOUT THEM

1. Martin Luther King: *King*
2. Edith Piaf: *Piaf*
3. Phineas T Barnum: *Barnum*
4. John Lennon: *Lennon*
5. Al Jolson: *Jolson*
6. Eva Peron: *Evita*
7. Joyce Grenfell: *Re: Joyce*
8. Annie Oakley: *Annie Get Your Gun*
9. Fanny Brice: *Funny Girl*
10. Buddy Holly: *Buddy*

10 PEOPLE WHO HAVE WRITTEN SHOWS

1. Petula Clark: *Someone Like You*
2. Suzi Quatro (with Willie Rushton and Shirley Roden): *Tallulah Who?*
3. Ben Elton: *Gasping; Silly Cow; Popcorn*
4. David Essex: *Beauty And The Beast*
5. Pope John Paul II: *The Goldsmith Shop*
6. Mike Read (with words by John Betjeman): *Betjeman*
7. Michael Praed: *Mac And Beth*
8. Melvyn Bragg (with Howard Goodall): *The Hired Man*
9. Jeffrey Archer: *Shadow of a Doubt*
10. Bjorn Ulvaeus and Benny Andersson (with Tim Rice): *Chess*

10 PLAYS WHICH BOMBED

1. *The Intimate Revue* (The Duchess Theatre, West End). Lasted just one night in 1930. Scene changes took up to 20 minutes each and even with the scrapping of seven scenes, it only just finished before midnight. This has to be the shortest ever run as it didn't even last for one full performance.

2. *Leonardo* (The Strand, West End). In 1993, this musical based on the life of Leonardo Da Vinci lasted four weeks but what guarantees its inclusion in this list is not so much the extent of the show's losses (£1.5 million) but the aptness of the show's source of finance. It was backed by the tiny South Pacific island of Nauru whose major source of income is derived from the er, 'excrement' of the island's sea-fowl. Rather like *Les Misérables* is known as 'The Glums', during its short life, *Leonardo* was known in the business as "Give us a smile, Mona".

3. *Carrie* (Broadway). In 1988, this Royal Shakespeare Company musical based on the Stephen King novel of the same title closed after just five performances with a loss estimated at $7 million.

4. *The Lady of Lyons* (The Shaftesbury Theatre, West End). Written by Lord Lytton, this opened on Boxing Day, 1888. Unfortunately, no one could open the safety curtain and so, after an hour, the audience left - thus ending the play's run before it had even begun.

5. *Eurovision* (The Vaudeville, West End) This comedy (starring Anita Dobson) about gays finding true love at the Eurovision Song Contest lasted for just three weeks in 1993 - although the decision to close the show was taken after just four days. What was surprising about its failure was that one of the co-producers was Sir Andrew Lloyd Webber. His only other flop had been *Jeeves* (a show he had written with Alan Ayckbourn) but which they later successfully revived.

6. *Thirteen For Dinner* (The Duke of York's Theatre, West End). There's a saying that 'Thirteen for dinner' is unlucky. Can't argue with that when you consider that this play closed after just one night in 1942 (though the War might just have had something to do with it).

7. *Little Johnny Jones* (Broadway). This play had what must have seemed like a major box office attraction: Donny Osmond. Unfortunately, this was 1982, not 1972, and the show closed after just one night.

8. *Valentine's Day* (The Globe Theatre, West End). This musical - written by Denis King and Benny Green - and based on George Bernard Shaw's play, *You Never Can Tell,* closed after nine days in 1992. The composers had had more luck with an earlier adaptation of a Shaw play (*The Admirable Bashville* in 1983) but couldn't match the success enjoyed by Lerner and Loewe when they turned Shaw's *Pygmalion* into the musical *My Fair Lady.*

9. *Top People* (The Ambassadors Theatre, West End). Having been home to *The Mousetrap* for so long, The Ambassadors is used to long runs. Unfortunately, this wasn't one of them, closing after just four days in 1984.

10. *King* (Piccadilly Theatre, West End) In 1990, this musical based on the life of Martin Luther King ran for (a comparatively respectable) six weeks but it still managed to lose a record £3 million. Unlike in New York's Broadway where bad notices can still close a play overnight, in the West End, things are kept on for a little longer, in case the critics have got it wrong and the coach parties show up. Recent examples of this include: *Which Witch, Bernadette; The Importance* (a musical based on Oscar Wilde's classic play featuring the song, *Born In A Handbag*); *Marilyn* (A musical based on the life of Marilyn Monroe); *Matador; Winnie* (a musical based on the life of Sir Winston Churchill); *Robin, Prince of Sherwood, Children of Eden;* and the appropriately entitled *Curtains.*

10 FILM ADAPTATIONS OF MUSICALS WHICH FLOPPED

1. *Hair* The ultimate 1960s' musical. It was enormously popular on both sides of the Atlantic - running for 1,750 performances on Broadway. It should have been obvious that it could never have been turned into a film. Obvious to everyone except director Milos Forman who tried and (spectacularly) failed in a 1979 attempt starring Treat Williams. People who appeared in the stage shows include Oliver Tobias, Joan Armatrading, Paul Nicholas and Diane Keaton (apparently the only woman never to take her kit off).

2. *The Best Little Whorehouse In Texas* Musical about a legendary Texas brothel known as the Chicken Ranch (so-called because in the Depression, men were allowed to pay with poultry). It ran for 1,703 performances on Broadway. It was turned into a 1982 film starring Dolly Parton and Burt Reynolds and duly stiffed. If you'll pardon the expression.

3. *A Chorus Line* The all-time longest running production (musical or dramatic) on Broadway, this is a show about showbusiness. As with *Evita,* it took many years (nine) to turn it into a film because no one knew how to develop it for the cinema. Richard Attenborough had a go in 1985 and made a fair attempt but it was still universally panned.

4. *Godspell* Almost as big a hit in New York as *Jesus Christ Superstar* was in London, this musical about the last seven days of Christ ran for 2,651 performances on and off-Broadway. It was turned into a 1973 film starring Victor Garber (who?) which, notwithstanding the fine music, was truly, truly awful.

5. *A Little Night Music* The Stephen Sondheim musical which boasts his most famous song *(Send In The Clowns)* ran for 600 performances on Broadway - some achievement for a not obviously commercial musical. As the musical was itself based on a film (Ingmar Bergman's *Smiles of A Summer Night*) it should have transferred seamlessly to the screen but the 1977 film starring Elizabeth Taylor and Diana Rigg was a critical and commercial disappointment.

6. *Annie* This musical - adapted from the cartoon strip *Little Orphan Annie* - ran for 2,377 performances on Broadway, making it the third longest running musical of the 1970s. The 1982 film, starring Albert Finney as Daddy Warbucks, was a total flop.

7. *The Boy Friend* This affectionate 1950s send-up of 1920s musical comedies made Sandy Wilson, its writer, the first Englishman since Noel Coward to conquer Broadway where his musical ran for 485 performances - starring a young Julie Andrews. In 1971, Ken Russell directed the film version (starring Twiggy) but his efforts were blasted by the critics.

8. *Jesus Christ Superstar* Andrew Lloyd Webber and Tim Rice's first big hit ran for 3,357 performances in the West End and 720 on Broadway. In 1973, it was turned into a critically panned film starring Ted Neeley (and whatever happened to him?). The movie was co-written by one Melvyn Bragg. Perhaps he should do a *South Bank Show* special on it. Perhaps not.

9. *Man Of La Mancha* This musical version of *Don Quixote* was a Broadway hit in the 1960s, running for 2,328 performances. However, the 1972 film - starring Peter O'Toole and Sophia Loren - merely served to prove that it is easier to suspend disbelief in a theatre than it is in a cinema. As *Variety* said at the time: "Needful of all the imagination the spectator can muster".

10. *The Wiz* This all-black rock version of *The Wizard of Oz* was a surprise Broadway hit, running for 1,672 performances. The 1978 film was an unsurprising flop - despite (because of?) the fact that it starred Diana Ross and Michael Jackson.

10 FORMER DANCERS

1. Madonna
2. Ken Russell
3. Clare Francis
4. Toyah Wilcox
5. Christopher Beeny
6. Victoria Principal
7. Brigitte Bardot
8. Tracey Ullman
9. Suzanne Vega
10. Betty Boothroyd

10 WINNERS OF PERRIER AWARDS AT THE EDINBURGH FESTIVAL

1. Dylan Moran (1996)
2. Jenny Eclair (1995)
3. Lano & Woodley (1994)
4. Lee Evans (1993)
5. Steve Coogan In Character With John Thomson (1992)
6. Frank Skinner (1991)
7. Sean Hughes (1990)
8. Simon Fanshawe (1989)
9. Jeremy Hardy (1988)
10. Cambridge Footlights (1981) The intervening years (between 1981 and 1987) produced the winners, Writers Inc. (1982), Los Trios Ringbarkus (1983), Brass Band (1984), Theatre De Complicité (1985), Ben Keaton (1986) and Brown Blues (1987) but none of them went on to enjoy as much fame as some of the Footlights team which included Hugh Laurie, Tony Slattery, Stephen Fry and Emma Thompson.

10 SONGS FROM MUSICALS WHICH REACHED NUMBER ONE IN BRITAIN

1. *Happy Talk* by Captain Sensible (from the musical *South Pacific*)
2. *Don't Cry For Me Argentina* by Julie Covington (*Evita*)
3. *You'll Never Walk Alone* by Gerry & The Pacemakers (*Carousel*) The Crowd also had a Number One with this song in 1985 in aid of the victims of the Bradford City FC fire.
4. *Mack The Knife* by Bobby Darin (*The Threepenny Opera*)
5. *Climb Ev'ry Mountain* by Shirley Bassey (*The Sound of Music*)
6. *I Know Him So Well* by Elaine Paige and Barbara Dickson (*Chess*)
7. *Cabaret* by Louis Armstrong (*Cabaret*) It was a Double A side with *What A Wonderful World*
8. *Summer Nights* by John Travolta and Olivia Newton-John (*Grease* - which had been a stage musical before it was turned into a movie)
9. *Begin The Beguine* by Julio Iglesias (*Jubilee*)
10. *On The Street Where You Live* by Vic Damone (*My Fair Lady*)

10 POETS YOU MIGHT NOT HAVE BEEN AWARE OF

1. Damon Albarn. The lead singer of Blur reckons that "a song is a form of poetry and poetry is an amalgamation of songs. They are inseparable". He has written poems like 'essex dogs' which includes the lines "6am is awash in violet dulux/and the essex dogs are all loved up".

2. Bob Hoskins. The man who tells us "it's good to talk" (and who, as Harold Shand in *The Long Good Friday,* offered his enemies a choice of "frostbite or verbals") writes poetry under the pseudonym of Robert Williams on the basis that "Well, I wouldn't want to own up to them, would I?"

3. Eric Cantona. The mercurial former Manchester United star is a keen poet - as befits a man who prattles on about seagulls and trawlers when asked questions about footie. "I write about liberty," he has been quoted as saying, "and the search for personal freedom." He is not the only rhyming sportsman: Muhammad Ali used to write odes before his fights and the England cricketer, John Snow, had a book of his poems published.

4. Jack Dee. The lugubrious comic - a former waiter - has confessed to writing poetry for his wife Jane but he has yet to publish a volume of his verse.

5. Enoch Powell. The former politician was also a published poet. He wrote his first book of poems while he was at Cambridge University. "Tis true I loved you from the first,/Yet had I turned away,/I should have soon forgot my thirst/And happier been today,/And now your face is graven deep/Upon my inward sight/And when I wake and when I sleep/I see you day and night."

6. Paul Gascoigne. In 1993, the boy Gazza was asked to submit his favourite childhood poem for a book which was being sold in aid of The Malcolm Sargent Cancer Fund For Children. Gazza sent in a poem entitled *Just Me*, a poem he had written two years ago while he was in hospital with an injured knee. He was, of course, ridiculed but he's probably no worse a poet than Poet Laureate Ted Hughes is a footballer.

7. Susan George. The British actress, who starred in *Straw Dogs* and once dated the Prince of Wales, started writing poetry when she was 24. It coincided with "the losing of a love". She has said that "I just woke up one morning and started writing about my feelings". With a line like that, maybe she should have become a blues musician instead.

8. Ray Davies. The lead singer of The Kinks is not only (probably) the greatest lyricist in the history of rock and roll, he is also a published poet. Along with fellow rock musicians Damon Albarn and Patti Smith, he took part in the 1996 Poetry Olympics at the Royal Albert Hall.

9. Bobby Ball. The pint-sized comic partner of Tommy Cannon writes poetry because it "clarifies things for me". He says that his poems are "personal, truthful and from the heart" but that although he enjoys writing poetry, he doesn't read any as he finds it "very boring".

10. Steven Berkoff. The multi-talented British actor - a heavy in such films as *McVicar, Beverly Hills Cop* and *The Krays* - wrote *America*, a 1988 book which combined poetry and prose.

Chapter 3

Music

THE LAST 10 CHRISTMAS NUMBER ONES

1. 1996: *2 Become 1* (The Spice Girls)
2. 1995: *Earth Song* (Michael Jackson)
3. 1994: *Stay Another Day* (East 17)
4. 1993: *Mr Blobby* (Mr Blobby)
5. 1992: *I Will Always Love You* (Whitney Houston)
6. 1991: *Bohemian Rhapsody/These Are The Days Of Our Lives* (Queen)
7. 1990: Saviour's Day (Cliff Richard)
8. 1989: *Do They Know It's Christmas?* (Band Aid II)
9. 1988: *Mistletoe And Wine* (Cliff Richard)
10. 1987: *Always On My Mind* (The Pet Shop Boys)

10 ROCK STARS WHO PRODUCED NO. 1 HITS FOR OTHER ROCK STARS

1. Mick Jagger - *Out Of Time* (Chris Farlowe)
2. Barry Gibb* - *Woman In Love* (Barbra Streisand)
3. Pete Townshend - *Something In The Air* (Thunderclap Newman)
4. Dave Stewart - *A Good Heart* (Feargal Sharkey)
5. Lenny Kravitz - *Justify My Love* (Madonna)
6. Nick Rhodes* - *Too Shy* (Kajagoogoo)
7. John Phillips* - *San Francisco (Be Sure To Wear Some Flowers In Your Hair)* (Scott McKenzie)
8. Chet Atkins: *Distant Drums* (Jim Reeves)
9. Bruce Welch: *We Don't Talk Anymore* (Clfff Richard)
10. Jeff Wayne: *Hold Me Close* (David Essex)

*= Co-produced

10 PEOPLE WHO APPEARED IN POP VIDEOS

1. Neil Kinnock: *My Guy* by Tracey Ullman
2. Ian McKellen: *Heart* by The Pet Shop Boys
3. French and Saunders: *That Ole Devil Called Love* by Alison Moyet
4. Chevy Chase: *You Can Call Me Al* by Paul Simon
5. Frances Tomelty: *Sister of Mercy* by The Thompson Twins
6. Donald Sutherland: *Cloudbusting* by Kate Bush
7. Diana Dors: *Prince Charming* by Adam and the Ants
8. Joss Ackland: *Always on my Mind* by The Pet Shop Boys
9. Danny de Vito: *When The Going Gets Tough* by Billy Ocean
10. Frankie Howerd: *Don't Let Me Down* by The Farm

10 SONGS WHICH INSPIRED FILMS

1. *Coward of The County:* Kenny Rogers' 1980 hit about a supposed coward who eventually learns to fight became a 1981 film starring Mr Rogers himself as a preacher whose nephew is the 'coward'.

2. *Convoy:* Back in 1976 at the height of the CB radio craze, C.W. McCall released *Convoy* about a trucker trying to run a police blockade. Two years later, Sam Peckinpah directed a film based on the song starring Kris Kristofferson and Ali MacGraw. You copy?

3. *Torn Between Two Lovers:* In 1977, Mary MacGregor had a Top 5 hit with this corny ballad. In a 1979 film of the same name, Lee Remick is similarly torn between George Peppard and Joseph Bologna.

4. *Rock Around The Clock:* Bill Haley And His Comets' hit record caused teenagers to rip up cinema seats when it was featured in the credits of the 1955 film *The Blackboard Jungle*. The following year, Bill and the boys starred in a cheap film named after their classic song.

5. *Mrs Brown, You've Got A Lovely Daughter:* In 1965, Herman's Hermits had a U.S. Number One with this song. Three years later, the lads were cast in a film of the same name which attempted to cash in on the whole Swinging London phenomenon.

6. *Harper Valley PTA:* In 1968, Jeannie C. Riley had a hit with this song about a woman who is ruled to be an unfit mother by her local PTA. The 1978 film of the same name - starring Barbara Eden - took this story and showed the heroine getting even by exposing the members of the PTA as hypocrites.

7. *Yellow Submarine:* The 1966 Beatles' song - the only one to feature Ringo on lead vocals - was the inspiration for the 1968 animated film (co-written by *Love Story* author, Erich Segal) which has become a cult classic.

8. *Ode To Billy Joe:* Bobbie Gentry released this haunting song about a love affair which ends in suicide in 1967. In 1976, a film of the same title opened up the story of Billy Joe and his jump off the Tallahatchee Bridge.

9. *Lili Marlene:* This extraordinary song's place in musical history was assured when it became the only song in World War II to be adopted by both the Germans and the British. The song subsequently inspired a 1980 film of the same name starring Hanna Schygulla.

10. *White Christmas:* The song *White Christmas* - written by Irving Berlin - was so popular when Bing Crosby sang it in the 1942 film *Holiday Inn* that it was used as the title of a 1954 film - also starring Bing Crosby.

10 BRITISH SONGS WHICH REACHED NUMBER 1 IN THE U.S. BUT NOT IN THE U.K.

1. *Praying For Time* (George Michael)
2. *Venus* (Bananarama)
3. *I'm Telling You Now* (Freddie And The Dreamers)
4. *Together Forever* (Rick Astley)
5. *Sunshine Superman* (Donovan)
6. *Two Hearts* (Phil Collins)
7. *Mrs. Brown You've Got A Lovely Daughter* (Herman's Hermits)
8. *To Sir With Love* (Lulu)
9. *Money For Nothing* (Dire Straits)
10. *Wild Thing* (The Troggs)

10 UPDATED BEATLES' SONGS FOR THE 1990s

1. *I Think I'd Better Hold Your Hand*
2. *Sergeant Pepper's Darby And Joan Club Band*
3. *Get Back Pain*
4. *Home Help!*
5. *Can't Find Me Glove*
6. *I've Felt Finer*
7. *Bus Pass To Ride*
8. *When I'm 94*
9. *Large Print Paperback Reader*
10. *The Ballad of Yoko*

10 SONGS WHICH, AMAZINGLY, WEREN'T BANNED

1. *You Can't Always Get What You Want* (The Rolling Stones) 1969 song which was the B-side of *Honky Tonk Women* (itself a song about prostitution). The song is about a heroin addict trying to make her 'connection' and settling for what she can get.

2. *Walk On The Wild Side* (Lou Reed) There are so many allusions to sex, transvestites and drugs in this 1973 song about Holly who "plucked her eyebrows on the way, shaved her legs and then he was a she" that it's extraordinary that it wasn't banned.

3. *Eight Miles High* (The Byrds) While the BBC were busy banning The Beatles' *A Day In The Life, Fixing A Hole* and *Lucy In The Sky With Diamonds* for supposedly being about drugs, they allowed this 1966 song to be played. Unfortunately, it wasn't about ballooning but, rather, about the (reportedly, m'lud) pleasurable effects of narcotics.

4. *Pictures of Lily* (The Who) A song about the old five-finger shuffle (aka masturbation) which no-one at the BBC picked up on.

5. *Blinded By The Light* (Manfred Mann's Earth Band) 1976 song - written by 'Boss' Bruce Springsteen - which is also a paean to self-abuse. "In the dumps with the mumps as the adolescent pumps his way into his hat". Naughty but nice.

6. *Itchycoo Park* (The Small Faces) Wonderfully evocative 1967 song but there's no doubt what Steve Marriott is referring to when he sings, "What will we do there?/We'll get high". Interestingly, the song takes its title from the nickname of a London park where courting couples risked nettle-rash if they lay down in the bushes. Again, *Here Comes The Nice* is about a drug pusher nicknamed 'the nice' (see also Bob Dylan's *Mighty Quinn*). If you listen carefully, you'll hear Steve Marriott singing the praises of speed.

7. *Lola* (The Kinks) Typically, the Beeb got its knickers in a twist over this 1970 song's references to 'Coca-Cola' - necessitating <u>two</u> trips across the Atlantic by Ray Davies to re-dub the words 'cherry-cola' - and promptly missed the fact that *Lola* is a song about a transsexual.

8. *Turning Japanese* (The Vapours) The song's title apparently refers to the look on the face of a man who is enjoying himself in an er, 'manly' way.

9. *Pass The Dutchie* (Musical Youth) The 'dutchie' in this 1982 Number One song confused a lot of people. What was it and why was it so important to pass it? All confusion ends when you realise that said dutchie is a euphemism for a joint.

10. *Brown Sugar* (The Rolling Stones) The 'brown sugar' Mick sings about in this incredibly sexist and racist 1971 song with overtones of violence and domination, is of course a type of heroin and not, as I'd always assumed, Demerara sugar.

10 SONGS WHICH WERE NO. 1 ON BOTH SIDES OF THE ATLANTIC AT THE SAME TIME

1. *I Just Called To Say I Love You* (Stevie Wonder)
2. *I Feel Fine* (The Beatles)
3. *Maggie May* (Rod Stewart)
4. *Honky Tonk Women* (The Rolling Stones)
5. *Without You* (Nilsson)
6. *I Will Survive* (Gloria Gaynor)
7. *We Are The World* (USA For Africa)
8. *Billie Jean* (Michael Jackson)
9. *Bridge Over Troubled Water* (Simon And Garfunkel)
10. *Night Fever* (The Bee Gees)

10 STARS WHO WROTE (OR CO-WROTE) BRITISH NO. 1s FOR OTHERS BUT NOT FOR THEMSELVES

1. Joni Mitchell (*Woodstock* which was No. 1 for Matthews' Southern Comfort)
2. Bob Dylan (*Mighty Quinn* for Manfred Mann; *Mr Tambourine Man* for The Byrds)
3. Neil Diamond (*I'm A Believer* for The Monkees; *Red Red Wine* for UB40)
4. Carole King (*I'm Into Something Good* for Herman's Hermits)
5. Herbie Flowers (*Grandad* for Clive Dunn)
6. David Gates (*If* for Telly Savalas; *Everything I Own* for Ken Boothe and for Boy George)
7. Melanie (*Combine Harvester (Brand New Key)* for The Wurzels)
8. John Phillips (of The Mamas And The Papas) (*San Francisco (Be Sure To Wear Some Flowers In Your Hair)* for Scott McKenzie)
9. Johnny Bristol (*Love Me For A Reason* for The Osmonds)
10. Kris Kristofferson (*One Day At A Time* for Lena Martell)

10 LENNON & McCARTNEY SONGS NEVER ACTUALLY RELEASED BY THE BEATLES (apart from on the anthologies)

1. *Bad To Me* (Billy J. Kramer And The Dakotas)
2. *Nobody I Know* (Peter And Gordon)
3. *Like Dreamers Do* (The Applejacks)
4. *Tip Of My Tongue* (Tommy Quickly)
5. *Step Inside Love* (Cilla Black)
6. *That Means A Lot* (P.J. Proby)
7. *A World Without Love* (Peter And Gordon)
8. *I'm In Love* (The Fourmost)
9. *One And One Is Two* (The Strangers With Mike Shannon)
10. *It's For You* (Cilla Black)

10 COVERS OF BEATLES' SONGS

1. *Lucy In The Sky With Diamonds* (William Shatner)
2. *She Loves You* (Peter Sellers)
3. *I Want You (She's So Heavy)* (Donald Pleasance)
4. *We Can Work It Out* (George Burns)
5. *When I'm 64* (Jon Pertwee)
6. *Hey Jude* (Tottenham Hotspur FC)
7. *Ob-La-Di Ob-La-Da* (Jack Wild)
8. *I Want To Hold Your Hand* (Metal Mickey)
9. *Mean Mr Mustard* (Frankie Howerd)
10. *Can't Buy Me Love* (Pinky And Perky)

10 BEATLES' SONGS AND THEIR WORKING TITLES

1. *Hello Goodbye:* Hello Hello
2. *A Day In The Life:* In The Life Of
3. *Yesterday:* Scrambled Eggs
4. *It's Only Love:* That's A Nice Hat
5. *Think For Yourself:* Won't Be There With You
6. *Flying:* Aerial Tour Instrumental
7. *Eleanor Rigby:* Miss Daisy Hawkins
8. *Thank You Girl:* Thank You Little Girl
9. *Love You To:* Granny Smith
10. *I Saw Her Standing There:* Seventeen

10 REAL PEOPLE MENTIONED IN BEATLES' SONGS

1. The Queen *(Penny Lane)*
2. Edgar Allen Poe *(I Am The Walrus)*
3. Edward Heath *(Taxman)*
4. Sir Matt Busby *(Dig It)*
5. Charles Hawtrey *(Two of Us)*
6. Mao Tse-tung *(Revolution)*
7. Sir Walter Raleigh *(I'm So Tired)*
8. Peter Brown *(The Ballad of John And Yoko)*
9. Harold Wilson *(Taxman)*
10. Bob Dylan *(Yer Blues)*

10 SONGS ABOUT THE BEATLES

1. *All I Want For Christmas Is A Beatle* (Dora Bryan) This is the most successful Beatles' tribute record - which isn't saying much. It reached No. 20 in the British charts in December 1963.
2. *We Love You Beatles* (The Carefrees) And this was the most successful Beatles' tribute song in the U.S. It reached No. 39 in 1964.
3. *My Girlfriend Wrote A Letter To The Beatles* (The Four Preps) And, guess what?, they didn't write back...
4. *I Wanna Be A Beatle* (Gene Cornish And The Unbeatables) Soon after recording this cash-in tosh, Gene and the boys changed their names to The Young Rascals and made some real records (including *Groovin'*).
5. *Ringo I Love You* (Bonnie Jo Mason) An undistinguished disc save for the fact that Bonnie Jo was actually a pseudonym for...Cher.
6. *A Beatle I Want To Be* (Sonny Curtis) Sonny was one of Buddy Holly's Crickets which is significant as The Fab Four had named themselves after The Crickets.
7. *I Hate The Beatles* (Allan Sherman) As if they could care... Sherman was an American 'humorous' singer. His only British hit was *Hello Muddah, Hello Faddah.*
8. *Get Back Beatles* (Gerard Kenny) Mr Kenny holds two claims to fame: he wrote the song *New York New York* (not the Sinatra one but the one that goes "New York New York, so good they named it twice") and he also wrote the music for the theme song for *Minder.*
9. *I'm Better Than The Beatles* (Brad Berwick And The Bugs) Er, history would suggest otherwise...
10. *The Beatles' Barber* (Scott Douglas) Another supposedly funny song - this time about a man who has been put out of work because the Fabs never have their mop tops cut. Or something.

10 BEATLES' SONGS AND WHO OR WHAT INSPIRED THEM

1. *A Hard Day's Night:* Although the title was inspired by a comment from Ringo (as indeed was *Eight Days A Week*), John wrote the song for Julian, his baby son ("But when I get home to you, I find the things that you do, will make me feel all right"). It was for Julian, of course, that Paul wrote *Hey Jude* - to cheer the lad up when his parents split up.

2. *Something:* Written by George for his wife Patti. "Something in the way she moves, attracts me like no other lover". Unfortunately, she had the same effect on Eric Clapton who wrote *Layla* for her and then married her. They are of course divorced now but Eric and George are still best mates. Women, who needs 'em, eh?.

3. *Eleanor Rigby:* Although Paul claimed that he made up the story and the name, there is a gravestone of a woman named Eleanor Rigby ("Died 10th Oct. 1939 Aged 44 Years. Asleep") in St Peter's, Woolton - where Paul first met John at a church fete. Could be one of the greatest coincidences of all time.

4. *Lucy In The Sky With Diamonds:* Long after it wouldn't have mattered anyhow, John always insisted that this song had nothing to do with the drug LSD but rather was inspired by a picture painted by a schoolfriend of John's son, Julian. The girl in question was Lucy O'Donnell, 4, and Julian's description of her picture "Lucy in the sky with diamonds" evidently inspired one of his father's greatest songs.

5. *A Day In The Life:* This song was about lots of things but the line, "He blew his mind out in a car" was inspired by the death in a car of Tara Browne, an Irish heir (he was male, despite the name) who was related to the Guinness family. Browne was friendly with Paul and other members of the rock aristocracy.

6. *Things We Said Today:* Written by Paul for Jane Asher. "We'll go on and on". Alas not. Though where would the world of music have been without Linda McCartney?

7. *We Can Work It Out:* Once again for Jane Asher. "Try to see it my way", begged Paul, but the future cake queen would have none of it. Paul also wrote *You Won't See Me* for her - again to no avail

8. *You've Got To Hide Your Love Away:* Supposedly written by John 'for' Brian Epstein. The love that Epstein had to "hide" was, of course, his homosexuality. Whether or not John was also referring to any such relationship he might have had with his manager is a matter of interpretation.

9. *She Said She Said:* Written by John during his acid phase. John got the line "I know what it's like to be dead" when he overheard the actor Peter Fonda talking about a near-death childhood experience to George.

10. *She's Leaving Home:* Paul read a story in the papers about teenage runaway, Melanie Coe. Her father was quoted as saying, "I cannot imagine why she should run away: she has everything here" which has its echo in Paul's line, "We gave her everything money could buy". Amazing coincidence: unknown to Paul, he had actually met the young girl when he had presented her with a competition prize on *Ready Steady Go* four years earlier.

10 ARTISTS WHO HAD BIGGER HITS WITH LENNON AND McCARTNEY SONGS THAN THE BEATLES

1. Billy J. Kramer and the Dakotas: *Do You Want To Know A Secret?*
2. Peter And Gordon: *A World Without Love*
3. The Overlanders: *Michelle*
4. Joe Cocker: *With A Little Help From My Friends*
5. Marmalade: *Ob-La-Di Ob-La-Da*
6. Earth Wind And Fire: *Got To Get You Into My Life*
7. Billy Bragg: *She's Leaving Home*
8. Steve Harley And Cockney Rebel: *Here Comes The Sun*
9. Emmylou Harris: *Here, There And Everywhere*
10. Kenny Ball And His Jazzmen: *When I'm 64*

10 THINGS NOEL GALLAGHER SAID ABOUT LIAM GALLAGHER

1. "You don't speak for the band."
2. "Liam is in love with himself. He loves himself so much he can't love another person."
3. "I'm really proud of his singing and the rest of it, but some of the stuff he says and does is a bit out of order."
4. "He's a bigmouth, you know, all front."
5. "He's the most famous person in Manchester. The poor lad can't walk outside the front door without being Liam Gallagher, if you know what I mean, and getting beaten up or threatened at least."
6. "I hear him giving it all this gobs (boasting) and I think, 'shut up, I baby-sat for you'."
7. "He wishes he was me."
8. "Liam's the star. He's the singer, and singers have always been conceited tossers."
9. "I've given up advising him...if you tell a child not to put his hand in the fire, he'll put his hand in the fire. And he'll get burnt."
10. "Liam's a genius frontman but he'd be nothing without me."

10 THINGS LIAM GALLAGHER SAID ABOUT NOEL GALLAGHER

1. "You don't speak for the band."
2. "I hate this bastard."
3. "Noel's up there next to John Lennon in my book."
4. "Never one day goes by without me wanting to see our kid."
5. "He knows nothing about me and my life."
6. "I do write my own songs but I never show them to him."
7. "I'm sick of being in this fucking silly band. I think I'd be better off without them and they'd be better off without me."
8. "We go out. He turns up in a Rolls-Royce and I come in a taxi."
9. "I'm more of this band than he is, I'm the talent..."
10. "There's a fuckin' line there and we're right on the edge of it."

10 COUNTRIES WHICH FAILED TO SCORE A SINGLE POINT IN THE EUROVISION SONG CONTEST

1. Norway (1978)
2. Turkey (1983)
3. Spain (1965)
4. Finland (1982)
5. Italy (1966)
6. Lithuania (1994)
7. Luxembourg (1970)
8. Austria (1988)
9. Belgium (1962)
10. Monaco (1966)

10 ROCK STARS WHO GUESTED ON RECORDS

1. Peter Gabriel: played flute on *Lady D'Arbanville* by Cat Stevens
2. Billy Joel: played piano on *Leader of The Pack* by The Shangri-Las
3. Elton John: played piano on *He Ain't Heavy, He's My Brother* by The Hollies
4. Jack Bruce: played bass on *Sorrow* by The Merseys
5. Brian Jones played oboe on *Baby You're A Rich Man* by The Beatles
6. Mick Jagger: did backing vocals on *You're So Vain* by Carly Simon
7. Paul Weller: played guitar on *Champagne Supernova* by Oasis
8. Jimmy Page: played guitar on *You Really Got Me* by The Kinks
9. Billy Idol: did backing vocals on *Dancin' Clown* by Joni Mitchell
10. Ritchie Blackmore: played guitar on *Just Like Eddie*

10 BRITISH ACTS WHICH FINISHED SECOND IN THE EUROVISION SONG CONTEST

1. Matt Monro: *I Love The Little Things* - 1964
2. Kathy Kirby: *I Belong* - 1965
3. Cliff Richard: *Congratulations* - 1968
4. Mary Hopkin: *Knock Knock Who's There?* - 1970
5. The New Seekers: *Beg Steal Or Borrow* - 1972
6. The Shadows: *Let Me Be The One* - 1975
7. Lynsey De Paul And Mike Moran: *Rock Bottom* - 1977
8. Scott Fitzgerald: *Go* - 1988
0. Live Report: *Why Do I Always Get It Wrong?* - 1989
10. Michael Ball: *One Step Out Of Time* - 1992

10 BANDS AND HOW THEY DERIVED THEIR NAMES

1. THE BEATLES: All The Beatles were fans of Buddy Holly and The Crickets and so John decided to call his band The Beetles. Then he changed it to Beatles - a suitable pun for a beat band.
2. WET WET WET: They took their name from a Scritti Politti song, *Getting, Having And Holding*.
3. LEVEL 42: Took their name from *The Hitchhiker's Guide To The Galaxy* by Douglas Adams in which the number 42 is the answer to the "meaning of life".
4. EVERYTHING BUT THE GIRL: Took their name from a second-hand shop where everything was for sale except for the people who worked there.
5. PINK FLOYD: They named themselves after legendary bluesmen, PINK Anderson and FLOYD Council.
6. PREFAB SPROUT: As a child, singer Paddy McAloon had misheard the words "pepper sprout" in a Nancy Sinatra song as "Prefab Sprout" and that's the name he always wanted to give his band
7. IRON MAIDEN: After a medieval torture device (consisting of a metal form with spikes on the inside).
8. THE JAM: Took their name from the jamming sessions Paul Weller and Rick Buckler used to have at school.
9. THE POGUES: Short for the Gaelic words "Pogue Mahone" which literally mean "Kiss my arse".
10. OASIS The name came from a sports centre in Swindon.

10 ROCK STARS WHO SERVED IN THE MILITARY

1. Jimi Hendrix (Army). The guitar virtuoso joined the 101st Airborne Paratroopers in 1961 when he was 18. As a member of the elite Screaming Eagles squad he made 26 jumps in a year before breaking his ankle in a jump and being honourably discharged.

2. Bill Wyman (RAF). You've got to be very old (at least late fifties) in order to have done National Service and the former Stones bassist easily falls into that category. Wyman – born William Perks – served as a Air Craftsman First Class.

3. The Everly Brothers (Marines). Like Elvis Presley, both Don and Phil Everly were called up for military service <u>after</u> becoming major stars with hits like *Bye Bye Love, Wake Up Little Susie* and *All I Have To Do Is Dream*. In 1961, they joined the US Marine Corps Reserve for six months' active service, working as artillerymen handling howitzers.

4. Johnny Cash (Air Force). The country singer known as The Man In Black joined the U.S. Air Force after graduating from high school at the age of 18 in 1950. He spent four years in the USAF, serving in Germany and developing his musical career by forming a group and having his song published in the services' newspaper *Stars And Stripes.*

5. Billy Bragg (Army). In 1981, at the age of 24, the self-styled Bard from Barking joined the British Army following the break-up of his punk band Riff Raff. He was posted to a tank division but didn't enjoy it and he bought himself out after ninety days.

6. Bill Withers (Navy). The American singer-songwriter who brought us *Lean On Me* and *Ain't No Sunshine* spent a record (for a rock star) <u>nine</u> years in the Navy. Even after leaving the military, he didn't go straight into the music business, being well into his thirties before he released his first album.

7. Marvin Gaye (Air Force). The great soul singer joined the U.S. Air Force straight from school as a volunteer. In 1957, at the age of 18, he was given an honourable discharge when he asked to leave to pursue a musical career.

8. Terence Trent D'Arby (Army). Served in Elvis Presley's old regiment before going AWOL – Absent Without Leave – in Germany in order to become a rock star.

9. Hammer (Navy). The rap star – born Stanley Burrell and formerly known as MC Hammer – joined the Navy after failing to finish a college degree in communications and also failing to become a professional baseball player. He served for three years, being stationed in California for two and a half years and in Japan for six months before leaving to form a religious rap duo.

10. Kris Kristofferson (Army). The versatile repetitively named singer-songwriter-actor joined the U.S. Army in 1960 after studying at Oxford University as a Rhodes Scholar where he won a Blue for Boxing. He served for five years – learning to fly helicopters – before leaving with the rank of Captain. Surely the highest ranking rocker of all time?

10 RECORDS WENT STRAIGHT INTO THE CHARTS AT NUMBER ONE

1. *Going Underground* (The Jam)
2. *Get Back* (The Beatles)
3. *The Fly* (U2)
4. *Don't Stand So Close To Me* (The Police)
5. *Do They Know It's Christmas?* (Band Aid & Band Aid II)
6. *I Love You, Love Me Love* (Gary Glitter)
7. *Innuendo* (Queen)
8. *The Young Ones* (Cliff Richard)
9. *Bring Your Daughter...To The Slaughter* (Iron Maiden)
10. *Jailhouse Rock* (Elvis Presley)

10 CLASSIC NO.2s – AND WHAT STOPPED THEM FROM GETTING TO NO. 1

NUMBER ONE	NUMBER TWO
1. *Release Me* (Engelbert Humperdinck)	*Penny Lane/ Strawberry Fields Forever* (The Beatles)
2. *Son Of My Father* (Chicory Tip)	*Telegram Sam* (T.Rex)
3. *The Carnival Is Over* (The Seekers)	*My Generation* (The Who)
4. *Shaddap You Face* (Joe Dolce Music Theatre)	*Vienna* (Ultravox)
5. *In The Summertime* (Mungo Jerry)	*All Right Now* (Free)
6. *Grandad* (Clive Dunn)	*Ride A White Swan* (T Rex)
7. *Billy Don't Be A Hero* (Paper Lace)	*The Air That I Breathe* (The Hollies)
8. *Knock Three Times* (Dawn)	*Brown Sugar* (The Rolling Stones)
9. *Ernie (The Fastest Milkman In The West)* (Benny Hill)	*Jeepster* (T. Rex)
10. *Mouldy Old Dough* (Lieutenant Pidgeon)	*Donna* (10 C.C.)

10 GENUINE SONG TITLES

1. *Who Ate Napoleons With Josephine When Bonaparte Was Away* (written by Alfred Bryan and E. Ray Gotz in 1920)
2. *I'd Rather Be A Lobster Than A Wiseguy* (Edward Madden and Theodore F. Morse, 1907)
3. *(Potatoes Are Cheaper - Tomatoes Are Cheaper) Now's The Time To Fall In Love* (Al Lewis And Al Sherman, 1931)
4. *Hey Young Fella Close Your Old Umbrella* (Dorothy Fields and Jimmy McHugh, 1933)
5. *I'm Gonna Hire A Wino To Decorate Our Home* (DeWayne Blackwell, 1982)
6. *Aunt Jemima And Your Uncle Cream of Wheat* (Johnny Mercer and Rube Bloom, 1936)
7. *Come After Breakfast, Bring 'Long Your Lunch And Leave 'Fore Supper Time* (J. Tim Bryman, Chris Smith and James Henry Burris, 1909)
8. *I Love To Dunk A Hunk of Sponge Cake* (Clarence Gaskill, 1928)
9. *Caldonia (What Makes Your Big Head So Hard)* (Fleecie Moore, 1946)
10. *All The Quakers Are Shoulder Shakers Down In Quaker Town* (Bert Kalmar, Edgar Leslie and Pete Wendling, 1919)

10 ROCK STARS' NICKNAMES

1. Michael Jackson: Smelly
2. George Harrison: The Quiet One
3. Eric Clapton: Slowhand
4. Aretha Franklin: The Queen of Soul
5. Garry Glitter: The Bacofoil Bulk
6. Jerry Lee Lewis: The Killer
7. George Michael: Yog
8. Bruce Springsteen: The Boss
9. Alison Moyet: Alf
10. Phil Collins: Thumper

10 SONGS BASED ON CLASSICAL MUSIC

1. *I Believe In Father Christmas* (Greg Lake): Based on Prokofiev's *Lieutenant Kije Suite*

2. *It's Now Or Never* (Elvis Presley): Based on de Capua's *O Sole Mio*

3. *Stranger In Paradise* (Tony Bennett): Based on Borodin's *Polotsvian Dances*

4. *Sabre Dance:* (Love Sculpture) Based on Aram Kachaturian's ballet *Gayaneh*

5. *Lady Lynda* (The Beach Boys): Based on Bach's *Jesu Joy of Man's Desiring*

6. *More Than Love* (Ken Dodd): Based on Beethoven's *Pathetique Sonata*

7. *Could It Be Magic* (Barry Manilow): Based on Chopin's *Prelude In C Major*

8. *Joybringer* (Manfred Mann's Earth Band): Based on Holst's *The Planets*

9. *A Lover's Concerto* (The Toys): Based on Bach's *Minuet In G*

10. *All By Myself* (Eric Carmen): Based on Rachmaninov's *Piano Concerto No. 2*

10 ACTS AND THEIR IMPERSONATORS

1. The Rolling Stones: The Counterfeit Stones

2. The Stranglers: The Men In Black

3. Queen: Kween

4. The Beatles: The Bootleg Beatles

5. Elton John: Elton Jack

6. U2: The Joshua Trio

7. Oasis: Noasis

8. The Doors: The Australian Doors

9. Abba: Bjorn Again

10. Led Zeppelin: Dread Zeppelin

10 ROCK ACTS WHICH NEVER HAD A NUMBER ONE SINGLE IN THE UK

1. The Who
2. Billy Fury
3. Tina Turner
4. Bananarama
5. Elvis Costello
6. Kim Wilde
7. Prince
8. The Carpenters
9. Depeche Mode
10. Free

10 FORMER DRUMMERS

1. Rick Astley
2. Jim Davidson
3. Madonna
4. Mark King
5. Chevy Chase
6. David Essex
7. Andrew Neil
8. Joe Cocker
9. Russ Abbot
10. Frank Zappa

10 ROLLING STONES' SONGS UPDATED

1. *Fade Away*

2. *Time Is Not on My Side*

3. *Gimme Sheltered Accomodation*

4. *(I Can't Get No)*

5. *Paint It A Nice Shade Of Magnolia*

6. *Undercover Of The Electric Blanket Of The Night*

7. *Street Fighting Gran*

8. *(I Can't Remember) The Last Time*

9. *You Can't Always Get What You Want These Days*

10. *I Wanna Be Your Nan*

10 SONGS BASED ON OTHER SONGS

1. *El Condor Pasa:* (1933) Based on a Peruvian folksong

2. *Love Me Tender:* (1956) Based on George Poulton's *Aura Lee* (1861)

3. *Waltzing Matilda:* (1903) Based on Robert Tannahill's *Craigielea*

4. *Those Were The Days:* (1968) Based on a traditional East European tune

5. *Don't Sit Under The Apple Tree:* (1942) Based on *Long Long Ago* (1833)

6. *It's All In The Game:* (1951) Based on *Melody* by Dawes (1912)

7. *She'll Be Comin' Round The Mountain (When She Comes):* (1899) Based on the hymn *When The Chariot Comes*

8. *Hello Dolly:* (1964) Based on *Sunflower* by Mack David (1948)

9. *Midnight In Moscow:* (1962) Based on the Russian song *Padrnas Koveeye Vietchera*

10. *My Sweet Lord:* (1971) Based on Ronald Mack's *He's So Fine* (1962)

10 CLASSIC SINGLES WHICH DIDN'T MAKE THE BRITISH TOP 20

1. *I Don't Believe In Miracles* (Colin Blunstone)

2. *We've Only Just Begun* (The Carpenters)

3. *Stop Your Sobbing* (The Pretenders)

4. *Last Train To Clarksville* (The Monkees)

5. *Someone Saved My Life Tonight* (Elton John)

6. *Wouldn't It Be Nice* (The Beach Boys)

7. *Rikki Don't Lose That Number* (Steely Dan)

8. *Angel of The Morning* (P.P. Arnold)

9. *Year of The Cat* (Al Stewart)

10. *What A Fool Believes* (The Doobie Brothers)

10 CLASSIC ALBUMS WHICH NEVER GOT TO NUMBER ONE

1. *Bat Out of Hell :* Meatloaf

2. *Off The Wall:* Michael Jackson

3. *Are You Experienced?:* Jimi Hendrix

4. *An Innocent Man:* Billy Joel

5. *Makin' Movies:* Dire Straits

6. *Hotel California:* The Eagles

7. *Dark Side of The Moon:* Pink Floyd

8. *Hunky Dory:* David Bowie

9. *Blonde On Blonde:* Bob Dylan

10. *Tapestry:* Carole King

10 SONGS WHERE YOU WON'T FIND THE TITLE IN THE ACTUAL WORDS

1. *Ballad of John And Yoko* (The Beatles)

2. *Bohemian Rhapsody* (Queen)

3. *Ball Park Incident* (Wizzard)

4. *A Day In The Life* (The Beatles)

5. *Space Oddity* (David Bowie)

6. *Excerpt From A Teenage Opera* (Keith West)

7. *The Logical Song* (Supertramp)

8. *Jilted John* (Jilted John)

9. *Subterranean Homesick Blues* (Bob Dylan)

10. *Pyjamarama* (Roxy Music)

10 ROCK RUMOURS – ALL OF THEM <u>UTTERLY UNTRUE</u>

1. **PAUL McCARTNEY IS DEAD!** Among the many pieces of evidence were: On the inside cover of *Sgt. Pepper's*, Paul has a black armband bearing the initials OPD (Officially Pronounced Dead). At the end of *Strawberry Fields Forever*, John sings "I buried Paul" (Lennon claims that he really said "Cranberry sauce.") On the cover of *Abbey Road,* Paul is barefoot and a VW in shot had the licence number 28IF (i.e. the age Paul would have been if he'd lived). So who is Linda McCartney married to then?

2. **ALL THE MEMBERS OF TAKE THAT WERE GAY!** This was a nasty rumour put about by jealous guys and bitchy non-fans. The truth is that when Nigel Martin-Smith, their manager, took them on, he decreed that they shouldn't have any <u>regular</u> girlfriends in case it upset their female fans. This was the same thinking which 30 years earlier saw John Lennon hiding his wife Cynthia from the world.

3. **KEITH RICHARDS REGULARLY WENT TO SWITZERLAND TO HAVE A COMPLETE BLOOD TRANSFUSION!** Keith had a well-documented heroin habit which was mitigated by the fact that he had enough money to ensure that a) he always got the best 'gear' and b) was looked after when he was stoned. This was obvious but fantasists preferred to believe that the reason he could still function was that he was drained of all his blood and given fresh stuff. Frankly, for me, Keith's excesses were always a major part of the Stones' appeal and if he gets to 60, I want my money back...

4. **MARIANNE FAITHFULL ONCE HAD A 'FOURSOME' WITH MICK JAGGER, KEITH RICHARDS AND A MARS BAR!** Once again Keith stars in a rock legend. The truth of the story was that there was a drugs bust and Marianne was indeed unclothed. The rest is pure fantasy - denied by all the participants (though not the Mars Bar) - made up by either a journalist, a policeman or Peter Cook for *Private Eye* (as he himself later claimed). This is the one story that everyone has always <u>wanted</u> to be true. Sadly it isn't.

5. **ELVIS PRESLEY LIVES!** Oh no he doesn't - but you'd be surprised by the number of people who will give you an argument on the subject. Indeed, before we started importing Canadian tennis players, the odds against the King's reappearance were shorter than those for a British man to win a Wimbledon Singles title. The truth is that the belarded cheeseburger-guzzling, pill-popping, nappy-wearing King died of heart failure on August 16 1977. Despite all the sightings (many in Britain!), that's all there is to it.

6. **JIM MORRISON DIDN'T DIE!** Another (story/man) which refuses to die. As (most of) the world knows, the lead singer of The Doors, moved to Paris, in March 1971 and, four months later, was found dead in a bathtub. He was buried at Père-Lachaise cemetery alongside Oscar Wilde and Edith Piaf. Unfortunately, Doors' fans won't let him lie (and constantly make pilgrimages to Paris) - hence the sad - but completely untrue - rumours and sightings. These got worse after Oliver Stone's 1991 film.

7. **PAUL SIMON & ART GARFUNKEL WERE ONCE MARRIED!** Don't be silly. Even if they were gay, why get "married"? For the record, they are both straight and married - though not to each other - and have children (Simon used to be married to Carrie Fisher). Duos are often prey to this sort of rubbish - the same un-founded story was told of Marc Bolan and his percussionist, Mickey Finn.

8. **JOHN LENNON WAS MURDERED ON THE ORDERS OF THE CIA!** What is tragically unavoidable is that Lennon was murdered by Mark David Chapman on December 8 1980. However, paranoid Americans, having exhausted all the conspiracy theories surrounding the deaths of John F. Kennedy, Robert F. Kennedy, Martin Luther King and Marilyn Monroe, decided to exploit Lennon's admittedly not-very-good relations with the U.S. establishment to come up with a ludicrous story. The truth is that Chapman was an evil man acting alone.

9. **THE PET SHOP BOYS NAMED THEMSELVES AFTER A BIZARRE SEXUAL PERVERSION!** You know those stories (all, sadly, untrue) about a Hollywood star and his romantic involvement with a gerbil and/or hamster? Well, legend has it that The Pet Shop Boys' name alludes to this. In fact, the truth is much more mundane: Neil Tennant and Chris Lowe had some friends who worked in an Ealing pet shop.

10. **MICHAEL JACKSON AND LATOYA JACKSON ARE ONE AND THE SAME PERSON!** This starts from the wonderful premise that they've never been seen together so it could be *possible*! The same, of course, could be said for <u>any</u> two lookalikes. Leaving aside the fact that LaToya is clearly all woman (and darker than her brother) and disregarding the question of why he would <u>want</u> to be two people when he has enough trouble as one person, Michael and LaToya were actually seen together during the recording of USA For Africa's *We Are The World*.

10 ROCK STARS' FORMER GROUPS

1. Roland Gift: Acrylic Victims
2. Debbie Harry: Wind in the Willows
3. Holly Johnson: Hollycaust
4. Mark Knopfler: Brewer's Droop
5. Eric Clapton: Casey Jones & the Engineers
6. Mick Hucknall: The Frantic Elevators
7. Van Morrison: Deanie Sands and the Javelins
8. Adam Ant: Bazooka Joe & his Rhythm Hot Shots
9. Billy Joel: The Hassles
10. Paul Young: Kat Kool and the Kool Kats

10 SONGS BY NON-HUMANS

1. *The Wombling Song* (The Wombles)
2. *Sugar Sugar* (The Archies)
3. *Mr Blobby* (Mr Blobby)
4. *Halfway Down The Stairs* (The Muppets)
5. *The Smurf Song* (Father Abraham And The Smurfs)
6. *The Birdie Song* (The Tweets)
7. *Ruff Mix* (The Wonder Dogs)
8. *Orville's Song* (Keith Harris And Orville)
9. *'Fraggle Rock'* Theme (The Fraggles)
10. *Do The Bartman* (The Simpsons)

10 'B' SIDES WHICH BECAME 'A' SIDES

1. *Use It Up And Wear It Out* (Odyssey)
2. *Maggie May* (Rod Stewart)
3. *Toast* (Streetband)
4. *Move It* (Cliff Richard)
5. *I Got You Babe* (Sonny And Cher)
6. *Smooth Operator* (Sade)
7. *Kung Fu Fighting* (Carl Douglas)
8. *Bachelor Boy* (Cliff Richard And The Shadows)
9. *The Girl Of My Best Friend* (Elvis Presley)
10. *Unchained Melody* (The Righteous Brothers)

10 DOUBLE 'A' SIDES

1. *Sacrifice/Healing Hands* (Elton John)
2. *Rivers Of Babylon/Brown Girl In The Ring* (Boney M)
3. *The Model/Computer Love* (Kraftwerk)
4. *Please Don't Go/Game Boy* (KWS)
5. *Let It Rock/Memphis Tennessee* (Chuck Berry)
6. *Mull Of Kintyre/Girls' School* (Wings)
7. *Walk Right Back/Ebony Eyes* (The Everly Brothers)
8. *I Don't Want To Talk About It/First Cut Is The Deepest* (Rod Stewart)
9. *Penny Lane/Strawberry Fields Forever* (The Beatles)
10. *A Town Called Malice/Precious* (The Jam)

THE CANNED MUSIC TOP 10

1. *Moon River*
2. *The Way We Were*
3. *Yesterday*
4. *It's Impossible*
5. *Love Is Blue*
6. *El Condor Pasa*
7. *Don't Cry For Me Argentina*
8. *Sailing*
9. *Chi Mai* Theme
10. *Strangers In The Night*

10 SONGS WHICH FEATURED STUTTERING

1. *Mama Weer All Crazee Now* (Slade)
2. *My Generation* (The Who)
3. *Nineteen* (Paul Hardcastle)
4. *Can That Boy Foxtrot* (Millicent Martin & Julia McKenzie)
5. *Peggy Sue* (Buddy Holly)
6. *Barbara Ann* (The Beach Boys)
7. *Changes* (David Bowie)
8. *S-S-S-Single Bed* (Fox)
9. *Jive Talkin'* (The Bee Gees)
10. *Bennie And The Jets* (Elton John)

10 SINGING DRUMMERS

1. Phil Collins
2. Kevin Godley
3. Don Henley
4. Dave Clark
5. Levon Helm
6. Ringo Starr
7. Stewart Copeland
8. Jim Capaldi
9. Karen Carpenter
10. Mickey Dolenz

A LITERAL TOP 10

1. *ONE* (U2)
2. *TWO Little Boys* (Rolf Harris)
3. *THREE Times A Lady* (The Commodores)
4. *FOUR Strong Winds* (Neil Young)
5. *FIVE Minutes* (The Stranglers)
6. *SIX Pack* (The Police)
7. *SEVEN Seas of Rhye* (Queen)
8. *EIGHT Miles High* (The Byrds)
9. *NINE Times Out of Ten* (Cliff Richard)
10. *TEN Thousand Miles* (Michael Holliday)

10 ROCK STARS WHO HAVE PROVIDED MUSIC FOR TV THEMES

1. Chas and Dave: *In Sickness And In Health*
2. Eric Clapton: *Edge of Darkness*
3. Squeeze: *Girls On Top*
4. Alan Price: *Chalkface*
5. Dexy's Midnight Runners: *Brush Strokes*
6. Elvis Costello: *Scully*
7. Deacon Blue: *Take Me Home*
8. Charles Aznavour: *The Seven Faces of Woman*
9. Simple Minds: *The Justice Game*
10. Clannad: *Robin of Sherwood*

10 BRITISH HITS IN FOREIGN LANGUAGES

1. *Joe Le Taxi* by Vanessa Paradis (1988)
2. *La Bamba* by Los Lobos (1987)
3. *Je T'aime ... Moi Non Plus* by Jane Birkin & Serge Gainsbourg (1969)
4. *Dominique* by The Singing Nun (1963)
5. *Guantanamera* by The Sandpipers (1966)
6. *Ca Plane Pour Moi* by Plastic Bertrand (1978)
7. *(Si Si) Je Suis Un Rock Star* by Bill Wyman (1981)
8. *Da Da Da* by Trio (1982)
9. *Quiereme Mucho (Yours)* by Julio Iglesias (1981)
10. *Begin The Beguine (Volver A Empezar)* by Julio Iglesias (1981)

10 BANDS WHICH CAME UP WITH SOMEWHAT UNIMAGINATIVE SONG TITLES

1. *Doop* (Doop 1994)
2. *Immaculate Fools* (Immaculate Fools 1985)
3. *Jilted John* (Jilted John 1978)
4. *Living in a Box* (Living in a Box 1987)
5. *Love and Money* (Love and Money 1987)
6. *Natural Life* (Natural Life 1992)
7. *The Singing Dogs* (The Singing Dogs 1955)
8. *Small Ads* (Small Ads 1981)
9. *Talk Talk* (Talk Talk 1982)
10. *Tricky Disco* (Tricky Disco 1990)

10 INSTRUMENTALS WHICH REACHED NUMBER ONE

1. *Albatross* (Fleetwood Mac)
2. *Apache* (The Shadows)
3. *Mouldy Old Dough* (Lieutenant Pigeon)
4. *Eye Level* (Simon Park Orchestra)
5. *Wonderful Land* (The Shadows)
6. *Amazing Grace* (The Pipes And Drums And Military Band Of The Royal Scots Dragoon Guards)
7. *Dance On!* (The Shadows)
8. *Nut Rocker* (B Bumble And The Stingers)
9. *Telstar* (The Tornados)
10. *Foot Tapper* (The Shadows)

10 ROCK STARS WITH ROCK STAR PARENTS

1. Zak Starkey (Ringo Starr)
2. Sam Brown (Joe Brown)
3. Chesney Hawkes (Chip Hawkes)
4. Julian Lennon (John Lennon)
5. Ziggy Marley (Bob Marley)
6. Carnie Wilson (Brian Wilson)
7. Jason Bonham (John Bonham)
8. Kim Wilde (Marty Wilde)
9. Jakob Dylan (Bob Dylan)
10. Nona Gaye (Marvin Gaye)

10 ROCK GROUPS' PREVIOUS NAMES

1. Spandau Ballet: The Makers
2. The Who: The High Numbers
3. Madness: The Invaders
4. The Beatles: Johnny And The Moondogs
5. Creedence Clearwater Revival: The Golliwogs
6. Sweet: Sweetshop
7. The Beach Boys: The Pendletones
8. The Shadows: The Drifters
9. The Temptations: The Elgins
10. The Grateful Dead: The Warlocks

10 CELEBRITIES WHO RECORDED SONGS

1. Clint Eastwood: *I Talk To The Trees*
2. Leonard Nimoy: *Proud Mary*
3. Barry Cryer: *Purple People Eater*
4. Mae West: *Twist And Shout*
5. Terry Wogan: *Floral Dance*
6. Richard Chamberlain: *Love Me Tender*
7. Bernard Bresslaw: *Mad Passionate Love*
8. Hayley Mills: *Let's Get Together*
9. William Shatner: *Mr. Tambourine Man*
10. David McCallum: *Louie Louie*

Chapter 4

Sport

AN ENGLAND XI OF CAPTAINS

1. Graham Gooch (Essex)
2. Michael Atherton (Lancashire)
3. Colin Cowdrey (Kent)
4. David Gower (Leicestershire)
5. Mike Gatting (Middlesex)
6. Ian Botham (Somerset)
7. Alec Stewart (Surrey) (Wicket-keeper)
8. Ray Illingworth (Yorkshire)
9. John Emburey (Middlesex)
10. Gubby Allen (Middlesex)
11. Bob Willis (Warwickshire)

10 GREAT CRICKETERS WHO WERE NEVER NAMED AS WISDEN'S CRICKETERS OF THE YEAR

1. Wes Hall
2. Richard Collinge
3. Tony Lewis
4. Phil Edmonds
5. Eddie Barlow
6. Wasim Bari
7. Pat Pocock
8. Gubby Allen
9. Bishen Bedi
10. Doug Walters

10 SETS OF BROTHERS WHO HAVE PLAYED IN THE VERY SAME TEST TEAM

1. Ian & Greg Chappell (Australia)
2. Gary & Peter Kirsten (South Africa)
3. Dayle & Richard Hadlee (New Zealand)
4. Steve & Mark Waugh (Australia)
5. Peter & Graeme Pollock (South Africa)
6. Hanif & Mushtaq Mohammad (Pakistan)
7. Jeff & Martin Crowe (New Zealand)
8. W.G. & E.M. Grace (England)
9. Wasim & Ramiz Raja (Pakistan)
10. Brendan & John Bracewell (New Zealand)

AN ENGLAND CRICKET XI OF ONE-CAP WONDERS

1. Mark Benson (Kent)
2. Alan Butcher (Glamorgan)
3. Andy Lloyd (Warwickshire)
4. Paul Parker (Durham)
5. John Whitaker (Leicestershire)
6. Alan Wells (Sussex)
7. Wilfred Price (Wicket-keeper) (Middlesex)
8. Ken Palmer (Somerset)
9. Arnie Sidebottom (Yorkshire)
10. Tony Pigott (Sussex)
11. Neil Williams (Middlesex)

10 BATSMEN DISMISSED BY THE FIRST BALL OF A TEST MATCH

1. Sunil Gavaskar (India v. West Indies 1983-84)
2. Jim Morrison (New Zealand v. England 1974-75)
3. Sunil Gavaskar (India v. England 1974)
4. Keith Stackpole (Australia v. New Zealand 1973-74)
5. Roy Fredericks (West Indies v. India 1970-71)
6. Eddie Barlow (South Africa v. Australia 1966-67)
7. Conrad Hunte (West Indies v. Pakistan 1957-58)
8. Tommy Worthington (England v. Australia 1936-37)
9. Herbert Sutcliffe (England v. New Zealand 1932-33)
10. Warren Bardsley (Australia v. England 1926)

THE 10 JOCKEYS WHO'VE WON THE GRAND NATIONAL THE MOST TIMES

1. George Stephens (5 times)
2. Tom Olliver (4 times)
3. Mr Thomas (3 times)
4. Jack Anthony (3 times)
5. Tommy Beasley (3 times)
6. Arthur Nightingall (3 times)
7. Ernie Piggott (3 times)
8. Brian Fletcher (3 times)
9. Fred Winter (2 times)
10. Pat Taaffe (2 times)

10 THINGS SAID ABOUT CRICKET

1. "Cricket is a second-guesser's game. Worse even than baseball." (Mike Brearley)
2. "Personally, I have always looked on cricket as organised loafing." (William Temple, British churchman)
3. "That's what cricket is all about – two batsmen pitting their wits against one another." (Fred Trueman)
4. "Remember selectors don't make cricketers, the system produces them – for better or worse." (Alec Bedser)
5. "Sunday League cricket - multi-coloured pyjamas, two-tone umpires, and white balls with black seams. There is nothing like traditional English sport." (David Hunn)
6. "Amateur players would rather sweep roads or sell newspapers in the street than pretend to be first-class umpires." (Cross-Arrow)
7. "A cricketer - a creature very nearly as stupid as a dog." (Bernard Levin)
8. "[There is] the need to teach people how to think. That is what is missing in English cricket". (Brian Close)
9. "If she [Mrs. Thatcher] had been running cricket, England would be better off than they are." (Ted Dexter)
10. "There's no more amateurish professional game in the world." (John Emburey)

10 LORD'S TAVERNERS

1. Barry Norman
2. Kevin Lloyd
3. Robert Powell
4. Chris Tarrant
5. Bill Tidy
6. Gary Lineker
7. Henry Kelly
8. Sir David Frost
9. Rory Bremner
10. Leslie Thomas

10 THINGS ALL GRAND NATIONAL WINNERS HAVE IN COMMON

1. A jockey who has overcome injury or ill-health
2. A tendency to be "a bit of a character at home"
3. An ability to race at the back of the field for three miles
4. A trainer who wears a ridiculous pork pie hat
5. The luck to avoid being tipped by any racing tipster
6. An owner who "fancied the horse at 100-1 and backed him all the way down to his starting price"
7. An owner's wife who has absolutely no dress sense
8. A stable lad older than the jockey
9. A name which, afterwards, turns out to be entirely appropriate
10. "A heart as big as 'isself"

10 GREAT DRIVERS WHO NEVER WON THE BRITISH GRAND PRIX

1. Ronnie Peterson
2. Mario Andretti
3. Jochen Mass
4. Gilles Villeneuve
5. Graham Hill
6. Rene Arnoux
7. John Surtees
8. Jacky Ickx
9. Didier Peroni
10. Mike Hawthorn

10 MEN WHO HAVE BEEN RACEHORSE OWNERS

1. Bryan Robson
2. Freddie Starr
3. Nigel Dempster
4. Sir Andrew Lloyd Webber
5. Peter Shilton
6. Enn Reitel
7. Niall Quinn
8. Henry Kelly
9. Jim Davidson
10. John Virgo

10 MEN WHO SCORED A HOLE-IN-ONE IN GOLF

1. Jimmy Tarbuck
2. Mike Reid
3. Freddie Garrity
4. Richard Nixon
5. Graham Gooch
6. Bob Hope
7. Brian Jacks
8. Bing Crosby
9. Cliff Michelmore
10. Henry Cooper

10 RACES FOR SUNDAY RACING

1. The Homebase Stakes
2. The Traffic Cones Hurdle
3. The Post-Brunch Bathroom Sprint
4. The In-Laws Handicap
5. The Pre-Lunch Whitbread Trophy
6. The Village Church Steeplechase
7. The Car Boot Sale Selling Plate
8. The Spoilt Brats Chase
9. The Afternoon Hollywood Classic
10. The Elderly Relatives Stayers Cup

10 THINGS SAID BY MURRAY WALKER

1. "I make no apologies for their absence - I'm sorry they're not here"

2. "So, with half the race gone there's half the race to go"

3. "Now excuse me while I interrupt myself"

4. "Either the car is stationary or it's on the move"

5. "Patrick Tambay's hopes, which were nil before, are absolutely zero now"

6. "I imagine that the conditions in those cars today are totally unimaginable"

7. "I wonder if he's in the relaxed state of mind that he's in"

8. "The atmosphere is so tense you could cut it with a cricket stump"

9. "The lead car is absolutely unique – except for the one behind it which is identical"

10. "Do my eyes deceive me or is Senna's Lotus sounding a bit rough?"

10 WIMBLEDON FAVOURITES WHO NEVER WON THE MEN'S SINGLES TITLE

1. Ken Rosewall

2. Ivan Lendl

3. Fred Stolle

4. Pancho Gonzales

5. Ilie Nastase

6. Tom Okker

7. Tony Roche

8. Roger Taylor

9. Vijay Amritraj

10. Roscoe Tanner

10 SPORTS WHICH WERE NOT INCLUDED IN THE FIRST MODERN OLYMPICS (1896)

1. Rowing

2. Hockey

3. Equestrianism

4. Soccer

5. Yachting

6. Boxing

7. Archery

8. Basketball

9. Archery

10. Modern Pentathlon

10 RELATIVES OF OLYMPIC COMPETITORS

1. Grace Kelly (Her father, John Kelly, Rowing 1920)

2. Roddy Llewellyn (His father, Sir Harry Llewellyn, Showjumping 1952)

3. Jean Simmons (Her father, Charles Simmons, Gymnastics 1952)

4. Jonathon Porritt (His father, Arthur Porritt, 100 metres 1924)

5. Bobby Davro (His father, Bill Nankeville, 1500 metres 1948)

6. Charlotte Rampling (Her father, Godfrey Rampling, 4x400 metres 1936)

7. Prince Rainier (His son, Prince Albert, Bobsleigh 1988)

8. Sir Rex Harrison (His son Noel, Alpine Skiing 1952)

9. Tara Palmer-Tomkinson (Her father, Charles Palmer-Tomkinson, Skiing 1964)

10. André Agassi (His father, Mike Agassi, Boxing 1948 & 1952)

10 EXTRAORDINARY OLYMPIC CHAMPIONS

1. Harold Abrahams (U.K. 100 metres 1924) The *Chariots of Fire* hero had been selected for the 100 metres, 200 metres and the 4X100 metres relay when, a month before the Olympics, he broke the English long jump record and was duly selected for the event. An anonymous letter then appeared in the *Daily Express* criticising the selection of Abrahams in the long jump. Its author was Abrahams himself who managed to withdraw from the event.

2. Wyndham Halswelle (U.K. 400 metres 1908) This British veteran of the Boer War won his gold medal - without any opponents. In the first, void race, Halswelle was obstructed by Carpenter, an American who crossed the line first but was disqualified. Carpenter's American team mates refused to take part in the re-run and so Halswelle ran a solo race.

3. Stanislawa Walasiewicz (Poland 100 metres 1932) Walasiewicz - or Stella Walsh as she was known in her adopted country of America - only ran for her native Poland because the U.S. couldn't support her financially. She also finished second in the 100 metres in 1936. However, when the athlete was shot dead in Cleveland in 1980, the autopsy revealed that she was actually... a man!

4. Jim Thorpe (U.S. Decathlon and Pentathlon 1912) Thorpe, part-Red Indian, became a hero when he won his gold medals but in 1913, it was revealed that in 1909 and 1910, he had earned $25 a week playing minor league baseball. This infringed his amateur status and he was stripped of his medals by the Amateur Athletic Union. In 1951, Thorpe was portrayed by Burt Lancaster in *Jim Thorpe - All-American*. In 1982, the IOC lifted the ban on Thorpe and the following year, 30 years after his death, his gold medals were given to his children.

5. Ralph Craig (U.S. 100 metres 1912) Competed again in the Olympics 36 years later at the age of 59 - as an alternate in the U.S. yachting team.

6. Volmari Iso-Hollo (Finland 3000 metres steeplechase 1932) Iso-Hollo crossed the line with a 40-yard lead but there was no tape on the line and the lap counter read '1' - because the lap checker had forgotten to change the lap counter after the first lap. So Iso-Hollo set off on another lap and duly won the race by 75 yards in a race which was, by default, extended to 3460 metres!

7. Eleanor Holm (U.S. 100 metres backstroke 1932) In 1936, Holm, unbeaten for seven years, was on the ship heading for the Berlin games in the expectation of retaining her title. However, because she went to parties on board ship, got very drunk and shot craps, she was expelled from the team. She still had a good time in Berlin - meeting Goering who gave her a silver swastika which she had a mould made of and into which she put a diamond (Jewish) star of David.

8. Abdon Pamich (Italy 50 km metres walk 1964) Pamich won the gold medal but only after stopping at 38 km to throw up.

9. Melvin Sheppard (U.S. 1500 metres 1908) Sheppard, who went on to win another three Olympic gold medals, had applied to become a policeman but was rejected - due to a "weak heart".

10. Thomas 'Eddie' Tolan (U.S. 200 metres 1932) Tolan is the only man to have won a sprint gold medal while chewing gum! Unlike Paavo Nurmi, the winner of nine gold medals in 1920, 1924 and 1928, who always ran with a stopwatch in his hand.

10 WAYS IN WHICH THE BRITS ALWAYS TRIUMPH AT WIMBLEDON

1. Curtseying to the Royal Box
2. Quaffing champagne in hospitality tents
3. Losing gracefully
4. Queuing
5. Having the most humourless officials in the world
6. Charging over the odds for strawberries
7. Rain commentaries
8. Receiving the most wild card entries
9. Accepting dodgy line calls
10. Ticket-touting

10 NEW BOXING WORLD TITLES

1. BHS Paperweight
2. WWF Swelterweight
3. MEP Deadweight
4. WBA Hawthornweight
5. TWA Excessweight (scrapped)
6. RAC Longweight
7. BMW Cruisingweight
8. BBC Overweight
9. JPS Playerweight
10. REM Lightweight

10 MAJOR-WINNING GOLFERS WHO HAVEN'T WON THE OPEN CHAMPIONSHIP

1. Hale Irwin
2. Ray Floyd
3. Ian Woosnam
4. Lanny Wadkins
5. Craig Stadler
6. Payne Stewart
7. Ben Crenshaw
8. Fuzzy Zoeller
9. Bernhard Langer
10. Jose-Maria Olazabal

THE ONLY 10 COUNTRIES WHICH HAVE HAD MEN'S SINGLES CHAMPIONSHIP WINNERS AT WIMBLEDON

1. U.K. (35 wins. The most recent: Fred Perry in 1936)
2. U.S.A. (30 wins. The most recent: Pete Sampras in 1997)
3. Australia (20 wins. The most recent: Pat Cash in 1987)
4. Sweden (7 wins. The most recent: Stefan Edberg in 1990)
5. France (7 wins. The most recent: Yvon Petra in 1946)
6. New Zealand (4 wins. The most recent: Tony Wilding in 1913)
7. Germany (4 wins. The most recent: Michael Stich in 1991)
8. Spain (1 win. Manuel Santana in 1966)
9. Czechoslovakia (1 win. Jan Kodes in 1973)
10. Holland (1 win. Richard Krajicek in 1996). In addition, Jaroslav Drobny won the men's title in 1954 representing Egypt. However, Drobny was in fact a Czech but he was playing as an Egyptian when he won the title as he was obliged to declare a nationality. He later became British.)

THE LAST TEN BRITISH SINGLES WINNERS AT WIMBLEDON

1. Virginia Wade 1977
2. Ann Jones 1969
3. Angela Mortimer 1961
4. Dorothy Round 1937
5. Fred Perry 1936
6. Kitty Godfree 1926
7. Dorothea Lambert Chambers 1914
8. Ethel Larcombe 1912
9. Arthur W Gore 1909
10. Dora Boothby 1909

10 BOXERS WHO APPEARED IN FILMS

1. Joe Louis: *Spirit of Youth*
2. Jack Dempsey: *The Prizefighter And The Lady*
3. Primo Carnera: *A Kid for Two Farthings*
4. Terry Downes: *A Study In Terror*
5. Sugar Ray Robinson: *Candy*
6. Jersey Joe Alcott: *The Harder They Fall*
7. Henry Cooper: *Royal Flash*
8. Ken Norton: *Mandingo*
9. Muhammad Ali: *The Greatest*
10. Freddie Mills: *Carry On Constable*

10 KEEN SKIERS

1. Roger Moore
2. Kim Wilde
3. Stirling Moss
4. Don Johnson
5. Nick Ross
6. Paul McCartney
7. Gloria Hunniford
8. Jeremy Paxman
9. Faith Brown
10. Jason Donovan

10 BOXERS AND THEIR NICKNAMES

1. Roberto Duran (Stone Fists)
2. Thomas Hearns (Hitman)
3. Jake La Motta (Raging Bull)
4. Cassius Clay (Louisville Lip)
5. Mike Tyson (Typhoon)
6. James Douglas (Buster)
7. Barry McGuigan (Clones Cyclone)
8. James Smith (Bonecrusher)
9. Rocky Marciano (Brockton Blockbuster)
10. Jack Dempsey (Manassa Mauler)

10 ENGLAND CAPTAINS WHO CAPTAINED ENGLAND IN 1-10 GAMES

1. Peter Beardsley (captained England in one game)
2. Mick Channon (two)
3. Bobby Charlton (three)
4. Martin Peters (four)
5. Ronnie Clayton (five)
6. Alan Ball (six)
7. Terry Butcher (seven)
8. Gerry Francis (eight)
9. Stuart Pearce (nine)
10. Ray Wilkins (ten)

10 FORMER BOXERS

1. Bob Hope
2. Kris Kristofferson
3. Chris Isaak
4. Colin Moynihan
5. Eamonn Andrews
6. Terence Trent D'Arby
7. Berry Gordy
8. Norman Wisdom
9. Billy Joel
10. Mark McManus

10 BORING THINGS SKIERS SAY

1. "We found a wonderful resort where there were absolutely *no* queues"

2. "I can't believe that anyone could dislike skiing"

3. "There's nothing better than a hot bath after a hard day's skiing"

4. "I think you just <u>have</u> to buy your own skis"

5. "Of course I don't bother with the *après-ski*"

6. "I hate it when the snow's too powdery"

7. "I don't think three holidays a year is overdoing it"

8. "You can't beat skiing off-piste"

9. "I regard the money I spend on my equipment as an investment"

10. "Oh it was great, we played Trivial Pursuit <u>every</u> night!"

10 BORING THINGS NON-SKIERS SAY

1. "I'd like to get away from the snow thank you very much"

2. "I'm not paying a fiver for a pint"

3. "I can't afford to be off work with a broken leg"

4. "What's the point of going up a mountain just to go down it again?"

5. "You definitely wouldn't catch me going in one of those ski-lifts"

6. "The only thing that appeals to me is the *après-ski*"

7. "I'd be embarrassed to go on the nursery slopes with all the kids"

8. "When I go on holiday, I like to wear fewer clothes – not more"

9. "What's this Glue Wine they all go on about then?"

10. "I'd rather stay at home"

10 SOCCER SONGS WHICH MADE THE TOP 10

1. Baddiel & Skinner And The Lightning Seeds: *Three Lions On A Shirt (Football's Coming Home)* (1) 1996

2. Englandneworder: *World In Motion* (1) 1990

3. England: *Back Home* (1) 1970

4. England: *This Time (We'll Get It Right)* (2) 1982

5. Liverpool: *Anfield Rap (Red Machine In Full Effect)* (3) 1988

6. Chelsea: *Blue Is The Colour* (5) 1972

7. Scotland: *We Have A Dream* (5) 1982

8. Tottenham Hotspur: *Ossie's Dream (Spurs Are On Their Way to Wembley)* (5) 1981

9. Leeds United: *Leeds United* (10) 1972

10. Manchester United: *We All Follow Man United* (10) 1985

10 COUNTRIES WHICH BEAT ENGLAND AT WEMBLEY

1. Austria 1965 (3-2)

2. Brazil 1981 (1-0)

3. Denmark 1983 (1-0)

4. Holland 1977 (2-0)

5. Italy 1973 (1-0)

6. USSR 1984 (2-0)

7. Spain 1981 (2-1)

8. Sweden 1959 (3-2)

9. West Germany 1972 (3-1)

10. Uruguay 1990 (2-1)

10 THINGS YOU NEED TO BE A SOCCER MANAGER

1. Optimism
2. A sheepskin overcoat
3. A thick skin
4. A limited vocabulary
5. A tracksuit which doesn't quite fit
6. A large collection of packing cases
7. A surname which is long enough to be shortened by tabloid newspaper sub-editors
8. A map of motorway service stations
9. No sense of irony
10. The ability to withstand votes of confidence from the board

10 GOALKEEPERS WHO HAVE SCORED GOALS

1. Peter Shilton (Leicester City v. Southampton 1967)
2. Ray Charles (East Fife v. Stranraer 1990)
3. Steve Ogrizovic (Coventry City v. Sheffield Wednesday 1986)
4. Ray Cashley (Bristol City v Hull City 1973)
5. Steve Sherwood (Watford v. Coventry City 1984)
6. Andy McLean (Cliftonville v. Linfield 1988)
7. Iain Hesford (Maidstone United v. Hereford United 1991)
8. Alan Paterson (Glentoran v. Linfield 1989)
9. Pat Jennings (Tottenham Hotspur v. Manchester United 1967)
10. Andy Goram (Hibernian v. Morton 1988)

10 THINGS SAID BY SOCCER MANAGERS

1. "If you're in the penalty area and aren't sure what to do with the ball, just stick it in the net, and we'll discuss your options afterwards" (Bill Shankly)
2. "You're not a real manager unless you've been sacked" (Malcolm Allison)
3. "There are only two basic situations in football. Either you have the ball or you haven't" (Ron Greenwood)
4. "I've had more clubs than Jack Nicklaus" (Tommy Docherty)
5. "Last time we got a penalty away from home, Christ was still a carpenter" (Lennie Lawrence)
6. "I am a firm believer that if you score one goal the other team have to score two to win" (Howard Wilkinson)
7. "There's no fun in soccer any more. It's all deadly serious. We'll end up playing in cemeteries" (Terry Venables);
8. "Managers get too much of the praise and too much of the blame" (Sir Alf Ramsey)
9. "I promise results, not promises" (John Bond)
10. "I should have forgotten all about trying to play more controlled, attractive football and settled for a real bastard of a team" (Don Revie)

10 UNLIKELY CLUBS WHICH HAVE SUPPLIED PLAYERS TO THE ENGLAND FOOTBALL SIDE

1. 1st Surrey Rifles
2. Barnes
3. Hertfordshire Rangers
4. Uxbridge
5. Harrow Chequers
6. Swifts
7. Owlerton
8. Sheffield Heeley
9. Upton Park
10. Pilgrims

10 CELEBRITY FOOTBALL DIRECTORS

1. Jim Davidson: Bournemouth 1981 - 1982
2. Delia Smith: Norwich City 1996 -
3. Michael Grade: Charlton Athletic 1997 -
4. Arthur English: Aldershot 1981 - 1990
5. Jasper Carrott: Birmingham City 1979 - 1982
6. Elton John: Watford 1976 - 1990; 1991 -
7. Tommy Cannon: Rochdale 1986 - 1987
8. Sir Richard Attenborough: Chelsea 1969-1982
9. Norman Wisdom: Brighton & Hove Albion 1970 - 1978
10. Steve Davis: Leyton Orient 1997-

THE 10 MEN WHO CAPTAINED ENGLAND THE MOST TIMES

1. Bobby Moore (90 matches as captain)
2. Billy Wright (90)
3. Bryan Robson (65)
4. Kevin Keegan (29)
5. Emlyn Hughes (24)
6. Johnny Haynes (22)
7. Robert Crompton (21)
8. Eddie Hapgood (19)
9. Gary Lineker (18)
10. Jimmy Armfield (15)
10. Norman Bailey (15)
10. Peter Shilton (15)

10 PLAYERS WHO ONLY EVER SCORED ONE GOAL FOR ENGLAND

1. Nobby Stiles (in 28 games)
2. Mike Summerbee (8)
3. Alan Mullery (35)
4. Rodney Marsh (9)
5. Brian Kidd (2)
6. Emlyn Hughes (62)
7. Peter Withe (11)
8. Kevin Beattie (9)
9. Phil Thompson (42)
10. Stan Bowles (5)

10 GREAT SOCCER PLAYERS WHO NEVER WON AN F.A. CUP-WINNER'S MEDAL

1. Martin Peters
2. Tom Finney
3. Gordon Banks
4. Johnny Haynes
5. Malcolm MacDonald
6. Terry Cooper
7. Alan Ball
8. Peter Shilton
9. Tommy Lawton
10. Nobby Stiles

10 TOWNS OR CITIES WHICH USED TO HAVE FOOTBALL LEAGUE CLUBS

1. Stalybridge (Stalybridge Celtic)
2. Nelson (Nelson)
3. Newport (Newport County)
4. Gateshead (Gateshead)
5. Barrow (Barrow)
6. Aberdare (Aberdare Athletic)
7. Gainsborough (Gainsborough Trinity)
8. Accrington (Accrington Stanley)
9. Durham (Durham City)
10. Ashington (Ashington)

10 PEOPLE WHO PLAYED FOR – OR HAD A SOCCER TRIAL WITH – FOOTBALL LEAGUE CLUBS

1. Sir David Frost (Nottingham Forest)
2. David Essex (Leyton Orient)
3. The Duke of Westminster (Fulham)
4. Des O'Connor (Northampton Town)
5. Bradley Walsh (Brentford)
6. Mike Gatting (Arsenal)
7. Eddie Large (Manchester City)
8. Stan Boardman (Liverpool)
9. Angus Deayton (Crystal Palace)
10. Rod Stewart (Brentford)

THE 10 CLUBS WHICH HAVE SPENT THE MOST SEASONS IN THE TOP FLIGHT (i.e. in the First Division and/or the Premiership up to and including season 1996–97)

1. Everton (94 seasons)
2. Aston Villa (87 seasons)
3. Liverpool (82 seasons)
4. Arsenal (80 seasons)
5. Manchester City (72 seasons)
6. Manchester United (72 seasons)
7. Sunderland (71 seasons)
8. West Bromwich Albion (68 seasons)
9. Newcastle United (67 seasons)
10. Sheffield Wednesday (66 seasons)

AN ENGLAND SOCCER XI OF CAPTAINS

1. Peter Shilton (Southampton)
2. Alf Ramsey (Spurs)
3. Mick Mills (Ipswich)
4. Gerry Francis (QPR)
5. Billy Wright (Wolves)
6. Bobby Moore (West Ham)
7. Bryan Robson (Manchester United)
8. Ray Wilkins (A.C. Milan)
9. Gary Lineker (Spurs)
10. Johnny Haynes (Fulham)
11. Martin Peters (Spurs)

10 KEEN AMATEUR SNOOKER PLAYERS

1. Dennis Waterman
2. The Queen Mother
3. Julian Barnes
4. Brenda Fricker
5. Nicky Henson
6. Frankie Dettori
7. Dennis Skinner
8. Martin Amis
9. Mark Ramprakash
10. Paul Nicholas

10 REAL TENNIS PLAYERS

1. David Gower
2. Sally Jones
3. David Troughton
4. Martina Navratilova
5. David Wynne
6. Prince Edward
7. Lord Willoughby De Broke
8. Gabriela Sabatini
9. Sir Clifford Chetwood
10. Alan Alda

10 FENCERS

1. Marcel Marceau
2. Neil Diamond
3. Anita Harris
4. Bryan Mosley
5. Rocco Forte
6. Gene Wilder
7. J.P. Donleavy
8. David Acfield
9. Mick Fleetwood
10. Bruce Dickinson

A ONE-TO-TEN OF SPORTS TEAMS

1. Boxing
2. Doubles Tennis
3. Coxed Pairs Rowing
4. Polo
5. Basketball
6. Volleyball
7. Netball
8. Tug-Of-War
9. Baseball
10. Men's Lacrosse

10 SPORTING FATHERS AND SONS

1. Brian and Nigel Clough
2. Harry and Jamie Redknapp
3. Michael and Peter Scudamore
4. Tony and Mark Hateley
5. Richard and Mark Pitman
6. Joe and Joseph Bugner
7. Graham and Damon Hill
8. Percy and Peter Alliss
9. Harvey and Robert Smith
10. Sir Len and Richard Hutton

A NEWCOMER'S 10-POINT GUIDE TO RUGBY UNION

1. Stand-off: Someone who is too aloof to join the scrum
2. Conversion: Recipient of corporate hospitality finds that he actually enjoys the game
3. Scrum: Absolutely no chance of getting to the bar at half-time
4. Going blind: What eventually happens to players who fantasise about the game
5. Ruck: What would be illegal off the field is perfectly legal on it
6. Kick-off: The attempt to part a player and his head (see also Ruck)
7. Overlap: What happens to a forward's belly when he retires from the sport
8. Maul: Only for British Lions
9. Prop: What players do to the bar after the game
10. Sidestep: What married players must do if they encounter rugby groupies

10 PEOPLE WHO'VE DONE THE CRESTA RUN

1. David Gower
2. Julian Wilson
3. Gunther Sachs
4. Sandy Gall
5. Errol Flynn
6. Allan Lamb
7. Gianni Agnelli
8. Emma Freud
9. Duke of Kent
10. Walter Swinburn

10 CELEBRITIES WHO EXCELLED AT SPORT

1. Sir Jimmy Savile (All-In Wrestler)
2. Kathy Tayler (Modern Pentathlon Champion)
3. Julio Iglesias (Professional Soccer Player)
4. Johnny Mathis (High Jump)
5. Burt Reynolds (American Footballer)
6. Jeffrey Archer (International Athlete)
7. Samuel Beckett (Cricketer)
8. Sir Alec Douglas-Home (Cricketer)
9. Mr T (Wrestler)
10. Hugh Laurie (Rowing)

10 SPORTING KNIGHTS

1. Stanley Matthews (Soccer)
2. Bobby Charlton (Soccer)
3. Gordon Richards (Horse Racing)
4. Don Bradman (Cricket)
5. Malcolm Campbell (Powerboating)
6. Matt Busby (Soccer)
7. Richard Hadlee (Cricket)
8. Jack Brabham (Motor Racing)
9. Gary Sobers (Cricket)
10. Alf Ramsey (Soccer)

10 SPORTING RECORDS (ALL WORTHY OF BEING BROKEN)

1. *True Love* (Harvey Smith)
2. *Fog On The Tyne* (Gazza And Lindisfarne)
3. *We Shall Not Be Moved* (Big Daddy)
4. *You'll Never Walk Alone* (Jack Charlton)
5. *147* (Alex Higgins)
6. *Head Over Heels In Love* (Kevin Keegan)
7. *Fly Eddie Fly* (Eddie Edwards)
8. *Knock Me Down With A Feather* (Henry Cooper)
9. *Diamond Lights* (Glenn And Chris)
10. *Snooker Loopy* (The Matchroom Mob With Chas And Dave)

10 PEOPLE WHO'VE RUN THE LONDON MARATHON

1. Sir James Savile
2. Susan Tully
3. Eric Morley
4. Peter Duncan
5. Stephanie Lawrence
6. Graham Taylor
7. John Conteh
8. Gavin Campbell
9. Alan Minter
10. Nigel Dempster

Chapter 5

Animals

10 DOG OWNERS

1. Barbra Streisand   (Poodle: Sadie)
2. Steffi Graf   (Boxer: Ben)
3. Olivia Newton-John (Great Dane: Zargon)
4. Clint Eastwood   (Basset Hound: Sidney)
5. Madonna   (Chihuahua: Chiquita)
6. Charlton Heston   (St. Bernard: Portia)
7. Michael Keaton   (Border Collie: Dusty)
8. Barry Manilow   (Beagle: Bagel)
9. Michael Barrymore (West Highland Terrier: Candy)
10. Kevin Costner   (Labrador: Rosalita)

10 CAT OWNERS

1. Billy Crystal (Mittens)
2. Marie Helvin (Susu)
3. Lauren Hutton (Miss Mais Oui)
4. Cybill Shepherd (Olga)
5. Martin Shaw (Korky)
6. Jill Gascoine (Dodger)
7. David Hasselhoff (Kitty Kat)
8. Dame P.D. James (Cuthbert)
9. Jack Nicholson (Sugar)
10. Brooke Shields (Jingles)

10 PEOPLE AND THEIR UNUSUAL PETS

1. Ricki Lake (Cockatoo: Dudley)
2. David Bellamy (Budgerigar: Harry - who miaowed and turned out to be a female)
3. Burt Reynolds (Alligator: Fred)
4. Luke Perry (Vietnamese Pot-Bellied Pig: Jerry Lee)
5. Michael Jackson (Chimpanzee: Bubbles)
6. Shelley Duvall (Iguana: Twiggy)
7. Kirstie Alley (Chicken: Billy Idol)
8. Shannen Doherty (Dove: Pissaro)
9. Kim Basinger (Calf: Henry)
10. Robin Williams (Parrot: Big Sal)

10 PEOPLE WHO ADOPTED ANIMALS AT LONDON ZOO

1. Anthony Hopkins (Blackfooted Penguin)
2. Paul Young (Fruit Bat)
3. George Cole (American Alligator)
4. Marie Helvin (Black Rhino)
5. Letitia Dean (Chimpanzee)
6. Fiona Fullerton (Asian Elephant)
7. Andy Crane (Crowned Crane)
8. Steve Davis (Camel)
9. Rolf Harris (Koala Bear)
10. Robert Kilroy-Silk (Black & White Ruffed Lemur)

10 ANIMAL RIGHTS

1. Not to be anthropomorphised in Disney movies

2. Not to have to smoke untipped cigarettes in laboratories

3. Not to be "rescued" from barbaric Spanish villages by the *Daily Star*

4. Not to be filmed in the throes of sexual passion by Sir David Attenborough

5. Not to be named after TV weathermen or soap stars

6. Not to have to live on a city farm

7. Not to be patronised by Linda McCartney

8. Not to be used in hamburgers (apart from beef cattle)

9. Not to appear on *Blue Peter*

10. Not to be used in political photo opportunities

10 ANIMALS WHICH BECAME VERBS

1. Fox (to trick someone)

2. Pig (to devour food hurriedly and without manners)

3. Dog (to follow someone - particularly their footsteps)

4. Wolf (to eat ravenously)

5. Badger (to pester someone)

6. Monkey (to play around with someone or something)

7. Snake (to crawl on your belly)

8. Hog (to take all of something or keep it for yourself)

9. Stag (to sell a new issue of shares immediately)

10. Ape (to impersonate someone or something)

10 THINGS SAID ABOUT DOGS

1. "To his dog, every man is Napoleon, hence the constant popularity of dogs". (Aldous Huxley)

2. "A dog teaches a boy fidelity, perseverance and to turn round three times before lying down". (Robert Benchley)

3. "Anybody who hates children and dogs can't be all bad". (W.C.Fields)

4. "The greatest pleasure of a dog is that you may make a fool of yourself with him and not only will he not scold you, he will make a fool of himself too". (Samuel Butler)

5. "The woman who is really kind to dogs is always one who has failed to inspire sympathy in men". (Max Beerbohm)

6. "I loathe people who keep dogs. They are cowards who haven't got the guts to bite people themselves". (August Strindberg)

7. "A dog is the only thing on Earth that loves you more than you love yourself". (Josh Billings)

8. "That indefatigable and unsavoury engine of pollution, the dog". (John Sparrow)

9. "It is a terrible thing for an old lady to outlive her dogs". (Tennessee Williams)

10. "The censure of a dog is something no man can stand". (Christopher Morley)

10 THINGS SAID ABOUT CATS

1. "If a dog jumps onto your lap it is because he is fond of you but if a cat does the same thing it is because your lap is warmer". (A.N.Whitehead)

2. "You always ought to have tom cats arranged, you know - it makes 'em more companionable". (Noel Coward)

3. "Cat, *n*. a soft, indestructible automaton provided by nature to be kicked when things go wrong in the domestic circle". (Ambrose Bierce)

4. "We've got a cat called Ben Hur. We called it Ben till it had kittens". (Sally Poplin)

5. "There is something going on now in Mexico that I happen to think is cruelty to animals. What I am talking about of course, is cat juggling". (Steve Martin)

6. "When I play with my cat, who knows whether she is not amusing herself more with me than I with her?" (Michel de Montaigne)

7. "What cats most appreciate in a human being is not the ability to produce food (which they take for granted) but his or her entertainment value". (Geoffrey Household)

8. "A cat that lives with a good family is used to being talked to all the time". (Lettice Cooper)

9. "A dog is like a liberal. He wants to please everybody. A cat really doesn't need to know that everybody loves him". (William Kunstler)

10. "I would never wound a cat's feelings, no matter how downright aggressive I might be to humans". (A.L.Rowse)

10 ANIMALS AND HOW LONG THEY'RE PREGNANT FOR

1. African elephant (two years)

2. Rhinoceros (one and a half years)

3. Giraffe (one and a quarter years)

4. Porpoise (one year)

5. Horse (eleven months)

6. Polar bear (eight months)

7. Cat (nine weeks)

8. Dog (nine weeks)

9. Rabbit (one month)

10. Hamster (two weeks)

Chapter 6

Births

10 PEOPLE BORN IN BRITAIN WHO BECAME FAMOUS IN AMERICA

1. Cary Grant
2. Alexander Graham Bell
3. Ronald Colman
4. Charlie Chaplin
5. Elizabeth Taylor
6. Stan Laurel
7. Alistair Cooke
8. Boris Karloff
9. Ray Milland
10. Bob Hope

10 PAIRS OF PEOPLE BORN ON THE SAME DAY OF THE SAME MONTH OF THE SAME YEAR

1. Geoffrey Boycott and Manfred Mann (21.10.40)
2. Yoko Ono and Bobby Robson (19.2.33)
3. Prince Andrew and Leslie Ash (19.2.60)
4. John Motson and Virginia Wade (10.7.45)
5. Maureen Lipman and Donovan (10.5.46)
6. Ian Dury and Susan Hampshire (11.5.42)
7. Harvey Smith and Jon Voight (29.12.38)
8. Sheila Hancock and The Duchess of Kent (22.2.33)
9. Virginia Bottomley and James Taylor (12.3.48)
10. John Major and Eric Idle (29.3.43)

10 FAMOUS PEOPLE BORN ON THE VERY SAME DAY AS ANOTHER FAMOUS PERSON DIED

1. Anthea Redfern and Ernest Bevin: 14.4.1951
2. Derek Dougan and King George V: 20.1.1956
3. Donna Summer and Sir Malcolm Campbell: 31.12.1948
4. Adam Ant and Henri Matisse: 3.11.1954
5. Telly Savalas and V.I. Lenin: 21.1.1924
6. Frank Zappa and F. Scott Fitzgerald: 21.12.1940
7. Che Guevara and Emmeline Pankhurst: 14.6.1928
8. Sir James Savile and Harry Houdini: 31.10.1926
9. Johnny Rotten and A.A. Milne: 31.1.1956
10. Barry Sheene and Field Marshal Jan Christian Smuts: 11.9.1950

10 AMERICANS WHO WERE BORN ON THE FOURTH OF JULY

1. President Calvin Coolidge
2. Louis Armstrong
3. James Bailey (of Barnum and Bailey)
4. Neil Simon
5. George M. Cohan
6. Pam Shrivor
7. Stephen Foster
8. Louis B. Mayer
9. Bill Withers
10. John Oates

10 BRITS BORN ABROAD

1. Terry Butcher (Singapore)
2. Nicola Pagett (Egypt)
3. Gyles Brandreth (Germany)
4. Thomas Dolby (Egypt)
5. Lionel Blair (Canada)
6. Katie Boyle (Italy)
7. Chris de Burgh (Argentina)
8. Pamela Armstrong (Borneo)
9. Ted Dexter (Italy)
10. Nicola Pagett (Egypt)

10 PEOPLE BORN ON APRIL FOOLS' DAY

1. David Gower
2. George Baker
3. Ali MacGraw
4. Phillip Schofield
5. Ronnie Lane
6. Otto von Bismarck
7. Debbie Reynolds
8. Carol White
9. Edgar Wallace
10. Michael Praed

10 PEOPLE BORN ON CHRISTMAS DAY

1. Stuart Hall
2. Annie Lennox
3. Sir Isaac Newton
4. Princess Alexandra
5. Quentin Crisp
6. Sissy Spacek
7. Kenny Everett
8. Anwar Sadat
9. Noele Gordon
10. Shane MacGowan

10 PEOPLE BORN IN GERMANY

1. John McEnroe
2. Andre Previn
3. Marsha Fitzalan
4. Charles Wheeler
5. Jackson Browne
6. Peter Alliss
7. Bruce Willis
8. Ruth Prawer Jhabvala
9. Paul Ackford
10. Andrew Sachs

10 PEOPLE BORN ILLEGITIMATE

1. T.E. Lawrence. Had an aristocratic father but was "born on the wrong side of the blanket".

2. William The Conqueror. Known as the Bastard of Normandy - for obvious reasons.

3. Richard Wagner. Because of his lowly birth his early life was characterised by financial struggle and he finished one of his operas whilst living in a debtors' prison.

4. Sophia Loren. Born illegitimate in 1934, she grew up in poverty in Naples - often eating nothing more in a day than a slice of bread and a teaspoon of sugar.

5. Willy Brandt. Born Karl Herbert Frahm, he changed his name after fleeing to Norway to escape the Nazis.

6. Sir Alec Guinness. The great actor only discovered his true father - and his surname - when he was 14.

7. Sarah Bernhardt. She had troubled schooldays (being suspended three times) which could possibly be linked to her illegitimacy.

8. Derek Jameson. He never knew his father and was brought up by a lady known as Ma Wren who, in his words, "raised over 70 children - rejects, abandoned waifs, some of them dumped on her doorstep - and never had a penny from anyone".

9. Leonardo da Vinci. The greatest artist in the history of the world? (discuss using both sides of the paper) was born the illegitimate son of a Florentine notary (a sort of lawyer).

10. Jeremy Beadle. The TV presenter and trivia-meister prefers to remember the wonderful mother who went out to work to provide for him rather than to dwell on the absent father who was married to another woman.

10 PEOPLE BORN ON LEAP YEAR DAY (February 29th)

1. James Ogilvy
2. Joss Ackland
3. Jimmy Dorsey
4. Mario Andretti
5. Gioacchino Rossini
6. Ranchhodji Desai (late Indian Prime Minister)
7. John Holland (Irish-American inventor of the submarine)
8. Gretchen Christopher (a member of The Fleetwoods, an American 'doo-wop' group famous in the 1950s)
9. William Wellman (late American director who won a writing Oscar for the 1937 version of *A Star Is Born*)
10. Ann Lee (founder of the American Society of Shakers)

10 PEOPLE BORN IN INDIA

1. Spike Milligan
2. Joanna Lumley
3. Angela Thorne
4. Cliff Richard
5. Nigel Dempster
6. Engelbert Humperdinck
7. Colin Cowdrey
8. Tiny Rowland
9. Lindsay Anderson
10. John Aspinall

10 PEOPLE BORN IN AFRICA

1. Fiona Fullerton (Nigeria)
2. Claudia Cardinale (Tunisia)
3. Derek Pringle (Kenya)
4. Glynis Barber (South Africa)
5. Alan Whicker (Egypt)
6. Stephanie Beacham (Morocco)
7. Patrick Allen (Nyasaland)
8. Freddie Mercury (Zanzibar)
9. Moira Lister (South Africa)
10. Phil Edmonds (Zambia)

10 PEOPLE BORN IN CANADA

1. Saul Bellow
2. David Jensen
3. William Shatner
4. k.d. lang
5. Joni Mitchell
6. Bryan Adams
7. Leonard Cohen
8. Margot Kidder
9. Michael J. Fox
10. Donald Sutherland

10 PARENTS OF TWINS

1. Michael Aspel
2. Dr. Hilary Jones
3. Margaret Thatcher
4. Mel Gibson
5. Mark Knopfler
6. Judy Finnigan
7. Stan Boardman
8. Jayne Irving
9. Sir Geoffrey Howe
10. Cybill Shepherd

10 PEOPLE BORN ON BOXING DAY

1. Thomas Gray (Poet, born in 1716)
2. Henry Miller (Writer, 1891)
3. Chairman Mao Tse-Tung (Leader of China, 1893)
4. Irene Handl (Actress, 1902)
5. Richard Widmark (Actor, 1914)
6. Denis Quilley (Actor, 1927)
7. Rohan Kanhai (Cricketer, 1935)
8. Phil Spector (Record producer, 1940)
9. Jane Lapotaire (Actress, 1944)
10. Richard Skinner (DJ, 1951)

Chapter 7

Deaths

10 ROCK AND ROLL SUICIDES

1. Bobby Bloom
2. Kurt Cobain (Nirvana)
3. Johnny Ace
4. Richard Manuel (The Band)
5. Ian Curtis (Joy Division)
6. Pete Ham (Badfinger)
7. Terry Kath (Chicago)
8. Ron 'Pigpen' McKernan (Grateful Dead)
9. Donnie Hathaway
10. Paul Williams (The Temptations)

10 PEOPLE WHO KILLED THEMSELVES

1. Cleopatra
2. Ronnie Scott
3. Ernest Hemingway
4. Brian Epstein
5. Joseph Goebbels
6. George Sanders
7. Tony Hancock
8. Terence Donovan
9. Ted Moult
10. Adolf Hitler

10 PAIRS OF PEOPLE WHO DIED ON THE SAME DAY OF THE SAME MONTH OF THE SAME YEAR

1. Orville Wright and Mahatma Gandhi (30.1.1948)
2. Clark Gable and Gilbert Harding (16.11.1960)
3. Josef Stalin and Sergei Prokofiev (5.3.1953)
4. Maria Callas and Marc Bolan (16.9.1977)
5. Sir Anthony Eden (the Earl of Avon) and Peter Finch (14.1.1977)
6. Joyce Grenfell and Zeppo Marx (30.11.1979)
7. David Niven and Raymond Massey (29.7.1983)
8. River Phoenix (actor) & Federico Fellini (film director) (31.10.93)
9. Orson Welles and Yul Brynner (10.10.1985)
10. Jim Laker and Otto Preminger (23.4.1986)

10 PEOPLE WHOSE 'PARTS' WERE PRESERVED AFTER THEIR DEATHS

1. Albert Einstein's brain
2. Percy Bysshe Shelley's heart
3. Galileo's finger
4. Lenin's brain
5. Joseph Haydn's head
6. Napoleon's penis
7. Dr. David Livingstone's heart
8. George Washington's tooth
9. King Richard II's jawbone
10. Thomas Hardy's heart

10 MUSICIANS WHO DIED IN PLANE CRASHES

1. Buddy Holly (1959) On February 2 1959, the 22-year old Holly played a gig in Iowa and then at 1.00 in the morning, he and his friends went to the airport and paid $36 for a light aircraft to take them to North Dakota for their next gig. The plane crashed into a field just minutes after take-off, thus killing the man who gave us *That'll Be The Day, Peggy Sue* and *Oh Boy!*.

2. J.P. Richardson (The Big Bopper) (1959) The Big Bopper, who had a classic hit with *Chantilly Lace,* wasn't meant to be on the plane that killed Buddy Holly. He had a bad cold at the time and, irked at the fact that the tour bus had broken down the day before, he asked Waylon Jennings (now of course a famous country-and-western star) if he could have his seat on the plane. Jennings obliged - luckily for him but tragically unluckily for Richardson who died at the age of 28.

3. Ritchie Valens (1959) Valens, the man who brought us *La Bamba*, was the third great rock star to lose his life on that flight. Like the Big Bopper, he hadn't originally planned to be on the plane. His place was originally going to be filled by guitarist Tommy Allsup but Valens persuaded him to toss a coin to see who would get the seat. Valens 'won'. He was just 17.

4. Glenn Miller (1944) As anyone who's seen *The Glenn Miller Story* will know, Miller was a trombonist who formed a bestselling band which had hits with *In The Mood* and *Moonlight Serenade*. On December 15 1944, following a visit to Britain, the 40-year old bandleader boarded a plane which disappeared over the English Channel. After his death (as with Elvis and Jim Morrison) there was much speculation as to whether he had actually died but the sad truth is that he did.

5. Jim Croce (1973) On September 20 1973, the 30-year old American star responsible for *Time In A Bottle* and *You Don't Mess Around With Jim*, performed a concert in Louisiana. He boarded a twin-engined chartered aircraft to take him to his second gig of the day. Unfortunately, the plane crashed on take-off, killing Croce and five other people. He had a posthumous hit with *I'll Have To Say I Love You In A Song*.

6. Otis Redding (1967) The great soul singer was just 26 years old when, on December 10 1967, the plane carrying him and his backing band, The Bar-Kays, crashed into Lake Monoma, Wisconsin - killing Redding and all the other passengers (save one of The Bar-Kays). Just three days earlier, Redding had recorded *(Sittin' On) The Dock of The Bay* which became a huge hit after his death.

7. Lynyrd Skynyrd (1977) The American band - named after a hated gym teacher - which had a huge worldwide hit with the haunting *Free Bird* was devastated by a plane crash on October 20 1977. The band were in a rented plane which ran short of fuel on a journey from Greenville, South Carolina to Baton Rouge, Louisiana and crashed into a swamp. Steve Gaines, his sister Cassie (a backing-singer with the band) and Ronnie Van Zant were all killed. The rest of the band survived.

8. Stevie Ray Vaughan (1990) This great American blues guitarist was killed in a helicopter crash at the age of 35. It occurred on August 27 1990 on a journey to Chicago following a gig in Wisconsin which had ended with a jam session featuring Eric Clapton and Robert Cray. At his memorial service four days later, Stevie Wonder, Jackson Browne and Bonnie Raitt sang *Amazing Grace*.

9. Rick Nelson (1985) The American singer - a teen idol of the 1950s - who had hits with *Poor Little Fool, It's Late, Hello Mary Lou* and *Garden Party*, died on New Year's Eve 1985, aged 45. The plane carrying him, his fiancee and members of his backing band and entourage from a gig in Alabama to one in Texas caught fire and crashed.

10. Jim Reeves (1964) Before his death at the age of 40, this American singer had hits with songs like *Welcome To My World* and *I Love You Because* but his only British Number One, *Distant Drums*, taken from a demo, was released after his death. Reeves was a reluctant flyer and so he got his own daytime pilot's licence. On July 31, he and his manager/pianist were in a single-engined plane which crashed into woods outside Nashville, Tennessee during a storm. Both men were killed.

10 PEOPLE WHO DIED IN ROAD ACCIDENTS

1. Eddie Cochran. The American rock star who had hits with *Summertime Blues, C'mon Everybody* and *Three Steps To Heaven*, was in a car crash on the A4 near Chippenham, Wiltshire on April 17 1960 on a journey from Bristol to London. He went through a car windscreen and died in hospital some hours later. Also injured was fellow rocker Gene Vincent. One of the local policemen on the scene was the 16-year old cadet David Harman, who later became Dave Dee of Dave Dee, Dozy, Beaky, Mick and Tich.

2. David Penhaligon. The exceptionally popular (with MPs and supporters from all parties) 42-year old Liberal MP for Truro died when a van hit his car in Cornwall on December 22nd 1986.

3. Albert Camus. The Nobel Prize-winning (for Literature) author and philosopher died on January 4th 1960 at the age of 46 in Villeneuve-La-Guyard in France. Camus played in goal for the Algerian national soccer team.

4. Marc Bolan. The British rock star who created and fronted the glam rock band T Rex - which had hits with songs like *Hot Love, Metal Guru* and *Get It On* - died on September 19th 1977 when the car he was in hit a tree in London. He was just 29 years old.

5. Margaret Mitchell. The American authoress, whose only novel was the phenomenally successful *Gone With The Wind*, died in a car crash on August 16th 1949 at the age of 49 in - where else? - Atlanta, Georgia.

6. Duane Allman. The 24-year old American rock star - a founder member of The Allman Brothers Band - died on October 29th 1971 after crashing his motor-cycle in an attempt to avoid colliding with a truck. He was rushed to hospital but after three hours of intensive surgery, he died. He's best remembered today for his slide guitar work on Eric Clapton's *Layla*.

7. Jayne Mansfield. The Hollywood actress was killed in a car accident near New Orleans, Louisiana, on June 29 1967 at the age of 34. Originally launched as a Marilyn Monroe lookalike, she was far funnier and much more talented than that.

8. James Dean. The 24-year old Hollywood star of films like *Rebel Without A Cause* died when his Porsche crashed in Cholame, California on September 30th 1955. Spookily, the British actor, Sir Alec Guinness had foretold Dean's death only a few days earlier.

9. General George S. Patton. The American General - known as 'Blood and Guts' Patton, survived World War II only to die in a car accident in Heidelberg, Germany on December 21 1945 at the age of 60. He was portrayed by George C. Scott in a film biography of his life.

10. Grace Kelly. The ice-cool beautiful Hollywood actress - who starred in films like *Rear Window* and *High Society* - and Princess of Monaco died at the age of 52 on September 15 1982 when the car she and her daughter, Princess Stephanie, were travelling in plunged off a mountain road near Monte Carlo. Neither she nor her daughter were wearing safety-belts.

10 PEOPLE WHO DIED YOUNG

1. Otis Redding (26)
2. Edward VI (15)
2. Lady Jane Grey (16)
3. Joan of Arc (19)
4. Duncan Edwards (21)
5. James Dean (24)
6. John Keats (25)
7. Aubrey Beardsley (25)
8. Buddy Holly (22)
9. Jean Harlow (26)
10. River Phoenix (23)

10 PEOPLE WHO ACHIEVED MORE AFTER DEATH THAN DURING THEIR LIFETIME

1. Jim Reeves
2. Anne Frank
3. James Dean
4. Steve Biko
5. Johann Sebastian Bach
6. Karl Marx
7. J. Sainsbury
8. Sigmund Freud
9. Vincent van Gogh
10. Jesus Christ

10 EXTRAORDINARY BEQUESTS

1. In 1987, Bob Fosse, the choreographer and film director (he won an Oscar for *Cabaret*) left $378.79 to each of 66 people to "go out and have dinner on me". These included Liza Minnelli, Dustin Hoffman, Melanie Griffith, Neil Simon, Ben Gazzara, Jessica Lange and Roy Scheider (who played a character based on Fosse in *All That Jazz*).

2. In 1950, George Bernard Shaw left a considerable portion of his estate for the purpose of replacing the standard English alphabet of 26 letters with a more efficient alphabet of at least 40 letters.

3. In 1946, W.C. Fields left money for a "W.C. Fields College for orphan white boys and girls, where no religion of any sort is to be preached". It never happened because Fields's estranged wife successfully contested the will.

4. In 1986, Cary Grant bequeathed all of his "wearing apparel, ornaments and jewellery" to Stanley E. Fox on condition that Mr Fox shared everything out among 14 specified people - one of whom was Frank Sinatra.

5. An unnamed Scotsman bequeathed each of his two daughters her weight in £1 notes. The elder, slimmer daughter received £51,200 while her younger, fatter sister got £57,433. Who says you can't be too slim?

6. In 1975, Edward Horley, a former Mayor of Altrincham, instructed his solicitors to buy a lemon, cut it in two and send one half to the income tax inspectorate and the other half to the tax collector with the message "Now squeeze this".

7. In 1964, Ian Fleming, the writer who created James Bond, left four friends £500 each with the wish that they should "spend the same within twelve months of receipt in some extravagance".

8. In 1856, Heinrich Heine, the German poet, left everything to his wife only on the condition that she remarried "so that there will be at least one man to regret my death".

9. In 1977, Joan Crawford left (nearly) all her estate to charities, writing, "It is my intention to make no provision herein for my son Christopher or my daughter Christina for reasons which are well known to them". Her daughter wrote the less than flattering biography, *Mommie Dearest*.

10. In 1962, Marilyn Monroe left all her "personal effects and clothing" to Lee Strasberg, her acting coach who was nominated for an Oscar in *The Godfather, Part 2*, "it being my desire that he distribute these, in his sole discretion, among my friends, colleagues and those to whom I am devoted". She also left Strasberg most of her estate.

10 INCREDIBLE COINCIDENCES BETWEEN THE ASSASSINATIONS OF PRESIDENTS LINCOLN AND KENNEDY

1. Lincoln was elected President in 1860; Kennedy was elected President in 1960.

2. Lincoln had a secretary named Kennedy; Kennedy had a secretary named Lincoln.

3. Both Presidents were shot in the head and both Presidents were with their wives when they were assassinated.

4. Both assassinations took place on a Friday and both Presidents were warned that they might be assassinated but both refused to change their schedules.

5. Lincoln was shot in a theatre by a man who hid in a warehouse; Kennedy was shot from a warehouse by a man who hid in a theatre.

6. Lincoln's assassin (John Wilkes Booth) was a Southerner in his twenties; Kennedy's assassin (Lee Harvey Oswald) was a Southerner in his twenties.

7. Booth and Oswald both died before they could be tried.

8. Lincoln was succeeded by his Vice-President, Andrew Johnson, who was born in 1808; Kennedy was succeeded by his Vice-President, Lyndon Johnson, who was born in 1908.

9. Lincoln and Kennedy each had seven letters in their names. John Wilkes Booth and Lee Harvey Oswald each had 15 letters in their names. Andrew Johnson and Lyndon Johnson each had 13 letters in their names.

10. Kennedy was riding in a Lincoln when he was shot.

THE 10 COUNTRIES IN THE WORLD WITH THE LOWEST LIFE EXPECTANCY

1. Sierra Leone, Africa (41)

2. Guinea-Bissau, Africa (42)

   Afghanistan, Asia (42)

3. Guinea, Africa (43)

   The Gambia, Africa (43)

4. Mali, Africa (44)

   Ethiopia, Africa (44)

5. Angola, Africa (45)

   Niger, Africa (45)

   Somalia, Africa (45)

THE AGE 10 DEAD PEOPLE WOULD HAVE REACHED IN THE YEAR 2000

1. President John F. Kennedy - died 1963 - (83)

2. James Dean - died 1955 - (69)

3. Anne Frank - died 1945 - (71)

4. Marilyn Monroe - died 1962 - (74)

5. Elvis Presley - died 1977 - (65)

6. John Lennon - died 1980 - (60)

7. Marc Bolan - died 1977 - (53)

8. Judy Garland - died 1969 - (78)

9. Dr. Martin Luther King - died 1968 - (71)

10. Jimi Hendrix - died 1970 - (58)

Chapter 8

Health

THE 10 MOST COMMON OPERATIONS IN BRITAIN

1. D & C (Dilatation and curettage - scraping of the womb)
2. Treatment of fractures
3. Cystoscopies
4. Tonsils and adenoids
5. Hysterectomies
6. Operations on the abdominal wall
7. Hernias
8. Eyes (cataracts)
9. Hip replacements
10. Appendectomies

10 PEOPLE WHO HAVE USED ACUPUNCTURE

1. Ben Kingsley
2. Roger Moore
3. Michael Aspel
4. Penelope Keith
5. Michael Crawford
6. Lindka Cierach
7. Charles Dance
8. Lulu
9. David Jacobs
10. Maureen Lipman

10 (GENUINE) AILMENTS

1. Painter's Colic (Lead poisoning)
2. Barbados Leg (Elephantitis)
3. Lumpy-Jaw (Bacterial infection of the jaw with weeping sores)
4. Iliac Passion (Enduring pain in the lower three-fifths of the small intestine)
5. Parrot Disease (Illness caused by inhaling dust contaminated by the droppings of infected birds)
6. Crab-Yaws (Tropical disease resembling syphilis with lesions on the foot)
7. Mad Staggers (Often fatal gastric paralysis in horses)
8. Farmer's Lung (Allergic reaction to fungi growing on hay, grain or straw)
9. Derbyshire Neck (Enlargement of the thyroid gland visible as swelling on the neck)
10. Soldier's Heart (Stress-related palpitations)

10 PEOPLE WHO SUFFERED FROM SERIOUS DEPRESSION

1. Billy Joel
2. Jill Gascoine
3. Charlotte Rampling
4. Judy Finnigan
5. Elton John
6. Countess Spencer
7. Diane Keen
8. Claire Rayner
9. Axl Rose
10. Spike Milligan

10 DOCTORS BETTER KNOWN FOR OTHER THINGS

1. Dr. Graeme Garden
2. Dr. Che Guevara
3. Dr. David Owen
4. Dr. Harry Hill
5. Dr. Rob Buckman
6. Dr. W. Somerset Maugham
7. Dr. Lady Isobel Barnett
8. Dr. J.P.R. Williams
9. Dr. Graham Chapman
10. Dr. Jonathan Miller

10 PEOPLE WHO SURVIVED HEART ATTACKS

1. George C. Scott
2. Sue Townsend
3. Bill Tarmey
4. Walter Matthau
5. Lonnie Donegan
6. Marcelle D'Argy Smith
7. Martin Sheen
8. Kerry Packer
9. Michael Heseltine
10. Omar Sharif

10 THINGS DOCTORS SAY...AND WHAT THEY ACTUALLY MEAN

1. "Come in and sit down, please"
   (You have precisely six minutes...five minutes fifty-nine seconds...fifty-eight...)

2. "And what seems to be the matter?"
   (Come on, get on with it)

3. "Can you be more specific?"
   (God give me strength)

4. "There's a lot of it about at the moment"
   (Why couldn't you have asked one of your neighbours about it instead of bothering me?)

5. "Doctors have to keep up with developments - in fact I was on a course all day yesterday"
   (And if it hadn't been for that double bogey on the eighth I'd have gone round in par)

6. "This won't hurt at all"
   (This won't hurt *me* at all)

7. "Well, I suppose there's something to be said for alternative medicine"
   (Not by me there isn't)

8. "I'd like to refer you to someone else"
   (I wish I could do that with all my patients)

9. "General practice is <u>real</u> medicine"
   (I drink too much to be a surgeon)

10. "You must try to relax more"
    (Why don't you stop being so neurotic)

10 THINGS SAID ABOUT HEALTH

1. "It is a fact that not once in all my life have I gone out for a walk. I have been taken out for walks; but that it is another matter" (Max Beerbohm)

2. "The only reason I would take up jogging is so that I could hear heavy breathing again" (Erma Bombeck)

3. "Exercise is bunk. If you are healthy, you don't need it: if you are sick, you shouldn't take it" (Henry Ford)

4. "I have always said that exercise is a short cut to the cemetery" (John Mortimer)

5. "Little good can come of regular exercise, which reduces life to a monotonous machine" (E.V. Knox)

6. "I like long walks, especially when they are taken by people who annoy me" (Fred Allen)

7. "Illness of any kind is hardly a thing to be encouraged in others. Health is the primary duty of life" (Oscar Wilde)

8. "Too much health is unhealthy" (Leo Rosten)

9. "Early to rise and early to bed, makes a male healthy, wealthy and dead" (James Thurber)

10. "There is no human activity, eating, sleeping, drinking or sex which some doctor somewhere won't discover leads directly to cardiac arrest" (John Mortimer)

10 THINGS SAID ABOUT PSYCHIATRISTS AND PSYCHIATRY

1. "Psychoanalysis is confession without absolution" (G. K. Chesterton)

2. "I'd rather go mad than see a psychiatrist" (Michael Caine)

3. "A psychiatrist is a man who goes to the Folies-Bergère and looks at the audience" (Mervyn Stockwood)

4. "One should only see a psychiatrist out of boredom" (Muriel Spark)

5. "Couches are for one thing only" (John Wayne)

6. "Anybody who goes to a psychiatrist ought to have his head examined" (Sam Goldwyn)

7. "I was in group analysis when I was younger because I couldn't afford private. I was captain of the Latent Paranoid Softball Team. We played all the neurotics on a Sunday morning: the Nail-biters against the Bed-wetters" (Woody Allen)

8. "My therapy was all Reichian, which is all sexual" (Jack Nicholson)

9. "I was in analysis for years because of a traumatic childhood: I was breast-fed through falsies" (Woody Allen)

10. "I don't go for this auto-cannibalism. Very damaging" (Peter O'Toole)

10 THINGS SAID ABOUT DOCTORS

1. "God heals, the doctor takes the fee" (Benjamin Franklin)

2. "A virus is a Latin word translated by doctors to mean 'your guess is as good as mine'" (Anon)

3. "Let no one suppose that the words 'doctor' and 'patient' can disguise from the parties the fact that they are employer and employee" (George Bernard Shaw)

4. "It is frightening how dependent on drugs we are all becoming and how easy it is for doctors to prescribe them as the universal panacea for our ills" (The Prince of Wales)

5. "Heaven defend me from a busy doctor" (Welsh proverb)

6. "The art of medicine consists of amusing the patient while nature cures the disease" (Voltaire)

7. "Physicians of the Utmost Fame,
   Were called at once but when they came
   They answered, as they took their fees,
   'There is no cure for this disease'" (Hilaire Belloc)

8. "I am dying with the help of too many physicians" (Alexander The Great)

9. "My doctor is wonderful. Once, when I couldn't afford an operation, he touched up the X-rays" (Joey Bishop)

10. "After two days in hospital, I took a turn for the nurse" (W.C. Fields)

10 PHOBIAS YET TO BE DISCOVERED

1. Jellophobia (Fear of children's parties)

2. Espressophobia (Fear of tiny cups)

3. Bolerophobia (Fear of ice-skating)

4. Tangophobia (Fear of being struck by an orange man)

5. Davrophobia (Fear of men grinning)

6. Allegrophobia (Fear of being caught driving an old banger)

7. Brandophobia (Fear of putting on weight)

8. Polophobia (Fear of confectionery)

9. Grouchophobia (Fear of advertising executives with pony-tails)

10. Rambophobia (Fear of men grunting)

10 PEOPLE WHO SUFFERED FROM EATING DISORDERS

1. The Princess of Wales (Bulimia)

2. Sinitta (Anorexia)

3. Zina Garrison (Bulimia)

4. Marina Mowatt (Ogilvy) (Anorexia)

5. Lysette Anthony (Bulimia)

6. Lena Zavaroni (Anorexia)

7. Uri Geller (Bulimia)

8. Karen Carpenter (Anorexia)

9. Jane Fonda (Bulimia)

10. Emma Thompson (Bulimia)

10 GENUINE PHOBIAS

1. Pogonophobia (Fear of Beards)

2. Chrometophobia (Fear of Money)

3. Linonophobia (Fear of String)

4. Kyphophobia (Fear of Stooping)

5. Peccatophobia (Fear of Sinning)

6. Triskaidekaphobia (Fear of the Number Thirteen)

7. Sciophobia (Fear of Shadows)

8. Cinophobia (Fear of Beds)

9. Dikephobia (Fear of Justice)

10. Phobophobia (Fear of Fear)

Chapter 9

"Quotes"

10 THINGS SAID ABOUT VICE

1. "Vice is its own reward" (Quentin Crisp)

2. "It is the restrictions based on vice by our social code which makes its pursuit so peculiarly agreeable" (Kenneth Grahame)

3. "Whenever I'm caught between two evils, I take the one I've never tried" (Mae West)

4. "Many are saved from sin by being so inept at it" (Mignon McLaughlin)

5. "Never support two weaknesses at the same time. It's your combination sinners - your lecherous liars and your miserly drunkards - who dishonour the vices and bring them into bad repute" (Thornton Wilder)

6. "Wickedness is a myth invented by good people to account for the curious attractiveness of others" (Oscar Wilde)

7. "Half the vices which the world condemns most loudly have seeds of good in them and require moderate use rather than total abstinence" (Samuel Butler)

8. "Public schools are the nurseries of all vice and immorality" (Henry Fielding)

9. "It takes a certain courage and a certain greatness even to be truly base" (Jean Anouilh)

10. "It is the function of vice to keep virtue within reasonable bounds" (Samuel Butler)

10 THINGS SAID ABOUT IGNORANCE

1. "From ignorance our comfort flows, the only wretched are the wise" (Matthew Prior)

2. "What you don't know would make a great book" (Sydney Smith)

3. "To be conscious that you are ignorant is a great step to knowledge" (Benjamin Disraeli)

4. "I wish you would read a little poetry sometimes. Your ignorance cramps my conversation" (Anthony Hope)

5. "Ignorance is like a delicate exotic fruit; touch it, and the bloom is gone" (Oscar Wilde)

6. "I count religion but a childish toy, and hold there is no sin but ignorance" (Christopher Marlowe)

7. "The fellow seems to me to posess but one idea, and that is the wrong one" (Samuel Johnson)

8. "Somebody else's ignorance is bliss" (Jack Vance)

9. "You've got the brain of a four-year-old boy, and I bet he was glad to get rid of it" (Groucho Marx)

10. "The ignorant man always adores what he cannot understand" (Cesare Lombroso)

10 THINGS SAID ABOUT CARS

1. "The car has become the carapace, the protective and aggressive shell, of urban and suburban man" (Marshall McLuhan)

2. "There are no liberals behind steering-wheels" (Russell Baker)

3. "The motor-car is as much an instrument of lawlessness as the jemmy" (Lord Chief Justice Parker)

4. "A pedestrian is a man who has two cars: one being driven by his wife, the other by one of his children" (Robert Bradbury)

5. "The automobile changed our dress, manners, social customs, vacation habits, the shape of our cities, consumer purchasing patterns, common tastes and positions of intercourse" (John Ketas)

6. "Take most people, they're crazy about cars...I don't even like *old* cars. I mean they don't even interest me. I'd rather have a goddamn horse. A horse is at least *human* for God's sake" (Holden Caulfield in *The Catcher In The Rye* by J.D. Salinger)

7. "Cars today are almost the exact equivalent of the great Gothic cathedrals" (Roland Barthes)

8. "We are nourishing at immense cost a monster of great potential destructiveness, and yet we love him dearly" (Professor Colin Buchanan)

9. "I just solved the parking problem. I bought a parked car" (Henny Youngman)

10. "Horsedrawn carriages used to average 11½ miles an hour in New York's midtown traffic; the average speed of automobiles is a bare six miles an hour" (Norman B. Geddes)

10 THINGS SAID BY PAUL NEWMAN

1. "There are two Newman's Laws. First, it's useless to put on your brakes when you're upside down. Second, just when things look darkest, they go black"

2. "I wasn't driven to acting by an inner compulsion. I was running away from the sporting goods business"

3. "Acting is like letting your pants down: you're exposed"

4. "America may be violent, greedy and colonialist, but by God it's interesting!"

5. "I stopped signing autographs when I was standing at a urinal at Sardi's and a guy came up with a pen and paper. I wondered: do I wash first and then shake hands?"

6. "Photographers are the most loathsome inconvenience. They're imbeciles. They're the pits"

7. "I wish I could sue *The New York Post* but it's awfully hard to sue a garbage can"

8. (Explaining why he stays faithful to his wife) "Why go out for a hamburger when you can have a steak at home?"

9. "The embarrassing thing is that the salad dressing is out-grossing my films"

10. (Suggested epitaph) "Here lies Paul Newman, who died a failure because his eyes turned brown"

10 THINGS SAID ABOUT CRIME

1. "I think crime pays. The hours are good, you travel a lot" (Woody Allen)

2. "A broad definition of crime in England is that it is any lower class activity that is displeasing to the upper class" (David Frost and Anthony Jay)

3. "If poverty is the mother of crime, stupidity is its father" (Jean de La Bruyère)

4. "Crime is a logical extension of the sort of behaviour that is often considered perfectly respectable in legitimate business" (Robert Rice)

5. "Thieves respect property; they merely wish the property to become their property that they may more perfectly respect it" (G.K. Chesterton)

6. "Being a thief is a terrific life, but the trouble is they do put you in the nick for it" (John McVicar)

7. "Crime, like virtue, has its degrees" (Jean Racine)

8. "I'm all for bringing back the birch. But only between consenting adults" (Gore Vidal)

9. "It's not the people in prison who worry me. It's the people who aren't" (Earl of Arran)

10. "If England treats her criminals the way she has treated me, she doesn't deserve to have any" (Oscar Wilde)

10 THINGS SAID ABOUT BEING 50

1. "At fifty everyone has the face he deserves" (George Orwell)

2. "Fifty is a nice number for the states in the Union or for a national speed limit, but it is not a number that I was prepared to have hung on me. Fifty is supposed to be my father's age." (Bill Cosby)

3. "The man who views the world at fifty the same as he did at twenty has wasted thirty years of his life" (Muhammad Ali)

4. "Anybody fifty years old can outsing himself when he was seventeen" (Smokey Robinson)

5. "Middle age is when your age starts to show around your middle" (Bob Hope)

6. "I wouldn't mind being called middle-aged if only I knew a few more 100-year-old people" (Dean Martin on turning 50)

7. "At fifty a man can be an ass without being an optimist but not an optimist without being an ass" (Mark Twain)

8. "You take all the experience and judgment of men over fifty out of the world and there wouldn't be enough left to run it" (Henry Ford)

9. "Now that I think of it, I wish I had been a hell-raiser when I was thirty years old. I tried it when I was fifty but I always got sleepy" (Groucho Marx)

10. "Once a man's fifty, he's entitled only to make large and serious mistakes" (Norman Mailer)

10 FAMOUS MISQUOTES

1. "We will fight them for the peaches" (Winston Churchill demonstrating his reluctance to queue at greengrocers' shops)

2. "I've been with nine Berliners" (John F Kennedy boasting about his sexual prowess again)

3. "We have nothing to lose but our change" (Karl Marx entering a penny arcade)

4. "I believe it is peas for our time" (Neville Chamberlain expressing his preference vegetable-wise)

5. "I have nothing to offer but Blood, Sweat and Tears..." (Winston Churchill trying in vain to arrange swaps for his record collection)

6. "There will be no eye-wash at the White House" (President Nixon dedicating himself to homeopathic medicine)

7. "If you can't stand the meat get out of the kitchen" (President Truman's solution to the problems faced by Americans who didn't have refrigerators)

8. "That's one small step for Iman, one giant leap forward for mankind" (Neil Armstrong commenting on David Bowie's new girlfriend)

9. "Reports of my debt are greatly exaggerated" (Mark Twain on leaving a bank)

10. "Father, I cannot sell a tie" (George Washington pleading with his dad not to make him go into the family menswear business)

10 THINGS SAID ABOUT DIETING

1. "Diets are for those who are thick and tired of it all" (Anon)

2. "I'm on a see-food diet. I eat all the food I see" (Martina Navratilova)

3. "There was only one occasion in my life when I put myself on a strict diet and I can tell you, hand on heart, it was the most miserable afternoon I have ever spent" (Denis Norden)

4. "My wife is on a diet. Coconuts and bananas. She hasn't lost any weight, but she can sure climb a tree" (Henry Youngman)

5. "A gourmet who thinks of calories is like a tart who looks at her watch" (James Beard)

6. "I went on a diet, swore off drinking and heavy eating, and in fourteen days I lost two weeks" (Joe E. Lewis)

7. "I've been on a constant diet for the last two decades. I've lost a total of 789 pounds. By all accounts, I should be hanging from a charm bracelet" (Erma Brombeck)

8. "A dieter is one who wishes others wouldn't laugh at his expanse" (Al Bernstein)

9. "Your diet won't make you live longer, it will just seem that way" (Kerry Packer)

10. "Dieting makes you fat" (Geoffrey Cannon)

10 THINGS SAID ABOUT SEX

1. "I believe that sex is a beautiful thing between two people. Between *five*, it's fantastic..." (Woody Allen)

2. "When women go wrong, men go right after them" (Mae West)

3. "My father told me all about the birds and the bees. The liar - I went steady with a woodpecker till I was 21" (Bob Hope)

4. "Sex is one of the nine reasons for reincarnation - the other eight are unimportant" (Henry Miller)

5. "I know it does make people happy but to me it is just like having a cup of tea" (Cynthia Payne)

6. "Sex is important, but by no means the only important thing in life" (Mary Whitehouse)

7. "Sex is about as important as a cheese sandwich. But a cheese sandwich, if you ain't got one to put in your belly, is extremely important" (Ian Dury)

8. "Whatever else can be said about sex, it cannot be called a dignified performance" (Helen Lawrenson)

9. "The only unnatural sexual behaviour is none at all" (Sigmund Freud)

10. "All this fuss about sleeping together; for physical pleasure I'd sooner go to my dentist any day" (Evelyn Waugh)

10 THINGS SAID ABOUT WAR

1. "There never was a good war, or a bad peace" (Benjamin Franklin, American statesman)

2. "Men love war because it allows them to look serious. Because it is the one thing that stops women laughing at them" (John Fowles, British novelist)

3. "War should belong to the tragic past, to history: it should find no place on humanity's agenda for the future" (Pope John Paul II)

4. "Wars, conflict, it's all business. One murder makes a villain; millions a hero. Numbers sanctify" (Charles Chaplin)

5. "History is littered with wars which everybody 'knew' would never happen" (Enoch Powell)

6. "This war, like the next war, is a war to end war" (David Lloyd George, Britain's Prime Minister during World War I)

7. "Wars make for better reading than peace does" (A.J.P. Taylor, historian)

8. "War is like love: it always finds a way" (Bertolt Brecht, playwright)

9. "In starting and waging a war, it is not right that matters but victory" (Adolf Hitler)

10. "I'm, sick of war for many reasons,/Three of them will do:/It's 1815,/I am French/And this is Waterloo" (Mel Brooks in *To Be Or Not To Be*)

10 THINGS SAID ABOUT MARILYN MONROE

1. "Anyone can remember lines but it takes an artist to come on the set and not know her lines and give the performance she did" (Billy Wilder, her director on *Some Like It Hot*, who also said of her, "she has breasts like granite and a brain like Swiss cheese" and "I have never met anyone as mean as Marilyn Monroe")

2. "She was good at being inarticulately abstracted for the same reason that midgets are good at being short" (Clive James)

3. "A natural phenomenon like Niagara Falls or the Grand Canyon. You can't talk to it; it can't talk to you. All you can do is stand back and be awed by it" (Nunnally Johnson)

4. "Kissing her is like kissing Hitler" (Tony Curtis, her co-star in *Some Like It Hot*)

5. "Of course, as a sex symbol she was stunning but, sadly, she must be one of the silliest women I have ever met" (Donald Sinden. Marilyn Monroe's opinion of him - if indeed she had one - is not recorded)

6. "(She was) a very Stradivarius of sex, so gorgeous, forgiving, humorous, compliant and tender that even the most mediocre musician would relax his lack of art in the dissolving magic of her violin" (Norman Mailer)

7. "A professional amateur" (Laurence Olivier, her co-star in *The Prince And The Showgirl*)

8. "If she was a victim, she was a victim of friends" (George Cukor)

9. "Directing her was like directing Lassie: you needed 14 takes to get each one of them right" (Otto Preminger, her director on *River of No Return* who also called her "a vacuum with nipples")

10. "You don't have to hold an inquest to find out who killed Marilyn Monroe: those bastards in the big executive chairs killed her" (Henry Hathaway)

10 THINGS SAID BY MARILYN MONROE

1. "A sex symbol becomes a thing. I hate being a thing"

2. "I've always felt those articles somehow reveal more about the writers than they do about me"

3. "It's not true that I had nothing on. I had the radio on" (about posing naked for a calendar)

4. "A career is born in public, talent in private"

5. "Hollywood's a place where they'll pay you a thousand dollars for a kiss and fifty cents for your soul"

6. "Being a sex symbol is a heavy load to carry - especially when one is tired, hurt and bewildered"

7. "I started as a dumb blonde whore. I'll end as one"

8. "I've been on a calendar but never on time" (talking about her notorious lack of punctuality)

9. "Sometimes I've been to a party where no one spoke to me a whole evening. The men, frightened by their wives or sweeties, would give me a wide berth and the ladies would gang up in a corner to discuss my dangerous character"

10. "No one ever called me pretty when I was a little girl"

10 THINGS SAID BY ALBERT EINSTEIN

1. "When you sit with a nice girl for two hours, you think it's only a minute. But when you sit on a hot stove for a minute, you think it's two hours. That's relativity"

2. "I never think of the future. It comes soon enough"

3. "The hardest thing in the world to understand is income tax"

4. "If my theory of relativity is proven successful, Germany will claim me as a German, and France will declare that I am a citizen of the world. Should my theory prove untrue, France will say that I am a German, and Germany will declare that I am a Jew"

5. "An empty stomach is not a good political adviser"

6. "Nationalism is an infantile disease. It is the measles of mankind"

7. "I can't believe that God plays dice with the universe"

8. "The discovery of the nuclear chain reaction need not bring about the destruction of mankind any more than did the discovery of matches"

9. "The fear of death is the most unjustified of all fears, for there's no risk of accident to someone who's dead"

10. "We should take care not to make the intellect our god, it's not a good political adviser"

10 THINGS SAID BY GROUCHO MARX

1. "I don't want to belong to any club that would accept me as a member"

2. "I eat like a vulture; unfortunately, the resemblance doesn't end there"

3. "I've been around so long, I knew Doris Day before she was a virgin"

4. "I never forget a face but I'll make an exception in your case"

5. "They say a man is as old as the woman he feels"

6. "Go – and never darken my towels again"

7. "Only one man in a thousand is a leader of men: the other 999 follow men"

8. "Groucho isn't my real name, I'm breaking it in for a friend"

9. "We in this industry know that behind every successful screenwriter stands a woman. And behind her stands his wife"

10. "Time wounds all heels"

10 THINGS SAID BY LES DAWSON

1. "My mother-in-law has come round to our house at Christmas seven years running. This year we're having a change: we're going to let her in"

2. "The mother-in-law thinks I'm effeminate; not that I mind because, beside her, I am"

3. "I'm feeling very lonely. I've been married for 15 years and yesterday my wife ran off with the chap next door. I'm going to miss him terribly"

4. "My mother-in-law? Lovely woman - face like a bag of spanners"

5. "I went to my doctor and asked for something for persistent wind. He gave me a kite."

6. "Our terraced house was so small the mice walked about on their back legs"

7. "Lazy? He used to ride his bike over cobblestones to knock the ash off his ciggie"

8. "We were so poor, I used to think knives and forks were jewellery"

9. "I've been in this business so long, I can remember *The Archers* when they had only an allotment"

10. "The day my mother-in-law called, the mice threw themselves on the traps"

10 INSULTS

1. "She is so stupid, she returns bowling balls because they've got holes in them" (Joan Rivers on Bo Derek)

2. "His (Michael Jackson's) album was only called *Bad* because there wasn't enough room on the sleeve for 'Pathetic'" (Prince)

3. "She loves nature in spite of what it did to her" (Bette Midler on the Princess Royal)

4. "He has the wit of an unflushed toilet" (Bernard Manning on Stephen Fry)

5. "He's a wimp in disguise: he should go home and shave" (Keith Richards on George Michael)

6. "He's an ugly bastard with huge flapping ears" (Robbie Coltrane on Frank Sinatra)

7. "I love her but her oars aren't touching the water these days" (Dean Martin on Shirley Maclaine)

8. "One day someone will join two Terry Christians together and make one long plank" (Rory Bremner)

9. "Kirk Douglas would be the first to tell you that he's a difficult man; I would be the second" (Burt Lancaster)

10. "He reminds me of an aubergine: all shiny and plump" (Paul Young on Boy George)

10 THINGS SAID ABOUT WOMEN

1. "Men have sight; women have insight" (Victor Hugo)

2. "Women should be obscene and not heard" (John Lennon)

3. "A woman is like a teabag: you can't tell how strong she is until you put her in hot water" (Nancy Reagan)

4. "Women are like elephants to me; they're nice to look at but I wouldn't want to own one" (W.C. Fields)

5. "Plain women know more about men than beautiful ones do" (Katharine Hepburn)

6. "There is no such thing as an ugly woman: there are only the ones who do not know how to make themselves attractive" (Christian Dior)

7. "When women kiss, it always reminds one of prize fighters shaking hands" (H.L. Mencken)

8. "A woman without a man is like a fish without a bicycle" (Gloria Steinem)

9. "Women who live for the next miracle cream do not realise that beauty comes from a secret happiness and equilibrium within themselves" (Sophia Loren)

10. "Give a woman an inch and she thinks she's a ruler" (Anon.)

10 PEOPLE WHO SAID DUMB THINGS

1. "My imagination refuses to see any sort of submarine doing anything but suffocating its crew" (H.G. Wells, the writer who was big on futuristic fiction but not so hot on futuristic fact)

2. "Smoking kills. If you're killed, you've lost a very important part of your life" (Brooke Shields, the actress, displaying an uncanny ability to speak the obvious)

3. "Get rid of the lunatic who says he's got a machine for seeing by wireless" (The then Editor of the *Daily Express* refusing to meet John Logie Baird - the man who invented television)

4. "Iran is an island of stability in one of the most volatile parts of the world" (President Jimmy Carter, speaking incredibly unpresciently just before the Shah was booted out and Iran went absolutely pear-shaped)

5. "Ah yes, Mohammed: that's one of the most common Christian names in the world" (David 'Kid' Jensen, the disc jockey with a knack for inter-faith relations)

6. "I'm astounded by people who take 18 years to write something. That's how long it took that guy to write *Madame Bovary* and was that ever on the bestseller list?" (Sylvester Stallone giving his considered views on Gustav Flaubert's *oeuvres*)

7. "So, Carol, you're a housewife and a mother. And have you got any children?" (Michael Barrymore, for once being completely 'awong')

8. "Come, come - why, they couldn't hit an elephant at this dist...." (John Sedgwick, American Civil War General, just before he was shot dead)

9. "We will make them grovel" (Tony Greig, the then captain of the England cricket team, on what he and his men were going to do to the West Indies in 1976. In the event, the West Indies won the series 3-0)

10. "This picture is going to be one of the biggest white elephants of all time" (Victor Fleming, the director of *Gone With The Wind*, assessing its likely prospects at the box office)

10 THINGS SAID ABOUT BARBRA STREISAND

1. "She's not really an actress, not even much of a comedienne. She's an impersonator... When she goes one way and the movie goes another, it's no contest. The movie is turned to junk" (Vincent Canby)

2. "She does her own schtick... but she doesn't do anything she hasn't already done. She's playing herself - and it's awfully soon for that" (Pauline Kael)

3. "Her work is pretentiously arty, overinvolved and overprojected, and made further intolerable by a vocal tone best described by the Irish word 'keening'" (John Indox)

4. "Her acting consists entirely of fishily thrusting out her lips, sounding like a cabbie bellyaching at breakneck speed, and throwing her weight around" (John Simon)

5. "She ought to be called 'Barbra Strident'" (Stanley Kaufman)

6. "I have more talent in my smallest fart than you have in your entire body" (Walter Matthau)

7. "She looks like a cross between an aardvark and an albino rat surmounted by a platinum-coated horse bun" (John Simon)

8. "The most pretentious woman the cinema has ever known" (Ryan O'Neal)

9. "I have no disagreement with Barbra Streisand. I was merely exasperated by her tendency to megalomania" (Walter Matthau)

10. "She's a ball buster. Protect me from her" (Nick Nolte)

10 THINGS SAID BY BARBRA STREISAND

1. "Success to me is having ten honeydew melons and eating only the top half of each one"

2. "I wanted to be Scarlett O'Hara and not Vivien Leigh"

3. "Women are superior to men. I don't even think we're equal"

4. "I just don't want to be hampered by my own limitations"

5. "Why am I so famous? What am I doing right? What are the others doing wrong?"

6. "Myths are a waste of time. They prevent progression"

7. "I've considered having my nose fixed. But I didn't trust anyone enough. If I could do it myself with a mirror..."

8. "I'm tired of malicious articles slandering me"

9. "I hated singing. I wanted to be an actress. But I don't think I'd have made it any other way"

10. "I knew that with a mouth like mine, I just had to be a star or something"

10 THINGS SAID BY GEORGE BURNS

1. "Too bad all the people who know how to run the country are busy driving taxi-cabs and cutting hair"

2. "I'd go out with women my age but there *are* no women my age"

3. "I smoke ten to fifteen cigars a day: at my age I have to hold on to something"

4. "Actually, it only takes one drink to get me loaded. Trouble is, I can't remember if it's the thirteenth or fourteenth"

5. "You have to have something to get you out of bed. I can't do anything in bed anyway"

6. "Retirement at 65 is ridiculous. When I was 65 I still had pimples"

7. "I was brought up to respect my elders and now I don't have to respect *anybody*"

8. "It's hard for me to get used to these changing times. I can remember when the air was clean and sex was dirty"

9. "I must be getting absent-minded. Whenever I complain that things aren't what they used to be, I always forget to include myself"

10. "I'm at that age now where just putting my cigar in its holder is a thrill"

10 THINGS SAID BY FRANK SINATRA

1. "I could go on stage and make pizza and they'd still come to see me"

2. "If I had as many love affairs as I've been given credit for, I'd be in a jar in the Harvard Medical School"

3. "All day long, Hollywood reporters lie in the sun, and when the sun goes down, they lie some more"

4. "I get an audience involved because I'm involved myself. If the song is a lament at the loss of love, I get an ache in my gut - I cry out the loneliness"

5. "When they (the press) have treated me unfairly, I struck back. I've turned the other cheek. Hell, I've turned all four cheeks and I still get the short end"

6. "Rock 'n' Roll fosters almost totally negative and destructive reactions in young people: it smells phoney and false"

7. "I'm supposed to have a PhD on the subject of women. Truth is, I've flunked more often than not. I'm very fond of women, I admire them. But, like all men, I don't understand them"

8. "I detest bad manners. If people are polite, then I am. They shouldn't try to get away with not being polite to me"

9. "It was my idea to make my voice work in the same way as a trombone or violin: not sounding like them but 'playing' the voice like those instruments"

10. "Basically, I'm for anything that gets you through the night - be it prayer, tranquillisers or a bottle of Jack Daniels"

10 DEVASTATING REPLIES

1. Oscar Wilde: "It's a pretty poor work of art"
   James Whistler: "Yes. And you're a pretty poor work of nature"

2. George Bernard Shaw: "Isn't it true, my dear, that male judgement is superior to female judgement?"
   Mrs Shaw: "Of course, dear. After all, you married me and I you"

3. Bessie Braddock: "Winston, you're drunk!"
   Winston Churchill: "Bessie, you're ugly. But tomorrow morning I shall be sober"

4. Convicted criminal: "As God is my judge - I am innocent"
   Judge Norman Birkett: "He isn't; I am, and you're not!"

5. Clare Booth Luce: (Opening a door) "Age before beauty"
   Dorothy Parker: (Going through first) "Pearls before swine"

6. Singer: "You know, my dear, I insured my voice for fifty thousand dollars"
   Miriam Hopkins: "That's wonderful. And what did you do with the money?"

7. Sir Lewis Morris: "The press are neglecting my poems. It is a conspiracy of silence. What ought I do Oscar?"
   Oscar Wilde: "Join it!"

8. Jacob Epstein: "Do you remember the days before we knew each other?"
   Mark Gertler: "Yes"
   Jacob Epstein: Well then, let's go back to them"

9. George Bernard Shaw: "Am reserving two tickets for you for my première. Come and bring a friend - if you have one"
   Winston Churchill: "Impossible to be present for the first performance. Will attend the second - if there is one"

10. Actor: "Last night I was a sensation at the Roxy. I had the audience glued to their seats"
    George Jessel: "How clever of you to think of it"

10 THINGS SAID BY NOEL GALLAGHER

1. "I've always sworn I'll never refuse an autograph"

2. "What I was bad at was spelling. Still am. Anything over six letters and that's me gone"

3. "I wish I'd never said some of the things I've said"

4. "I'm not Morrissey. I'm not Bob Dylan. I'm not Brett Anderson. They are better lyricists than I'll ever be"

5. "The people in my band, we'll be working-class till we die. We were brought up socialists and we'll die socialists"

6. "We do take too many drugs, though, and I wish I'd never started"

7. "What people have got to understand is that we are lads. We have burgled houses and nicked car stereos and we like girls and swear"

8. "If I could write a song half as good as *This Guy's In Love With You* or *Anyone Who Had A Heart*, I'd die a happy man"

9. "I think we sparked something in a generation of 14- and 15-year-olds who were just waiting for their Beatles"

10. "I'm in it for my name in the brackets. I always wanted to be a songwriter because songs last for ever. It's a form of immortality"

10 THINGS SAID ABOUT VEGETARIANISM

1. "You are what you eat and who wants to be a lettuce?" (Peter Burns)

2. "I have known many meat-eaters to be far more non-violent than vegetarians." (Mahatma Gandhi)

3. "A meal without flesh is like eating grass" (Indian Proverb)

4. "The thought of two thousand people crunching celery at the same time horrified me" (G. B. Shaw, refusing an invitation to a vegetarian dinner)

5. "Vegetarianism is harmless enough, though it is apt to fill a man with wind and self-righteousness" (Sir Robert Hutchinson)

6. "Vegetarianism isn't simply a distaste for animal products. It's a way of life: faddish, cranky and holier-than-thou" (Harriet van Horne)

7. "A vegetarian diet may be best for those who would be beautiful but it does not seem to have done much for the elephant" ('Punch')

8. "Vegetarians have wicked, shifty eyes and laugh in a cold, calculating manner. They pinch little children, steal stamps, drink water, favour beards" (J. B. Morton)

9. "The first time I tried organic wheat bread, I thought I was chewing on roofing material" (Robin Williams)

10. "I did not become a vegetarian for my health. I did it for the health of the chickens" (Isaac Bashevis Singer)

10 THINGS SAID BY ZSA ZSA GABOR

1. "Husbands are like fires - they go out when unattended"

2. "The Women's Movement hasn't changed my sex life at all: it wouldn't dare"

3. "The only place men want depth in a women is in her *décolletage*"

4. "You never really know a man until you have divorced him"

5. "I never really hated a man enough to give him his diamonds back"

6. "I want a man who's kind and understanding. Is that too much to ask of a millionaire?"

7. "If they had as much adultery going on in New York as they said in the divorce courts, they would never have a chance to make the beds at the Plaza"

8. "I am a marvellous housekeeper, every time I leave a man I keep his house"

9. "Getting divorced just because you don't love a man is almost as silly as getting married just because you love him"

10. "I believe in large families: every woman should have at least three husbands"

10 THINGS SAID BY MICHAEL CAINE

1. "When you reach the top, that's when the climb begins"

2. "I live in Beverly Hills so I took the Beverly Hills diet. I ate a lot of pineapple. It made me spotty - so I ate a lot of Nivea Cream"

3. "I'm a sort of boy-next-door. If that boy has a good scriptwriter"

4. "John Wayne once advised me, talk low, talk slow and don't talk too much. And then I went and made *Sleuth*"

5. "I'm not interested in directing. Now, producing - I noticed when it starts to rain, the only person who goes back to the hotel is the producer"

6. "People who break their word in Japan kill themselves. People who break their word here (Hollywood) kill you"

7. "I read books like mad, but I am careful not to let anything I read influence me"

8. "To qualify for a Los Angelean, you need three things: a) a driver's licence; b) your own tennis court; c) a preference for snorting cocaine"

9. "I can tell you that Christopher Reeve is not homosexual. When we kissed in *Deathtrap*, he didn't close his eyes"

10. "I'll always be there because I'm a skilled professional actor. Whether or not I've any talent is beside the point"

10 THINGS SAID ABOUT SCIENCE

1. "A good scientific theory should be explicable to a barmaid" (Ernest Rutherford)

2. "What science cannot tell us, mankind cannot know" (Bertrand Russell)

3. "Whenever science makes a discovery, the devil grabs while the angels are debating the best way to use it" (Alan Valentine)

4. "The great tragedy of Science - the slaying of a beautiful hypothesis by an ugly fact" (Thomas Huxley)

5. "Science knows only one commandment - contribute to science" (Bertolt Brecht)

6. "Science may be described as the art of systematic over-simplification" (Karl Popper)

7. "Science is not just the fruit of the tree of knowledge, it is the tree itself" (Derek Price)

8. "Science cannot stop while ethics catches up - and nobody should expect scientists to do all the thinking for the country" (Elvin Stackman)

9. "Science has done more for the development of Western civilization in one hundred years than Christianity did in 18 hundred" (John Burroughs)

10. "That is the essence of science: ask an impertinent question, and you are on the way to a pertinent answer" (Jacob Bronowski)

10 THINGS SAID BY PETER USTINOV

1. "Comedy is simply a funny way of being serious"

2. "Playwrights are like men who have been dining for a month in an Indian restaurant. After eating curry night after night, they deny the existence of asparagus"

3. "Glamour in the theatre is usually twenty chorus girls in a line all doing the same thing. It is assumed that twenty women are more glamorous than one"

4. "I do not believe that friends are necessarily the people you like best, they are merely the people who got there first"

5. "Acting on television is like being asked by the captain to entertain the passengers while the ship goes down"

6. "A diplomat these days is nothing but a head-waiter who's allowed to sit down occasionally"

7. "Parents are the bones on which children sharpen their teeth"

8. "As for being a General, well, at the age of four with paper hats and wooden swords we're all Generals. Only some of us never grow out of it"

9. "He (the recruiting officer) asked me 'Why tanks?' I replied that I preferred to go into battle sitting down"

10. "Books, I don't know what you see in them...I can understand a person reading them, but I can't for the life of me see why people have to write them"

10 THINGS SAID BY TALLULAH BANKHEAD

1. "Cocaine isn't habit-forming - I should know. I've been using it for years"

2. "I'll come and make love to you at five o'clock. If I'm late start without me"

3. "The only thing I regret about my past life is the length of it. If I had my past life over again I'd make all the same mistakes - only sooner"

4. "It's one of the tragic ironies of the theatre that only one man in it can count on steady work - the night watchman"

5. "It's the good girls who keep the diaries; the bad girls never have the time"

6. "There is less in this than meets the eye"

7. "I've been called many things but never an intellectual"

8. "I've tried several varieties of sex. The conventional position makes me claustrophobic. And the others either give me a stiff neck or lockjaw"

9. "I'm as pure as the driven slush"

10. "I'd rather be strongly wrong than weakly right"

10 THINGS SAID ABOUT ADULTERY

1. "If you were married to Marilyn Monroe - you'd cheat with some ugly girl" (George Burns)
2. "The minute you start fiddling around outside the idea of monogamy, nothing satisfies any more" (Richard Burton)
3. "It's a game I never play" (Sophia Loren)
4. "Why fool around with hamburger when you have steak at home?" (Paul Newman)
5. "I couldn't stand that my husband was unfaithful. I am Raquel Welch - understand?" (Raquel Welch)
6. "Accursed from their birth they be/Who seek to find monogamy./ Pursuing it from bed to bed -/ I think they would be better dead" (Dorothy Parker)
7. "On a sofa upholstered in human skin/Mona did researches in original sin" (William Plomer)
8. "You know, of course, that the Tasmanians, who never committed adultery, are now extinct" (W. Somerset Maugham)
9. "I've looked on a lot of women with lust. I've committed adultery in my heart many times. God recognises I will do this and forgives me" (Jimmy Carter)
10. "Merely innocent flirtation,/ Not quite adultery, but adulteration" (George Byron)

10 THINGS SAID ABOUT THE COUNTRYSIDE

1. "That's the trouble with the country; there's too much public world between the private ones" (Dylan Thomas)
2. "I have never understood why anybody agreed to go on being a rustic after about 1400" (Kingsley Amis)
3. "It is pure unadulterated country life. They get up early because they have so much to do and go to bed early because they have so little to think about" (Oscar Wilde)
4. "There is nothing good to be had in the country, or, if there be, they will not let you have it" (William Hazlitt)
5. "It is only in the country that we can get to know a person or a book" (Cyril Connolly)
6. "No country home is complete without a surly figure seated in the kitchen like Rodin's thinker, wishing she was back in a hot little room under the Third Avenue Elevated" (S.J. Perelman)
7. "I am not the type who wants to go back to the land; I am the type who wants to go back to the hotel" (Fran Lebowitz)
8. "Anybody can be good in the country; there are no temptations there" (Oscar Wilde)
9. "The country has charms only for those not obliged to stay there" (Edouard Manet)
10. "I am at two with nature" (Woody Allen)

10 THINGS SAID BY MARK TWAIN

1. "When angry, count to four; when very angry, swear"
2. "Familiarity breeds contempt...and children"
3. "It takes your enemy and your friend - working together - to hurt you to the heart: the one to slander you and the other to get the news to you"
4. "I can live for two months on a good compliment"
5. "I was born modest. Not all over but in spots"
6. "I am opposed to millionaires - but it would be dangerous to offer me the position"
7. "Fewer things are harder to put up with than the annoyance of a good example"
8. "Cauliflower is nothing but cabbage with a college education"
9. "Man is the only animal that blushes or needs to"
10. "If you tell the truth you don't have to remember anything"

10 THINGS SAID BY JOAN RIVERS

1. "I hate housework. You make the beds, you do the dishes and six months later you have to start all over again"
2. "I was so flat I used to put 'x's on my chest and write 'you are here'"
3. "I was born in 1962. And the room next to me was 1963"
4. "Madonna is so hairy that when she lifted her arm I thought it was Tina Turner in her armpit"
5. "Who fits in any more? I was invited to a pot party and I brought Tupperware"
6. "(Bo Derek) turned down the role of Helen Keller because she couldn't remember the lines"
7. "I don't work out. If God wanted us to bend over he'd put diamonds on the floor"
8. "(Elizabeth Taylor's) got more chins than the Chinese telephone directory"
9. "Boy George is all England needs: another Queen who can't dress"
10. "(Mick Jagger) has got child-bearing lips"

10 THINGS SAID ABOUT THE CITY

1. "There is no solitude in the world like that of the big city" (Kathleen Norris)
2. "If you would know and not be known, live in a city" (Charles Caleb Colton)
3. "As a remedy to life in society I would suggest the big city. Nowadays it is the only desert within our means" (Albert Camus)
4. "Hell is a city much like London - a populous and smoky city" (Percy Bysshe Shelley)
5. "God made the country, and man made the town" (William Cowper)
6. "Cities, like cats, will reveal themselves at night" (Rupert Brooke)
7. "The city is not a concrete jungle, it is a human zoo" (Desmond Morris)
8. "Farmers worry only during the growing season, but town people worry all the time" (Edgar Watson Howe)
9. "A great city is that which has the greatest men and women" (Walt Whitman)
10. "The chicken is the country's, but the city eats it" (George Herbert)

10 THINGS SAID BY CLIVE JAMES

1. "A TV programme can never be worse than its viewers; for the more stupid it is, the more stupid they are to watch it"

2. "All you have to do on television is be yourself, provided, that is, you have a self to be"

3. "It is an American characteristic not to stop running even if after you have arrived"

4. "You can never get a woman to sit down and listen to a drum solo"

5. "I've got a *monumental* conceit, *look* at me - conceit on the rampage. I seriously believe this: you've got to keep your conceit well-brushed and ready to operate at all times"

6. "At the Harvest Festival in church the area behind the pulpit was piled high with tins of IXL fruit for the old-age pensioners. We had collected the tinned fruit from door to door. Most of it came from old-age pensioners"

7. "You should never trust anyone who listens to Mahler before they're 40"

8. "...we did one of those quick, awkward kisses where each of you gets a nose in the eye"

9. "The Sydney opera house looks like a typewriter full of oyster shells...like a broken Pyrex casserole dish in a brown cardboard box"

10. "All full time writers, even if they can't tell a tonic solfa from a ton of sulphur should stay in touch with music if they can, if only to remind themselves that compared with musicians they are in a low state of training"

10 THINGS SAID ABOUT GARDENING

1. "My garden will never make me famous/I'm a horticultural ignoramus" (Ogden Nash)

2. "The more help a man has in his garden, the less it belongs to him" (W.H. Davies)

3. "Observing the ancient housekeeper wrestling with the plantlife in the garden, I occasionally point out a weed and encourage her from the deck-chair" (Arthur Marshall)

4. "God Almighty first planted a garden. And indeed it is the purest of human pleasures" (Sir Francis Bacon)

5. "I've had enough of gardening: I'm just about ready to throw in the trowel" (Anon.)

6. "Nature, to be commanded, must be obeyed" (Sir Francis Bacon)

7. "What a man needs in gardening is a cast-iron back with a hinge in it" (Charles Dudley Warner)

8. "You must not praise the elegance of an Englishman's house though you may always be impressed by the garden" (George Mikes)

9. "To create a little flower is the labour of ages" (William Blake)

10. "Oh Adam was a gardener and God who made him sees/That half a proper gardener's work is done upon his knees" (Rudyard Kipling)

10 THINGS SAID ABOUT BOREDOM

1. "When you're bored with yourself, marry and be bored with someone else" (David Pryce-Jones)

2. "Society is now one polish'd horde, form'd of two mighty tribes, the bores and the bored" (Lord Byron)

3. "Punctuality is the virtue of the bored" (Evelyn Waugh)

4. "I wanted to be bored to death, as good a way to go as any" (Peter De Vries)

5. "You ought not to be ashamed of being bored. What you ought to be ashamed of is being boring" (Lord Hailsham)

6. "He was not only a bore; he bored for England" (Malcolm Muggeridge of Anthony Eden)

7. "A bore is a man who, when you ask him how he is, tells you" (Bert Leston Taylor)

8. "Somebody's boring me - I think it's me" (Dylan Thomas)

9. "The secret of making one's self tiresome is not to know when to stop" (Voltaire)

10. "'I believe I take precedence,' he said coldly; 'you are merely the club Bore; I am the club Liar'" (Saki)

10 THINGS SAID BY NOEL COWARD

1. "I can take any amount of criticism, so long as it is unqualified praise"

2. "Sunburn is very becoming - but only when it is even - one must be careful not to look like a mixed grill"

3. "Never trust a man with short legs - brains too near their bottoms"

4. "I have a memory like an elephant. In fact elephants often consult me"

5. "I love the weight of American Sunday newspapers. Pulling them up off the floor is good for the figure"

6. "I've over-educated myself in all things I shouldn't have known at all"

7. "I don't believe in astrology. The only stars I can blame for my failures are those that walk about the stage"

8. "I don't know what London's coming to - the higher the buildings the lower the morals"

9. "I have not felt it necessary to be with it. I am all for staying in my place"

10. "Wit ought to be a glorious treat, like caviar. Don't spread it about like marmalade"

10 THINGS SAID ABOUT HOLLYWOOD

1. "If you say what you mean in this town, you're an outlaw." (Kevin Costner)
2. "If you stay in Beverly Hills too long, you become a Mercedes." (Dustin Hoffman)
3. "Hollywood is not my cup of tea - nor am I its cup of tea." (Peter O'Toole)
4. "They're all so jealous in Hollywood. It's not enough to have a hit. Your best friend should also have a failure." (Peter Bogdanovich)
5. "A rotten gold-plated sewer of a town." (James Woods)
6. "Hollywood's a place where they'll pay you a thousand dollars for a kiss and fifty cents for your soul." (Marilyn Monroe)
7. "Hollywood is simply geared to cheat you left, right and bloody centre." (John Hurt)
8. "There'll always be an England, even if it's in Hollywood." (Bob Hope)
9. "The only community in the world where the entire population is suffering from rumourtism." (Anon.)
10. "In Hollywood the eternal triangle consists of an actor, his wife and himself." (Anon.)

10 THINGS SAID BY GORE VIDAL

1. "I'm all for bringing back the birch - but only between consenting adults."
2. "Any American who is prepared to run for President should automatically, by definition, be disqualified from ever doing so."
3. "Commercialism is doing well that which should not be done at all."
4. "Never have children, only grandchildren."
5. "It is not enough to succeed; others must fail."
6. "Never miss a chance to have sex or appear on television."
7. "A narcissist is someone better looking than you are."
8. "Whenever a friend succeeds, a little something in me dies."
9. "Television is now so desperately hungry for material that they're scraping the top of the barrel."
10. "For certain people, after fifty, litigation takes the place of sex."

10 THINGS SAID BY MEL BROOKS

1. "Some critics are emotionally desiccated, personally about as attractive as a year-old peach in a single girl's refrigerator."
2. "If Presidents don't do it to their wives, they do it to their country."
3. "If Hollywood keeps gearing movie after movie to teenagers, next year's Oscar will develop acne."
4. "My Uncle Joe was a philosopher, very deep, very serious. Never eat chocolate after chicken, he'd tell us, wagging his finger."
5. "You're always a little disappointing in person because you can't be the edited essence of yourself."
6. "Success helps you ease up."
7. "Vulgarity is in the hand of the beholder."
8. "Comedy is serious - deadly serious. Never, never try to be funny! The actors must be serious. Only the situation must be absurd."
9. "I only direct in self-defence."
10. "I had a dream. A vision. Of money in the bank. And I said: 'If I make a big picture that everybody laughs at they'll give me money ... and when I'm an old man, I'll go visit my money in the bank.'"

10 THINGS SAID BY STEVEN SPIELBERG

1. "I always think of the audience when I'm directing - because I am the audience."
2. "Oh, torture. Torture. My pubic hairs went grey." (on shooting *E.T.*)
3. "When I grow up, I still want to be a director."
4. "The most expensive habit in the world is celluloid not heroin and I need a fix every two years."
5. "Failure is inevitable. Success is elusive."
6. "When I'm 60, Hollywood will forgive me. I don't know for what, but they'll forgive me."
7. "I'm a Democrat with Republican underpinnings. I'm liberal about a lot of things but I'm bullish about America."
8. "I'd rather direct. Any day. And twice on Sundays."
9. "I love *Rambo* but I think it's potentially a very dangerous movie. It changes history in a frightening way."
10. "The more and more terrified people get of making Westerns, the more I want to do one."

10 THINGS SAID BY CLINT EASTWOOD

1. "My old drama coach used to say: 'Don't just do something, stand there.'"
2. "I don't seem to have the gift it takes to enjoy fame the way it should be enjoyed."
3. "I've always thought of myself as a character actor rather than a leading man."
4. "I squint because I can't take too much light."
5. "I've always had the ability to say to the audience: 'Watch this if you like and if you don't - take a hike.'"
6. "Movies are fun. But they're not a cure for cancer."
7. "I hate imitation. I've a reverence for individuality. I got where I am by coming off the wall."
8. "The reason I started Malpaso was I saw a lot of inefficiencies and thought I can screw up as good as the next person."
9. "A lot of actors who play *Henry V* can't play my characters."
10. "I'm not too thrilled with the idea of talking about myself."

10 THINGS SAID BY BOB HOPE

1. "The good news is that Jesus is coming back. The bad news is that he's really pissed off."
2. "They said I was worth $500 million. If I was worth that much, I wouldn't have visited Vietnam, I'd have sent for it."
3. "*Deep Throat* - I thought it was about a giraffe."
4. "The only time to believe any kind of rating is when it shows you at the top."
5. "Zsa Zsa Gabor got married as a one-off and it was so successul she turned it into a series."
6. "People who throw kisses are hopelessly lazy."
7. "If you watch a game it's fun. If you play it, it's recreation. If you work at it, it's golf."
8. "A bank is a place that will lend you money if you can prove that you don't need it."
9. "Concorde is great. It gives you three extra hours to find your luggage."
10. "There'll always be an England, even if it's in Hollywood."

10 THINGS SAID BY JACK NICHOLSON

1. "I've been physically dissected more than any frog in a biology class - my eyebrows, my eyes, my teeth. And now it's my stomach."
2. "The whole thing is to keep working and pretty soon they'll think you're good."
3. "I'd like to win more Oscars than Walt Disney (who won 32) and I'd like to win them in every category."
4. "The only reason that cocaine is such a rage today is that people are too dumb and lazy to get themselves together to roll a joint."
5. "If I could only be a star rather than an actor, I'd probably stop acting."
6. "It's good for people to think I'm a womaniser. I've no motivation to deny it."
7. "Once you've been really *bad* in a movie, there's a certain kind of fearlessness you develop."
8. "I'm preoccupied with sex - an area of human behaviour that's underexplored, in general. And I like virgin territory."
9. "They literally spring out of the parking lots at you with scripts - nobody can read a thousand scripts a year and still work."
10. "My best feature's my smile. And smiles - pray heaven - don't get fat."

10 THINGS SAID BY JOHN CLEESE

1. "People try to change the world - instead of themselves."

2. "I've spent two years of my life in America and I've married Americans...but I still feel insecure about making jokes there."

3. "I get bored easily. I've been bored most of my life."

4. "A director friend - I won't name him - was obliged to have a special $750,000 cocaine budget for his actors. I saw the film and said: 'All the money's on the screen'."

5. "Tension is wonderful for making people laugh."

6. "I've done commercials in Australia I'd pay you not to see."

7. "I'm the worst singer in Western Europe. I mean, horrendous. I was in *Half A Sixpence* on Broadway in 1965 on condition that I mime."

8. "I'm getting very curious about what I'm going to be doing *after* I'm dead."

9. "I hate two towns. Edmonton and Aswan. I've enjoyed all the rest. Even New Zealand."

10. "If I finish being married five times for seven years each time, that for me will probably be more interesting than one for 35 years. I know you're not supposed to say it, but why not?"

10 THINGS SAID ABOUT CHILDREN

1. "The trouble with children is that they are not returnable." (Quentin Crisp)

2. "Insanity is hereditary: you can get it from your children." (Sam Levenson)

3. "It was no wonder that people were so horrible when they started life as children." (Sir Kingsley Amis)

4. "My mother loved children - she would have given anything if I had been one." (Groucho Marx)

5. "I love children - especially when they cry, for then someone takes them away." (Nancy Mitford)

6. "This would be a better world for children if parents had to eat the spinach." (Groucho Marx)

7. "Never have children, only grandchildren." (Gore Vidal)

8. "The quickest way for a parent to get a child's attention is to sit down and look comfortable." (Lane Olinghouse)

9. "The main purpose of children's parties is to remind you that there are children more awful than your own." (Katherine Whitehorn)

10. "Whenever a child lies you will always find a severe parent. A lie would have no sense unless the truth were felt to be dangerous." (Alfred Adler)

Chapter 10

People

10 PEOPLE WITH BEAUTY SPOTS

1. Madonna
2. Robert De Niro
3. Cheryl Ladd
4. Roger Moore
5. Cindy Crawford
6. Lisa Stansfield
7. Sherilyn Fenn
8. Lynsey De Paul
9. Chesney Hawkes
10. Marilyn Monroe

10 PEOPLE WHO NEVER MARRIED

1. Greta Garbo
2. Sir Isaac Newton
3. Florence Nightingale
4. Ludwig van Beethoven
5. Cecil Rhodes
6. Frederic Chopin
7. Dame Flora Robson
8. Queen Elizabeth I
9. Ivor Novello
10. Jane Austen

10 PEOPLE WHO MARRIED SIX OR MORE TIMES

1. Mike Love (of The Beach Boys): 9 Marriages
2. Zsa Zsa Gabor: 9
3. Stan Laurel: 8
4. Lana Turner: 8
5. Mickey Rooney: 8
6. Elizabeth Taylor: 7
7. Sir Rex Harrison: 6
8. Johnny Weissmuller: 6
9. Gloria Swanson: 6
10. Hedy Lamarr: 6

10 SHORT-LIVED MARRIAGES

1. Rudolph Valentino and Jean Acker (One day)
2. Drew Barrymore and Jeremy Thomas (Six weeks)
3. Dennis Hopper and Michelle Phillips (One week)
4. Germaine Greer and Paul Du Feu (Three weeks)
5. Gloria Swanson and Wallace Beery (Three weeks)
6. Burt Lancaster and June Ernst (Less than one month)
7. Katharine Hepburn and Ludlow Ogden Smith (Three weeks)
8. Greer Garson and Edward Snelson (Five weeks)
9. John Milton and Mary Powell (One month)
10. Dennis Wilson and Karen Lamm (Seven months first time; Two weeks second time)

10 PEOPLE AND THE AGE AT WHICH THEY LOST THEIR VIRGINITY

1. Joan Rivers (20)
2. James Caan (13)
3. Don Johnson (12)
4. Bob Geldof (13)
5. Cher (14)
6. George Bernard Shaw (29)
7. Tina Turner (15)
8. Joan Collins (17)
9. Bobby Davro (15)
10. George Michael (13)

10 COUPLES WHO REMARRIED EACH OTHER AFTER GETTING DIVORCED

1. Elizabeth Taylor & Richard Burton
2. Melanie Griffith & Don Johnson
3. Sarah Miles & Robert Bolt
4. Elliott Gould & Jenny Bogart
5. Robert Wagner & Natalie Wood
6. Dorothy Parker & Alan Campbell
7. George Peppard & Elizabeth Ashley
8. Jane Wyman & Fred Karger
9. Dionne Warwick & Bill Elliott
10. Paul Hogan & Noelene Edwards

10 BEST MEN

	GROOM	BEST MAN
1.	David Bailey	Mick Jagger
2.	Kenneth Clarke	John Selwyn Gummer
3.	Jeremy Irons	Christopher Biggins
4.	Bob Geldof	Dave Stewart
5.	Kenneth Branagh	Brian Blessed
6.	John McEnroe	Bjorn Borg
7.	John Lennon	Brian Epstein
8.	Viv Richards	Ian Botham
9.	Tommy Steele	Lionel Bart
10.	Jimmy Mulville	Rory McGrath

10 PEOPLE WHO MARRIED BEFORE THE AGE OF 16

1. Emma Ridley (15)
2. Mahatma Gandhi (13)
3. Myra Gale Brown (Mrs Jerry Lee Lewis) (13)
4. Mary, Queen of Scots (15)
5. Zsa Zsa Gabor (15)
6. Catherine the Great (15)
7. Annie Oakley (15)
8. Loretta Lynn (13)
9. Jihan Sadat (Mrs Anwar Sadat) (15)
10. Marie Antoinette (14)

10 PEOPLE WITH FAMOUS FATHERS IN-LAW

	DAUGHTERS/ SONS-IN-LAW	FATHERS-IN-LAW
1.	Barry Humphries	Sir Stephen Spender
2.	Loyd Grossman	Sir David Puttnam
3.	Anthony Quinn	Cecil B. De Mille
4.	Axl Rose	Don Everly
5.	Charles Chaplin	Eugene O'Neill
6.	Karen Dotrice	Wilfred Hyde-White
7.	Richard Wagner	Franz Liszt
8.	Belinda Carlisle	James Mason
9.	Sir David Frost	The Duke of Norfolk
10.	John McEnroe	Ryan O'Neal

10 WOMEN WHO HAD CHILDREN AFTER THE AGE OF 40

1. Priscilla Presley
2. Goldie Hawn
3. Esther Rantzen
4. Elkie Brooks
5. Britt Ekland
6. Lucille Ball
7. Jan Leeming
8. Audrey Hepburn
9. Gloria Vanderbilt
10. Ursula Andress

10 MEN WHO WERE HOMOSEXUALS

1. Cole Porter. Tried marriage but it was doomed to failure given the great songwriter's leanings. Porter paid for gay sex but his most 'famous' homosexual relationship was with John 'Black Jack' Bouvier, the father of Jackie Onassis.

2. Leonardo da Vinci. The greatest artist of all time was a lifelong homosexual. At the age of 24, he was arrested for going with a 17-year old male prostitute and was jailed for a short time before his friends could release him.

3. King Edward II. King Eddie had a 14-year relationship with Piers Gaveston and was later murdered with a red-hot poker up his, er, 'fundament'.

4. John Maynard Keynes. The great British economist was a practising homosexual. In fact, he and the prominent biographer, Lytton Strachey, used to compete for male conquests. It was Strachey who, when asked by an army tribunal what he would do if he found a German soldier raping his sister, replied that he would take her place.

5. Julius Caesar. Unlike his wife, the great Roman geezer was NOT 'above suspicion' - indulging in all sorts of homosexual practices. But then the ancient world was like that: Alexander The Great, Socrates, Sophocles and Hadrian were all homo- or bi-sexual. No wonder Caesar was surprised when Brutus stabbed him...

6. Peter Tchaikovsky. The great Russian composer so detested his homosexuality that he married his student. Unfortunately, she was a psychopathic nymphomaniac. The marriage was never consummated and Tchaikovsky went back to the gay and narrow.

7. Hans Christian Andersen. The Danish writer was a notorious homosexual. Gives a new meaning to the expression 'fairy tale'. Interestingly, Andersen died falling out of bed.

8. Tennessee Williams. The American playwright was 28 when he first had gay sex - with a soldier in New Orleans. He was exclusively homosexual for the rest of his life.

9. E.M. Forster. Like Tennessee Williams, Forster was a late starter - recording his first gay encounter at the age of 31 on the living-room sofa. He too was resolutely homosexual.

10. James Dean. Although his sexual proclivities were hushed up in his lifetime, he was once quoted as saying "well I'm not going through life with one hand tied behind my back" when asked if he was homosexual. He himself confessed to five homosexual relationships.

10 MEN WHO FATHERED A CHILD LATE IN LIFE

1. Anthony Quinn (81)
2. Charlie Chaplin (73)
3. Clint Eastwood (66)
4. John Mortimer (61)
5. Cary Grant (62)
6. Yves Montand (67)
7. Bruce Forsyth (58)
8. Marlon Brando (65)
9. Pablo Picasso (62)
10. Arthur English (61)

10 VEGETARIANS

1. Joe Longthorne
2. Clare Francis
3. Tony Blackburn
4. Victoria Wood
5. Gaby Roslin
6. Gary Glitter
7. Captain Sensible
8. Kate Bush
9. Kate O'Mara
10. Elvis Costello

10 VEGANS

1. Carl Lewis
2. Uri Geller
3. k.d. lang
4. Dannii Minogue
5. Sinead O'Connor
6. Heather Small (M-People)
7. Yazz
8. Benjamin Zephaniah
9. Sophie Ward
10. William Shatner

110 WOMEN WHO POPPED THE QUESTION

1. Zsa Zsa Gabor. The much (9) married actress proposed to her first husband when she was just 15 years old. He accepted and they married before her 16th birthday. "Dahlink" Zsa Zsa had recently been disqualified from the Miss Hungary title for being under 16.

2. Pamela Stephenson. The comedienne and the comedian Billy Connolly lived together and had three children before deciding to tie the knot. During that time, she has said that they "went through periods of proposing to each other".

3. Countess Spencer. The former model proposed to the late Princess of Wales's brother in the days when he was plain Viscount Althorp. Apparently, he asked her to marry him but she wouldn't answer because she thought he might be tiddly. The next morning, she asked him.

4. Joan Collins. The actress (and novelist) proposed to Anthony Newley after deciding that he was the man for her. They had both been married before and their marriage too broke up but they have remained friends.

5. Queen Victoria. Victoria became Queen of England at the age of 18 and quickly realised that she had an obligation to produce an heir. She decided to marry her German cousin, Prince Albert. She duly summoned him and proposed marriage - telling him that it would make her "too happy" if he would accept.

6. Jerry Hall. 13 years before they tied the knot, the Bovril-drinking Texan-born model had given Mick Jagger an ultimatum that they had to get married within ten years. The three years' grace obviously helped to concentrate the Rolling Stone's mind.

7. Edwina Currie. Of all the women in this list - even including the two Queens - the MP is the least surprising. She has said of her husband that she "found out he was very close to his parents" and so "asked him to marry me".

8. Janet Brown. The comedienne and impressionist has said that instead of her intended asking for her "hand in marriage", it was "the other way round".

9. Queen Elizabeth II. Although no one has ever been told whether the Queen proposed to Philip or whether he proposed to her, it is thought likely that she was the one who popped the question as royal protocol demanded it.

10. Maureen Lipman. The *Agony* actress proposed to husband Jack Rosenthal, the playwright and former *Coronation Street* writer. He had been married before and she says that it took her four years to persuade him to tie the knot.

10 PEOPLE WHO HAVE BEEN THE VICTIMS OF STALKERS

1. Steffi Graf
2. Jodie Foster
3. Michaela Strachan
4. Lady Helen Taylor
5. Cliff Richard
6. Chris Evert
7. Ben Elton
8. Michael Crawford
9. Geena Davis
10. Helena Bonham Carter

10 PEOPLE WHO INSURED PARTS OF THEIR BODIES

1. Michael Flatley: Legs for £25 million
2. David Seaman: Hands for £1 million
3. Bruce Springsteen: Voice for £3.5 million
4. Dolly Parton: Bust for £2 million
5. Ken Dodd: Teeth for £4 million
6. Jamie Lee Curtis: Legs for £1.5 million
7. Nigel Benn: Fists for £10 million
8. Keith Richards: Third finger of his left hand for £1 million
9. Merv Hughes: Moustache for £200,000
10. Mark King: Hands for £1 million

10 OLD ETONIANS

1. Jonathon Porritt
2. Sir Ludovic Kennedy
3. Christopher Cazenove
4. Sir Ranulph Fiennes
5. Patrick Macnee
6. Tam Dalyell
7. Ian Fleming
8. Guy Burgess
9. George Orwell
10. Aldous Huxley

10 PEOPLE WHO WENT BANKRUPT

1. Kevin Maxwell
2. Margot Kidder
3. Walt Disney
4. Alan Bond
5. Eddie Fisher
6. Grace Jones
7. Mark Twain
8. Mickey Rooney
9. Peter Adamson
10. Lionel Bart

10 OLD HARROVIANS

1. Patrick Lichfield
2. Lord Byron
3. Terence Rattigan
4. Sir Robert Peel
5. Cecil Beaton
6. Sir Winston Churchill
7. John Profumo
8. Mark Thatcher
9. John Mortimer
10. Edward Fox

10 PEOPLE WHO LAUNCHED THEIR OWN PRODUCTS

1. Burt Reynolds: Jewellery
2. Joan Collins: Jeans
3. Paula Yates: Underwear
4. Paul Newman: Salad dressing
5. Fran Cotton and Steve Smith: Sportswear
6. Jerry Hall: Swimwear
7. Pepsi and Shirlie: Girls' clothes
8. Linda McCartney: Vegetarian frozen food
9. Princess Stephanie: Swimwear
10. Ken Kercheval: Popcorn

10 PEOPLE WHO LAUNCHED PERFUMES

1. Linda Evans: *Forever Krystle*
2. Elizabeth Taylor: *White Diamonds*
3. Englebert Humperdinck: *Release Me*
4. Omar Sharif: *Omar Sharif*
5. Sophia Loren: *Sophia*
6. Bjorn Borg: *Signature*
7. Cynthia Lennon: *Cynthia Lennon's Woman*
8. Joan Collins: *Scoundrel*
9. Luciano Pavarotti: *Luciano Pavarotti Parfum For Men*
10. Catherine Deneuve: *Deneuve*

10 PEOPLE WE'VE NEVER MET

1. Mrs Mainwaring (the wife of *Dad's Army's* Captain Mainwaring)
2. Everard and Slack Alice (pals of the late Larry Grayson)
3. Mrs Columbo (the wife of the raincoat-clad detective)
4. Kilroy (as in 'Kilroy Was Here')
5. Charlie (of *Charlie's Angels*)
6. 'Er Indoors (the trouble and strife of Arthur Daley)
7. Godot (as in *Waiting For Godot*)
8. Norman Everage (The Dame's late unlamented husband)
9. Carlton the doorman (in *Rhoda*)
10. Abigail (the eponymous heroine of Mike Leigh's *Abigail's Party* who doesn't show up no matter how many times you watch the video)

10 FORMER MINERS

1. Paul Shane
2. Sir Jimmy Savile
3. Dennis Skinner
4. Charles Bronson
5. Anthony & Peter Shaffer
6. Fred Trueman
7. Jeffrey Bernard
8. Jocky Wilson
9. Harold Larwood
10. Ray Reardon

10 PEOPLE AND WHAT THEY DID BEFORE

1. Belinda Carlisle: Petrol-pump attendant
2. Eric Bristow: Furniture salesman
3. Jeremy Irons: Social Worker
4. Ali MacGraw: Journalist
5. Chris Waddle: Sausage factory worker
6. Craig McLachlan: Plumber's assistant
7. Burt Lancaster: Circus Acrobat
8. Gloria Estefan: Interpreter
9. Terry Griffiths: Bus conductor
10. Simon Le Bon: Lumberjack

10 PEOPLE AND WHAT THEIR FATHERS DID FOR A LIVING

1. Michael Jackson (Crane Driver)
2. Faye Dunaway (U.S. Army Sergeant)
3. Barry McGuigan (Singer)
4. Ruby Wax (Sausage-skin manufacturer)
5. Roger Moore (Policeman)
6. Noel Edmonds (Headmaster)
7. Mel Smith (Bookmaker)
8. Sting (Milkman)
9. Jimmy Nail (Professional Soccer Player)
10. Patricia Hodge (Hotelier)

10 FORMER BOY SCOUTS

1. Michael Barrymore
2. George Michael
3. Melvyn Bragg
4. Ken Dodd
5. John Major
6. Paul McCartney
7. Jim Davidson
8. Ronnie Corbett
9. Sir Cliff Richard
10. Chris Tarrant

10 FORMER TEACHERS

1. Tom O'Connor
2. Sarah Kennedy
3. Sting
4. Gareth Hale
5. Bryan Ferry
6. Brian Glover
7. Ian Dury
8. Patricia Hodge
9. George C. Scott
10. Jim Bowen

10 FORMER GIRL GUIDES

1. Sarah Greene
2. Mandy Rice-Davies
3. Carol Vorderman
4. Anneka Rice
5. Delia Smith
6. Kim Wilde
7. Carol Smillie
8. Cherie Blair
9. The Queen
10. Gloria Hunniford

10 FORMER HAIRDRESSERS

1. Chuck Berry
2. Lewis Collins
3. Alison Moyet
4. Mike McGear
5. Yazz
6. Limahl
7. Danny De Vito
8. Sid James
9. Michael Barrymore
10. Twiggy

10 DYSLEXICS

1. Tom Cruise
2. Ruth Madoc
3. Michael Heseltine
4. Leslie Ash
5. Susan Hampshire
6. Duncan Goodhew
7. Cher
8. Henry Winkler
9. Sarah Miles
10. Jackie Stewart

10 PEOPLE WHO DIDN'T GO TO UNIVERSITY

1. Richard Branson
2. Sir James Goldsmith
3. Joanna Lumley
4. Sir John Harvey-Jones
5. Jilly Cooper
6. Patrick Moore
7. Alan Sugar
8. Anita Roddick
9. Peter De Savary
10. Sue Townsend

10 PEOPLE WITH NATIVE AMERICAN BLOOD

1. Burt Reynolds
2. Johnny Depp
3. Waylon Jennings
4. Cher
5. Mike McShane
6. Tiger Woods
7. Johnny Cash
8. Lena Horne
9. Jimi Hendrix
10. James Garner

10 PEOPLE WHO USED TO WORK IN SHOPS

1. Gary Numan (W.H. Smith)
2. Russ Abbot (Hepworths)
3. Mick Fleetwood (Liberty)
4. Betty Boo (Marks & Spencer)
5. Glenda Jackson (Boots)
6. Wendy Richards (Fortnum & Mason)
7. George Michael (BHS)
8. Annie Lennox (Mothercare)
9. Ted Rogers (W.H. Smith)
10. Bobby Davro (Bentalls)

10 THINGS PEOPLE DID

1. Jim Dale co-wrote the song *Georgy Girl*
2. Clive James once worked cleaning out a lion's cage
3. Shirley Williams screen-tested for the lead role in *National Velvet*
4. Lord Weidenfeld once fought a duel
5. Melvyn Bragg co-wrote the film of the musical *Jesus Christ Superstar*
6. Hugh Laurie rowed for Cambridge in the Boat Race
7. Simon Le Bon has kept bees
8. David Bellamy wrote a ballet (*Heritage*)
9. Debbie Harry used to be a Playboy bunny
10. When he was Viscount Althorp, Earl Spencer appeared in the film *Another Country*

10 MEMBERS OF MENSA

1. Sir Clive Sinclair (Inventor)
2. Sir Jimmy Savile (Broadcaster and Charity Worker)
3. Geena Davis (Actress)
4. Carol Vorderman (Mathematician and TV Presenter)
5. Leslie Charteris (Author of *The Saint*)
6. Garry Bushell (TV Critic of *The Sun*)
7. Carol Smillie (TV Presenter)
8. Sir Terence Beckett (Former Director of The CBI)
9. Jeremy Hanley (MP)
10. Adrian Moorhouse (Champion Swimmer)

10 PEOPLE WHO LOST AN EYE

1. Gordon Banks (Former England Goalkeeper)
2. Sir Rex Harrison (Actor)
3. Herbert Morrison (Former Deputy Leader of the Labour Party)
4. Joe Davis (Legendary Snooker Player)
5. James Thurber (Celebrated American Humourist)
6. Colin Milburn (Former England Cricketer)
7. John Ford (American Film Director)
8. Moshe Dayan (Israeli General)
9. Peter Falk (Actor)
10. John Milton (English writer who wrote *Paradise Lost*)

10 PEOPLE WHO HAVE SWITCHED ON THE OXFORD STREET LIGHTS

1. Lenny Henry (1994. In 1995, the cast of *Coronation Street* did it; In 1996, The Spice Girls did it).
2. Richard Branson (1993)
3. Linford Christie (1992)
4. Cliff Richard (1990. In 1991, disabled children from Westminster Children's Hospital performed the ceremony)
5. Gorden Kaye (1989)
6. Terry Wogan (1988)
7. Derek Jameson (1987)
8. Bob Geldof (1985. In 1986, 'Den & Angie' - Leslie Grantham and Anita Dobson - of *EastEnders* had done it)
9. Esther Rantzen (1984)
10. Pat Phoenix (1983 - succeeding Daley Thompson who had switched on the lights the year before)

10 PEOPLE WHO HAVE SWITCHED ON THE BLACKPOOL LIGHTS

1. George Formby (1953)
2. Gracie Fields (1964)
3. Lisa Stansfield (1992)
4. Shirley Bassey (1994)
5. The Bee Gees (1995)
6. Stanley Matthews (1951)
7. Sir Matt Busby (1968)
8. Gordon Banks (1973)
9. Frank Bruno (1989)
10. Jayne Mansfield (1959)

10 PEOPLE WITH UNIMAGINATIVE FIRST NAMES

1. Eddie Edwards
2. Kris Kristofferson
3. Jerome K. Jerome
4. Bobby Robson
5. Dave Davies
6. Magnus Magnusson
7. Bev Bevan
8. Sirhan Sirhan
9. Mitch Mitchell
10. Boutros Boutros-Ghali

10 PEOPLE WHO DID VSO (Voluntary Services Overseas)

1. Michael Brunson
2. Lord Skelmersdale
3. Jeremy Corbyn
4. Anton Lesser
5. David Essex (as an Ambassador)
6. Lord Bradford
7. Brian Hanrahan
8. Jon Snow
9. Robert Lacey
10. Robin Denselow

10 PEOPLE AND THE FOREIGN LANGUAGES THEY CAN SPEAK

1. Clive James (Japanese)
2. Prince Philip (German)
3. Gary Lineker (Spanish)
4. Sir John Harvey-Jones (Russian)
5. Kate Adie (Swedish)
6. Shirley Maclaine (Japanese)
7. Susannah York (French)
8. Alan Bennett (Russian)
9. Lord Denis Healey (Italian)
10. Prunella Scales (French)

10 PEOPLE AWARDED HONORARY DEGREES

1. Sue Lawley (LLD, Bristol University)
2. Sir Richard Attenborough (DLitt, Sussex University)
3. Tessa Sanderson (BSc, Birmingham)
4. Sean Connery (DLitt, Heriot-Watt)
5. Kenneth Branagh (DLitt, Belfast)
6. Dame Maggie Smith (DLitt, London)
7. Bob Geldof (MA, Kent)
8. Patrick Moore (DSc, Birmingham)
9. Gary Lineker (MA, Leicester)
10. Sir Anthony Hopkins (DLitt, University of Wales)

10 WOMEN WHO WERE BEAUTY QUEENS

1. Gina Lollobrigida (Miss Italy 1946)
2. Debbie Greenwood (Miss Great Britain 1984)
3. Sophia Loren (Miss Elegance 1950)
4. Michelle Pfeiffer (Miss Orange County 1976)
5. Raquel Welch (Miss Photogenic 1953)
6. Debbie Reynolds (Miss Burbank 1948)
7. Lauren Bacall (Miss Greenwich Village 1942)
8. Zsa Zsa Gabor (Miss Hungary 1936)
9. Dyan Cannon (Miss West Seattle 1957)
10. Cybill Shepherd (Miss Teenage Memphis 1966)

10 RAILWAY ENTHUSIASTS

1. Frank Sinatra
2. Peter Snow
3. Chris Donald
4. Jim Bowen
5. Keith Floyd
6. Timothy West
7. Phil Collins
8. Michael Palin
9. Pete Waterman
10. Jools Holland

10 QUALIFIED LAWYERS

1. Margaret Thatcher
2. Clive Anderson
3. Osvaldo Ardiles
4. Mahatma Gandhi
5. Sir Robin Day
6. John Mortimer
7. Hoagy Carmichael
8. Tony Blair
9. Fidel Castro
10. David Mellor

10 THINGS PEOPLE COLLECT

1. Old photographs (Brian May)
2. Dolls' houses and furniture (Dame Judi Dench)
3. Literary autographs (Sir Tom Stoppard)
4. Ornamental ducks (Josie Lawrence)
5. Comics (Jonathan Ross)
6. Old radios (Steve Wright)
7. Koi carp (Jim Davidson)
8. Motor racing books (George Harrison)
9. Porcelain pigs (Janet Jackson)
10. Old tin-plate toys (Michael Barrymore)

10 MEN WHO WERE DECORATED FOR THEIR PART IN WORLD WAR II

1. Viscount Whitelaw (MC)
2. Sir Edward Heath (MBE)
3. Dr Robert Runcie (MC)
4. Lord Carrington (MC)
5. John Profumo (OBE)
6. Denis Healey (MBE)
7. Audie Murphy (the most decorated American soldier in World War II, he won 36 medals for battlefield bravery including the Congressional Medal of Honor)
8. Enoch Powell (MBE)
9. Brian Johnston (MC)
10. Robert Maxwell (MC)

10 MEN WHO WERE PILOTS IN WORLD WAR II

1. Hughie Green
2. James Stewart
3. Ted Croker
4. Ian Smith
5. Kenneth Wolstenholme
6. George Bush
7. Bill Edrich
8. Raymond Baxter
9. Sir Rex Hunt
10. Dick Francis

10 PEOPLE AWARDED THE FREEDOM OF THE CITY OF LONDON

1. Billy Walker
2. Angela Rippon
3. Ernie Wise
4. Martyn Lewis
5. Sir Cliff Richard
6. Clare Francis
7. Lionel Bart
8. Terry Venables
9. Prunella Scales
10. Mike Oldfield

10 WORLD WAR II POWs

1. Clive Dunn
2. Denholm Elliott
3. Robert Kee
4. Angus Maude
5. Sam Kydd
6. Donald Pleasance
7. Roy Dotrice
8. The Earl of Harewood
9. Ronald Searle
10. E.W. Swanton

10 PEOPLE EXPELLED FROM SCHOOL

1. Roger Daltrey (Acton Grammar School)
2. Peter De Savary (Charterhouse)
3. Rupert Everett (Ampleforth)
4. Humphrey Bogart (Phillips Academy)
5. Boy George (Eltham Green School)
6. Jackie Collins (Francis Holland School)
7. Jade Jagger (St. Mary's Calne)
8. Richard Pryor (Central High School)
9. Raymond Baxter (Ilford County High School)
10. Stephen Fry (Uppingham)

O LEVELS 1-10

1. Peter de Savary
2. Betty Boo
3. John McCririck
4. Gary Lineker
5. Paul Daniels
6. Phillip Schofield
7. Kim Wilde
8. Amanda de Cadenet
9. Prince Edward
10. Anneka Rice

10 HARLEY DAVIDSON OWNERS

1. Alison Holloway
2. Viscount Linley
3. Midge Ure
4. Arnold Schwarzenegger
5. Whitney Houston
6. Burt Reynolds
7. Eric Clapton
8. Sylvester Stallone
9. Billy Idol
10. Jon Bon Jovi

10 UNICEF AMBASSADORS

1. Roger Moore
2. Julio Iglesias
3. Emmanuelle Beart
4. Sir Edmund Hillary
5. Imran Khan
6. Liam Neeson
7. George Weah
8. Lord Richard Attenborough
9. Liv Ullmann
10. Sir Peter Ustinov

10 NON-DRIVERS

1. Marianne Faithfull
2. Morrissey
3. Barry Cryer
4. Bernard Levin
5. Michael Jackson
6. Simon Gray
7. Sir David Attenborough
8. Gillian Clarke (wife of Ken)
9. David Copperfield
10. Kate Saunders

10 MEN WHO HAD AIRPORTS NAMED AFTER THEM

1. John Wayne (U.S.)
2. John F. Kennedy (U.S.)
3. Charles de Gaulle (France)
4. David Ben-Gurion (Israel)
5. Leonardo da Vinci (Italy)
6. King Khalid (Saudi Arabia)
7. Jan Smuts (South Africa)
8. Owen Roberts (U.S.)
9. Marco Polo (Italy)
10. Joshua Logan (U.S.)

10 PEOPLE WHO CHANGED CITIZENSHIP

1. Warren Mitchell (from British to Australian)
2. Joe Bugner (from British to Australian)
3. Martina Navratilova (from Czech to American)
4. Nadia Comaneci (from Romanian to American)
5. Yehudi Menuhin (from American to British)
6. Greta Scacchi (from British to Australian)
7. Andrew Sachs (from German to British)
8. Zola Budd (from South African to British to South African)
9. Ivan Lendl (from Czech to American)
10. Allan Lamb (from South African to British)

10 PEOPLE KNOWN BY THEIR INITIALS

1. O. J. (Orenthal James) Simpson
2. H. G. (Herbert George) Wells
3. k. d. (Kathryn Dawn) lang
4. P.D. James (Phyllis Dorothy)
5. J. P. R. (John Peter Rhys) Williams
6. J.M. Barrie (James Matthew)
7. W. C. (William Claude) Fields
8. P. J. (Patrick Jake) O'Rourke
9. D. H. (David Herbert) Lawrence
10. J. R. R. (John Ronald Reuel) Tolkien

10 PEOPLE WHO'VE DONE PARACHUTE JUMPS WITH THE RED DEVILS

1. Jim Davidson
2. Phillip Schofield
3. Tom Baker
4. Ian Ogilvy
5. Matthew Kelly
6. Jeremy Beadle
7. Suzanne Dando
8. Sarah Kennedy
9. Tony Blackburn
10. Roddy Llewellyn

10 MEN WHO TURNED DOWN KNIGHTHOODS

1. Graham Greene
2. Alastair Sim
3. J.B. Priestley
4. Augustus John
5. Henry Moore
6. Francis Bacon
7. T.S. Eliot
8. Michael Faraday
9. E.M. Forster
10. Joe Gormley (although he accepted a peerage)

10 HONORARY KNIGHTS

1. Ronald Reagan (1989)
2. Sidney Poitier (1974)
3. André Previn (1996)
4. Colin Powell (1993)
5. President Mitterrand (1984)
6. Alistair Cooke (1973)
7. Magnus Magnusson (1989)
8. Bob Geldof (1986)
9. Douglas Fairbanks Jr. (1949)
10. Lech Walesa (1991)

10 LIVING LEFT-HANDED PEOPLE

1. David Gower
2. Bill Clinton
3. Sarah Greene
4. Uri Geller
5. Jimmy White
6. George Bush
7. Nerys Hughes
8. Paul McCartney
9. Esther Rantzen
10. Terence Stamp

10 LEFT-HANDED PEOPLE IN HISTORY

1. Horatio Nelson
2. King George II
3. Sir Charles Chaplin
4. Leonardo da Vinci
5. Judy Garland
6. Cole Porter
7. Danny Kaye
8. Harpo Marx
9. Sir Rex Harrison
10. Michelangelo

10 KEEN ORNITHOLOGISTS

1. Bill Oddie
2. Norman Lamont
3. Peter Cushing
5. Judith Chalmers
6. Jack Cunningham
7. Nigel Planer
8. Magnus Magnusson
9. Daryl Hall
10. Bernard Cribbins

10 WINNERS OF THE GUILD OF PROFESSIONAL TOASTMASTERS BEST AFTER-DINNER SPEAKER OF THE YEAR AWARD

1. Clement Freud (1972)
2. Denis Norden (1991)
3. Sheila Hancock (1969)
4. Lord Tonypandy (1988)
5. Margaret Thatcher (1989)
6. Jimmy Tarbuck (1997)
7. Sir Peter Ustinov (1990)
8. Rachael Heyhoe Flint (1973)
9. Harold Wilson (1968)
10. Bob Monkhouse (1987)

10 PEOPLE WHO WERE IN THE NAVY

1. George Melly
2. Sir Alec Guinness
3. Hammer (MC Hammer)
4. Sean Connery
5. Ludovic Kennedy
6. Sir John Harvey-Jones
7. Richard Baker
8. Lord Callaghan
9. Ken Russell*
10. Tommy Steele*

*=Merchant Navy.

10 PEOPLE WHO HAVE FLOWN HELICOPTERS

1. Ian Botham
2. The Duchess of York
3. The Duke of York
4. Adam Faith
5. Mark Thatcher
6. Kenny Jones
7. Noel Edmonds
8. The Prince of Wales
9. Barry Sheene
10. David Essex

10 WOMEN WHO HAVE BEEN 'REAR OF THE YEAR'

1. Felicity Kendal
2. Lulu
3. Ulrika Jonsson
4. Elaine Paige
5. Su Pollard
6. Marina Ogilvy
7. Anneka Rice
8. Barbara Windsor
9. Anita Dobson
10. Suzi Quatro

10 PEOPLE WITH SUITABLE NAMES

1. Fred Housego
2. Quentin Crisp
3. Valerie Singleton
4. Melvyn Bragg
5. Janet Street-Porter
6. Cher
7. Tony Swift
8. Victor Mature
9. Steve Bull
10. Christopher Biggins

10 PEOPLE WITH UNSUITABLE NAMES

1. Jimmy Young
2. Chris Waddle
3. Simon Callow
4. Cilla Black
5. Barry White
6. Olivia Hussey
7. Sharon Stone
8. Katie Boyle
9. Sir David Steel
10. Madonna

10 FAMOUS COUSINS

1. Ginger Rogers and Rita Hayworth
2. Jon Snow and Peter Snow
3. Christopher Lee and Ian Fleming
4. Richard Briers and Terry-Thomas
5. Cyrille Regis and John Regis
6. Whitney Houston and Dionne Warwick
7. Peter Townsend (Princess Margaret's former 'boyfriend') and Hugh Gaitskell
8. Natasha Richardson and Jemma Redgrave
9. Patrick Macnee and David Niven
10. Rip Torn and Sissy Spacek

10 PEOPLE AND THE SUBJECTS THEY STUDIED AT UNIVERSITY

1. Rowan Atkinson: Electrical Engineering
2. William Roache: Medicine
3. Paul Simon: English
4. Chris Lowe: Architecture
5. Jonathan Ross: East European Modern History
6. Donald Fagen: English
7. Victoria Principal: Law
8. Harry Enfield: Politics
9. Chrissie Hynde: Art
10. Anna Ford: Economics

10 PAIRS OF PEOPLE WHO ATTENDED THE SAME SCHOOL

1. Salman Rushdie and Robert Hardy (Rugby)
2. Noel Edmonds and Griff Rhys-Jones (Brentwood)
3. Shane MacGowan and Sir Andrew Lloyd Webber (Westminster)
4. Baroness Lynda Chalker and Sarah Miles (Roedean)
5. Tom Stoppard and Ade Edmondson (Pocklington)
6. Ben Kingsley and Robert Powell (Manchester Grammar)
7. Barry Davies and Brian Moore (Cranbrook)
8. John Patten and Paul Merton (Wimbledon College)
9. Keith Floyd and Lord Jeffrey Archer (Wellington (Somerset))
10. Hugh Grant and Mel Smith (Latymer Upper)

10 PEOPLE AND WHAT THEY HAD ACHIEVED BY THE AGE OF 10

1. At the age of 3, Elizabeth Taylor danced in front of King George V
2. At the age of 5, Sergei Prokofiev composed his first piece of music
3. At the age of 4, Gustav Mahler composed his first piece of music
4. At the age of 5, Natalie Wood appeared in her first film
5. At the age of 3, the 19th Century English philosopher John Stuart Mill was able to read Greek
6. At the age of 8, Wolfgang Mozart composed his first symphony
7. At the age of 7, Fred Astaire was performing in vaudeville
8. At the age of 9, Ruth Lawrence passed 'A' Level Maths
9. At the age of 6, Shirley Temple was awarded an honorary Oscar "in grateful recognition of her outstanding contribution to screen entertainment during the year 1934"
10. At the age of 9, Macaulay Culkin was cast as the lead character in *Home Alone*, the movie which made him famous

10 PEOPLE WHO WERE ADOPTED

1. George Cole
2. Wendy James
3. Fatima Whitbread
4. Eric Clapton
5. Ex-President Gerald Ford
6. Daley Thompson
7. Dame Kiri Te Kanawa
8. Rob Newman
9. Debbie Harry
10. Mike McShane

10 PEOPLE WHO DROPPED OUT OF COLLEGE

1. Richard Dreyfuss
2. Carly Simon
3. David Gower
4. Bill Cosby
5. Jon Snow
6. Warren Beatty
7. Mick Jagger
8. Jane Fonda
9. Michael Douglas
10. Candice Bergen

10 THINGS ACHIEVED BY ELDERLY PEOPLE

1. At the age of 85, Mae West starred in the film *Sextet*
2. At the age of 84, W. Somerset Maugham published a collection of essays entitled *Points Of View*
3. At the age of 95, the American pianist Artur Rubinstein gave a public concert
4. At the age of 87, Francis Rous was awarded the 1966 Nobel Prize for Medicine
5. At the age of 87, Sir John Gielgud starred in the film *Prospero's Books*
6. At the age of 91, Eamon De Valera was President of Ireland
7. At the age of 84, William Gladstone was Prime Minister of Britain
8. At the age of 82, Sir Winston Churchill published part one of his four-part *History Of The English Speaking Peoples*
9. At the age of 80, George Burns won an Oscar for his role in *The Sunshine Boys*. He died at the age of 100 having only retired from live performing three years previously
10. At the age of 88, Michelangelo was still sculpting

10 PEOPLE EDUCATED AT HOME

1. Agatha Christie
2. Gerald Durrell
3. Molly Keane
4. C. S. Lewis
5. Sir Yehudi Menuhin
6. Ruth Lawrence
7. Alexander Graham Bell
8. Caitlin Moran
9. The Queen
10. George Bernard Shaw

10 CONSCIENTIOUS OBJECTORS

1. President Bill Clinton
2. Paul Eddington
3. Sir Michael Redgrave
4. Carl Wilson (of The Beach Boys)
5. Muhammad Ali
6. Lord Soper
7. Dom Mintoff
8. Donald Swann
9. Richard Dreyfuss
10. Harold Pinter

10 INSOMNIACS

1. Sir Winston Churchill
2. Marilyn Monroe
3. Derek Jameson
4. Vincent Van Gogh
5. Margaret Thatcher
6. Napoleon Bonaparte
7. Michael Aspel
8. Charles Dickens
9. Phil Edmonds
10. Cary Grant

10 NAMES PEOPLE GAVE TO THEIR CHILDREN

1. Moon Unit (Frank Zappa)
2. Dandelion (Keith Richards)
3. Rain (Richard Pryor)
4. Elijah Blue (Cher)
5. Dakota Mayi (Don Johnson & Melanie Griffith)
6. Navarone (Priscilla Presley)
7. Dog (Sky Saxon)
8. Scout (Bruce Willis & Demi Moore)
9. Aphra Kendal (Gyles Brandreth)
10. Free (Barbara Hershey)

10 TWINS

1. Matt Goss (Luke)
2. Alec Bedser (Eric)
3. Gayle Blakeney (Gillian)
4. Roger Black (Julia)
5. Reggie Kray (Ronnie)
6. Carol Thatcher (Mark)
7. Angela Tooby (Susan)
8. Babs Beverley (Teddy)
9. Henry Cooper (George)
10. Anthony Shaffer (Peter)

10 PEOPLE WHO HAD ROSES NAMED AFTER THEM

1. Sir Jimmy Savile
2. Sue Lawley
3. Julie Andrews
4. Sir Bobby Charlton
5. Anne Diamond
6. Arthur Scargill
7. Jimmy Greaves
8. Michael Crawford
9. Dame Catherine Cookson
10. Sir Cliff Richard

10 PEOPLE WHO HAVE 'SEEN' UFOs

1. David Bowie. The rock star reckons that he's seen many alien craft. Indeed, as a teenager, the then David Jones even edited a UFO magazine.

2. Muhammad Ali. The former heavyweight boxing champion of the world has also had many experiences of seeing UFOs - particularly in the early morning. He makes a point of talking about it so that other "sighters" won't feel isolated.

3. Reg Presley. The former lead singer of The Troggs is convinced that there's something out there - so much so that he's prepared to put his money where his mouth is. From the fortune he earned from Wet Wet Wet's re-release of his hit *Love Is All Around*, he has funded research into the links between UFOs and corn circles. He agrees that 75% of crop circles are hoaxes but reckons that the other 25% are "due to extra-terrestrials".

4. Michael Bentine. The former founder member of The Goons claims that he once "saw a bright white light behind a plane" which "shot up like a rocket" as the plane landed. Unable to find any other explanation, he decided it had to be a UFO.

5. Jimmy Carter. The former President of the US once saw a UFO which was "bluish at first, then reddish but not solid". Interestingly, he was with other men at the time who also saw the same thing.

6. Glenn Ford. The veteran Hollywood actor was staying at his beach house in California when he saw a strange object in the sky shaped like a pair of discs which hovered for eleven minutes before shooting off.

7. David Jacobs. The radio presenter was once driving on a motorway when he saw "an extraordinary light" crossing overhead. He mentioned it on his radio programme the next day and several people phoned in to say that they'd seen it too.

8. Mel Tormé. The American singer once saw an object in the sky "performing" extraordinary feats. As a licensed pilot, he knew that it couldn't be anything man-made and is therefore convinced that it was a UFO.

9. William Shatner. The actor who made his name as Captain Kirk in *Star Trek* reckons that he was once led to safety in the desert when his motor-bike wouldn't start and a craft appeared to guide him to safety.

10. The Krankies. The comic pair were on an aeroplane on their way to Glasgow when they saw an unexplained "tubular light". Janet said, "it wasn't like anything I'd seen before".

10 PEOPLE WHO DECIDED TO USE THEIR MIDDLE NAMES AS FIRST NAMES

1. James PAUL McCartney

2. Michael JEREMY Bates

3. Mary FARRAH Fawcett

4. Michael COLIN Cowdrey

5. William CLARK Gable

6. Michael TERRY Wogan

7. Nigel KEITH Vaz

8. Henry WARREN Beatty

9. Christopher ROB Andrew

10. Michael SYLVESTER Stallone

10 PEOPLE WHO HAVE "SEEN" GHOSTS

1. The Queen. When they were children, the Queen and her sister, Princess Margaret, reckon that they saw the ghost of Queen Elizabeth I at Windsor Castle.

2. Daniel Day-Lewis. The Oscar-winning star thought he had seen the ghost of his father (the late Poet Laureate Cecil Day-Lewis) when he was acting in *Hamlet* in 1989. When the actor playing the ghost of Hamlet's father said "I am thy father's spirit", Daniel Day-Lewis went off stage and wouldn't come back - convinced that he'd "seen" his father.

3. Jim Davidson. The Cockney comedian once lived with a girlfriend in the Old Kent Road in a flat which was said to be haunted by the ghost of a woman who'd been murdered there many years before. Jim was properly sceptical but was bothered when he couldn't find a rational explanation for all the strange noises which went on throughout the night. Eventually, after "seeing" crucifixes moving around the room, Jim and his girlfriend moved out.

4. Sting. The rock star awoke to "find" a "figure" dressed in Victorian clothes. He thought it was his wife but she was in bed next to him. She also saw this apparition and they held each other tight, staring at it until it simply faded away, never to return.

5. Patti Boulaye. In 1992, the singer was about to take on the lead role in the show *Carmen Jones* at the Old Vic and so was watching it from a private box. Suddenly, she felt a draught as though someone had opened the door to the box. However, when she turned round, no one was there. She mentioned it to someone who told her that it was the ghost of the late manager of the theatre, Lilian Baylis.

6. Bob Hoskins. Before finding fame, the Cockney actor was working as a porter in Covent Garden and was in a cellar when he "saw" a nun. She held her hands out to him and spoke but he didn't understand. Later he was told that Covent Garden had formerly been <u>Convent</u> Garden and had been owned by the Benedictines. The legend was that anyone who saw a nun's ghost would have a lucky life. As Bob now says, "it's good to talk".

7. Cilla Black. Cilla would be in bed at home when a teenage girl ghost would visit her regularly. The "girl", who would wear a Victorian night-dress, had a mournful expression on her face. It later turned out that the land on which Cilla's house was built had been farmland worked in the 19th century by a gardener who died leaving a young daughter who herself died at the age of 13.

8. June Brown. The actress who found fame as Dot Cotton in *EastEnders* saw something worse than a ghost, she saw a ghostly tunnel. She was walking with a friend along an abandoned single-track railway line and saw a tunnel which they started to walk down. Realising that the tunnel had no end and feeling a little spooked, they turned and ran back. The next day, they went back to where they had entered the tunnel and found that the tunnel had mysteriously vanished.

9. Miriam Karlin. The actress who plays a ghost in the TV sit. com. *So Haunt Me* believes that she herself is "haunted" by her father's ghost whenever she has to make a speech in public. Her father was a barrister and she is convinced that he "feeds" her her lines and makes her much more articulate than she would otherwise be.

10. Prince Andrew. In 1975, the Prince woke up three female guests who were sharing a room to tell them he had seen a ghost in his room and to ask them if he could spend the night in their room. Nice try, Andy, but the girls led him back to his own room - although the Prince did seem to believe that he had seen a ghost.

10 PEOPLE WHO ARE, WERE OR BECAME BLIND

1. Stevie Wonder
2. David Blunkett
3. John Milton
4. Ray Charles
5. Louis Braille
6. Claude Monet
7. Helen Keller
8. Jose Feliciano
9. James Thurber
10. Joseph Pulitzer

10 WINNERS OF THE PIPE SMOKER OF THE YEAR AWARD

1. Ian Botham (1988)
2. Rod Hull (1993)
3. Warren Mitchell (1967)
4. Jimmy Greaves (1985)
5. Jethro (1995)
6. Henry Cooper (1984)
7. Tony Benn (1992)
8. Eric Morecambe (1970)
9. Barry Norman (1987)
10. Sir Harold Wilson (1965 and 1976 when he was named Pipeman of the Decade - the only man to have won twice)

10 PEOPLE WHO HAVE STARTED THE DRAW FOR THE NATIONAL LOTTERY

1. Andi Peters
2. David Copperfield
3. Dale Winton
4. Virginia Bottomley
5. Terry Wogan
6. Meatloaf
7. Samantha Fox
8. Henry Cooper
9. Carol Smillie
10. Danny La Rue

10 WOMEN WHO ADOPTED CHILDREN

1. Jamie Lee Curtis
2. Mia Farrow
3. Dawn French
4. Shirley Bassey
5. Jilly Cooper
6. Dame Kiri Te Kanawa
7. Kirstie Alley
8. Penelope Keith
9. Nicole Kidman
10. Julie Andrews

Chapter 11

Royalty

10 THINGS SAID ABOUT THE QUEEN

1. "A piece of cardboard that they drag round on a trolley." (Johnny Rotten)

2. "She is frumpish and banal." (Malcolm Muggeridge)

3. "If you find you are to be presented to the Queen, do not rush up to her. She will eventually be brought around to you like a dessert trolley at a good restaurant." (*Los Angeles Times*)

4. "The personality conveyed by the utterances which are put into her mouth is that of a priggish school-girl, captain of the hockey team, a prefect and a recent candidate for confirmation." (John Grigg)

5. "She was just like a mum to us." (Paul McCartney after she handed him his MBE)

6. "She has a lovely laugh. She laughs with her whole face and she just can't assume a mere smile because she's a very spontaneous person." (Richard Crossman)

7. "She is a woman who acts her age, which is 50. She has, in fact, acted that age since she was little more that 20." (Fern Marja Eckman in 1976)

8. "A very pleasant middle to upper-class type of lady, with a talkative, retired Navy husband." (Malcolm Muggeridge)

9. "It always frightens me that people should love her so much." (Queen Elizabeth, the Queen Mother)

10. "Ein fabelhaftes Kind." ("a marvellous child") (Adolf Hitler)

10 PEOPLE THE QUEEN HAS TO LOOK AFTER HER

1. Keeper of The Queen's Swans
2. Mistress of The Robes
3. The Queen's Raven Master
4. The Clerk of The Closet
5. Lady of The Bedchamber
6. Woman of The Bedchamber
7. Hereditary Grand Falconer
8. Royal Bargemaster
9. The Queen's Racing Pigeon Manager
10. Grand Almoner

10 THINGS THAT THE QUEEN MIGHT CLAIM AS TAX-DEDUCTIBLE

1. Diamond-encrusted pooper-scoopers
2. Jeanette Charles's wages
3. Cigars for Sir Jimmy Savile
4. The Pro-Plus for use during the Royal Variety Show
5. Twenty-year-old dresses
6. Fire extinguishers
7. The *Hello!* subscription
8. Lord St. John of Fawsley's Christmas present
9. Trainer fees
10. Anti-bugging devices

10 THINGS SAID BY THE QUEEN

1. "Oh dear, have I got on what my family call my piggy face?" (when asked to smile by a portrait painter)

2. "I have been trained since childhood never to show emotion in public."

3. "More history for children to learn in a hundred years' time." (on being told of the outbreak of World War II)

4. "Manchester, that's not such a nice place." (what she said in 1994 to a Russian student who told her that she had been to Britain and stayed in Manchester)

5. "I should like to be a horse." (her reply when, as a child, she was asked her ambition)

6. "It is not a year on which I will look back with undiluted pleasure." (describing 1992, her "annus horribilis")

7. "Oh come on, get a bloody move on," (to the policeman who arrived to get rid of the intruder, Michael Fagan)

8. "I think everybody really will concede that on this, of all days, I should begin my speech with the words, 'My husband and I'." (at a banquet to mark her Silver Wedding anniversary)

9. "She's more royal than the rest of us." (of Princess Michael of Kent)

10. "I have to be seen to be believed."

AFTER THE ROYAL FAMILY...THE 10 TOP PEOPLE IN THE COUNTRY'S TABLE OF PRECEDENCE

1. The Archbishop of Canterbury

2. The Lord High Chancellor

3. The Archbishop of York

4. The Prime Minister

5. The Lord High Treasurer (although no such office exists at the moment)

6. Lord President of The Council

7. The Speaker of The House of Commons

8. The Lord Privy Seal

9. Ambassadors

   High Commissioners

10 TITLES HELD BY PRINCE PHILIP

1. Admiral of the Royal Yacht Squadron

2. Knight of the Thistle

3. Privy Councillor

4. Grand Master of the Guild of Air Pilots and Air Navigators

5. Field-Marshal

6. Marshal of the RAF

7. Chancellor of the University of Edinburgh

8. Admiral of the Fleet

9. Knight of the Garter

10. Chancellor of the University of Cambridge

10 THINGS THE QUEEN CAN DO

1. Drive without taking a driving-test.
2. Disobey the laws of the land because they are, of course, *her* laws. She could also refuse to give evidence in court as the courts are *her* courts. She also can't be sued.
3. Declare war on another country (the armed forces are under her command). She could also disband the army and sell all the navy's ships.
4. Send letters without putting stamps on (her letters carry the royal cipher).
5. Give away as many honours - including peerages and knighthoods - as she likes.
6. Declare a State of Emergency (which she once did - on May 31 1955 - because of the railway strike)
7. Turn any parish in the country into a university
8. Pardon any (or all) prisoners in *her* jails
9. Dismiss the Government
10. Get rid of the Civil Service (now *there's* a thought)

THE 10 LONGEST SERVING BRITISH MONARCHS SINCE 1066

1. Queen Victoria (64 years; 1837-1901)
2. King George III (60 years; 1760-1820)
3. King Henry III (56 years; 1216-1272)
4. King Edward III (50 years; 1327-1377)
5. Queen Elizabeth I (45 years; 1558-1603)
   Queen Elizabeth II (45 years: 1952-)
7. King Henry VI (39 years; 1422-1461)
8. King Henry VIII (38 years; 1509-1547)
9. King Henry I (35 years; 1100-1135)
   King Henry II (35 years; 1154-1189)
   King Edward I (35 years; 1272-1307)

10 KINGS AND THEIR UNFORTUNATE NICKNAMES

1. King Ivan the Terrible
2. King Louis the Sluggard
3. King William the Silent
4. King Ferdinand the Inconstant
5. King Charles the Mad
6. King Louis the Fat
7. King Charles the Simple
8. King Charles the Bad
9. King Louis the Quarreller
10. King Ethelred the Unready

10 PEOPLE DISTANTLY RELATED TO PRINCESS DIANA

1. Sir Winston Churchill (fourth cousin, twice removed)
2. Humphrey Bogart (seventh cousin, twice removed)
3. Louisa May Alcott (seventh cousin, four times removed)
4. T.E. Lawrence (fourth cousin, three times removed)
5. Otto Von Bismarck (eighth cousin, five times removed)
6. Oliver Cromwell (first cousin, eleven times removed)
7. Jane Austen (seventh cousin, six times removed)
8. Franklin D. Roosevelt (seventh cousin, three times removed)
9. Lord Lucan (second cousin, once removed)
10. Orson Welles (eighth cousin, twice removed)

10 THINGS THE QUEEN HATES

1. Garlic. She banned garlic from her kitchens.
2. Cats. She loves dogs but hates cats.
3. Tennis. She hates going to Wimbledon, preferring to leave that "job" to the Duchess of Kent (not to mention Fergie).
4. The cold. We all hate the cold but she is particularly sensitive to it, always taking her own hot-water bottle with her when she goes abroad on a royal visit.
5. Snails. She once asked Prince Philip "How can you eat those beastly things?"
6. Smoking. Particularly the smell of cigar smoke. Prince Philip gave up smoking the night before they got married.
7. Mathematics. She was hopeless at the subject when she was a girl.
8. Hearing the name of King Edward VIII. His abdication pushed her father on to the throne, the stress of which (or so the Queen Mother has always believed) caused his early death.
9. Pomposity. When a journalist once suggested that Diana should send a footman to buy her winegums if she wanted to escape media attention, the Queen said, "What a pompous remark, if I may say so."
10. Dictating letters.

10 THINGS TO TERRIFY THE QUEEN

1. She gets a letter from the Inland Revenue
2. Max Bygraves agrees to host the Royal Variety Show
3. The plants start talking back to Prince Charles
4. Prince Edward drops Sophie
5. Lady Helen Taylor announces her separation
6. Camilla changes her surname by deed poll to "Windsor"
7. Prince Andrew finds a new girl
8. Prince Charles doesn't
9. Fergie publishes her *unexpurgated* memoirs
10. *Terminator 3* is chosen for the Royal Command Performance

10 THINGS THE QUEEN LOVES

1. Music. She likes military march music and popular classical works but her favourite music comes from musicals. People who go to the Palace to receive their honours are often surprised to find a band playing selections from Hollywood musicals.
2. Champagne. Although the Queen drinks very moderately (certainly by comparison with her sister), she enjoys a glass of bubbly. She also enjoys sweet white wines.
3. Dogs. She owns and breeds corgis but only keeps female ones - passing the male dogs on to others. Names she has given her dogs include Shadow, Fable, Diamond and Myth.
4. Watching television. She enjoys watching telly with her supper on a tray. Her favourite TV programmes include *Dad's Army, Brideshead Revisited* and *The Good Life.*
5. Horse racing. She not only enjoys watching this sport, she also owns several horses. Her ambition - as yet unfulfilled - is to win the Derby.
6. Crossword puzzles. She does the crossword in the *Daily Telegraph* every day.
7. Impersonations. Not only does she enjoy watching impressionists but she is also a gifted impressionist and has done accurate impressions of family members and even politicians.
8. Charades. Royal get-togethers are notorious for the games of charades in which everyone has to take part.
9. Fancy dress. Not content with having to change her clothes an average of three times a day, the Queen also likes dressing up in fancy dress. When she was first married, she went to a fancy dress ball dressed as a maid and in 1962, she dressed up as a "beatnik" when she went to a "Come-As-A-Beatnik" party at Balmoral.
10. Barley water. It is the Queen's favourite drink and whenever she goes away, she always takes some with her.

Chapter 12

Movies

10 FILM SOUNDTRACKS WHICH WENT TO NUMBER ONE IN THE ALBUM CHARTS

1. *Batman* (1989)
2. *South Pacific* (1958)
3. *West Side Story* (1962)
4. *G.I. Blues* (1961)
5. *Grease* (1978)
6. *A Star Is Born* (1977)
7. *Summer Holiday* (1963)
8. *Fame* (1982)
9. *Saturday Night Fever* (1978)
10. *The Sound of Music* (1965)

10 ACTRESSES WHO TESTED FOR THE ROLE OF SCARLETT O'HARA

1. Lana Turner
2. Bette Davis
3. Norma Shearer
4. Miriam Hopkins
5. Tallulah Bankhead
6. Claudette Colbert
7. Katharine Hepburn
8. Loretta Young
9. Jean Harlow
10. Carole Lombard

THE 10 HIGHEST GROSSING FILMS OF ALL TIME (ALLOWING FOR INFLATION)

1. *Star Wars* (1977)
2. *Gone With The Wind* (1939)
3. *The Ten Commandments* (1958)
4. *The Sound of Music* (1965)
5. *Jaws* (1975)
6. *E.T., The Extra-Terrestrial* (1982)
7. *Doctor Zhivago* (1965)
8. *The Jungle Book* (1967)
9. *Snow White* (1937)
10. *101 Dalmatians* (1961)

10 RELATIONSHIPS WHICH STARTED ON A FILM SET

1. Jeff Goldblum & Laura Dern (on the set of *Jurassic Park*)
2. William Hurt & Marlee Matlin *(Children of A Lesser God)*
3. Humphrey Bogart & Lauren Bacall *(To Have And Have Not)*
4. Warren Beatty & Madonna *(Dick Tracy)*
5. Laurence Olivier & Vivien Leigh *(Fire Over England)*
6. Steve McQueen & Ali MacGraw *(The Getaway)*
7. Paul Hogan & Linda Koslowski *(Crocodile Dundee)*
8. Richard Burton & Elizabeth Taylor *(Cleopatra)*
9. Burt Reynolds & Sally Field *(Smokey And The Bandit)*
10. Tom Cruise & Nicole Kidman *(Days of Thunder)*

10 ACTORS WHO STARTED OUT AS EXTRAS

1. Dustin Hoffman
2. Marilyn Monroe
3. Ronald Reagan
4. Clint Eastwood
5. Donald Sutherland
6. John Wayne
7. Robert De Niro
8. Bill Cosby
9. Clark Gable
10. Robert Duvall

10 QUESTIONS STILL NOT RESOLVED AFTER INNUMERABLE VIEWINGS OF *THE GREAT ESCAPE*

1. Why is Steve McQueen dressed in 1960s casual clothing?

2. Given that everyone knows that Richard Attenborough is 'Big X', why bother giving him a codename?

3. Why does Charles Bronson try to join the Russian POWs at the start of the film?

4. Wasn't there a kinder way for Richard Attenborough to point out Donald Pleasance's myopia than to trip him up?

5. And if Donald Pleasance was so short-sighted, what was he doing going up in a plane for a joyride in the first place?

6. Why don't we actually see Christian Dior designing David McCallum's suit?

7. If Steve McQueen can escape under the wire so easily, why do they go to the bother of digging a huge tunnel?

8. Given that there are Americans in the camp, why is James Coburn cast as an Australian?

9. Why does Gordon Jackson always fall for that 'Have a nice day' trick?

10. Why didn't the Germans merely apprehend the escaped prisoners at the local station?

10 HOLLYWOOD STARS WHO STARTED IN SOAP OPERAS

1. Demi Moore *(General Hospital)*

2. Kevin Kline *(Search For Tomorrow)*

3. Alec Baldwin *(The Doctors)*

4. Tommy Lee Jones *(One Life To Live)*

5. Morgan Freeman *(Another World)*

6. Kevin Bacon *(Guiding Light)*

7. Meg Ryan *(As The World Turns)*

8. Ted Danson *(Somerset)*

9. Tom Selleck *(The Young And The Restless)*

10. Christian Slater *(Ryan's Hope)*

10 ROCK STARS WHO HAVE BEEN IN FILMS

1. John Lennon in *How I Won The War* (1967)

2. Mick Jagger in *Freejack* (1992)

3. Bob Dylan in *Pat Garrett And Billy The Kid* (1973)

4. Debbie Harry in *Videodrome* (1982)

5. Adam Ant in *Slamdance* (1988)

6. Phil Collins in *Buster* (1988)

7. Tina Turner in *Mad Max Beyond Thunderdome* (1986)

8. Bob Geldof in *The Wall* (1982)

9. James Taylor in *Two Lane Blacktop* (1971)

10. Roy Orbison in *The Fastest Guitar Alive* (1966)

10 WRITERS WHO DIRECTED FILMS

1. Norman Mailer: *Tough Guys Don't Dance* (1987)
2. Ruth Prawer Jhabvala: *The Courtesan of Bombay* (1985)
3. Tom Stoppard: *Rosencratz & Guildenstern Are Dead* (1990)
4. Nora Ephron: *Sleepless In Seattle* (1993)
5. Michael Crichton: *Westworld* (1973)
6. Clive Barker: *Night Breed* (1990)
7. Stephen King: *Maximum Overdrive* (1986)
8. William Peter Blatty: *The Exorcist III* (1990)
9. James Clavell: *To Sir, With Love* (1967)
10. Sidney Sheldon: *Dream Wife* (1953)

10 ROCK GROUPS IN FILMS

1. The Dave Clark Five: *Catch Us If You Can*
2. Madness: *Take It Or Leave It*
3. Led Zeppelin: *The Song Remains The Same*
4. The Who: *The Kids Are Alright*
5. Slade: *Flame*
6. Bill Haley and His Comets: *Rock Around The Clock*
7. T Rex: *Born To Boogie*
8. The Sex Pistols: *The Great Rock 'N' Roll Swindle*
9. The Monkees: *Head*
10. Gerry and The Pacemakers: *Ferry Cross The Mersey*

10 MOVIE THEMES THAT WENT TO NUMBER ONE

1. *The Shoop Shoop Song* by Cher *(Mermaids)*
2. *A Groovy Kind Of Love* by Phil Collins *(Buster)*
3. *Everything I Do (I Do It For You)* by Bryan Adams *(Robin Hood: Prince of Thieves)*
4. *Fame* by Irene Cara *(Fame)*
5. *Take My Breath Away* by Berlin *(Top Gun)*
6. *The One And Only* by Chesney Hawkes *(Buddy's Song)*
7. *Stand By Me* by Ben E. King *(Stand By Me)*
8. *Call Me* by Blondie *(American Gigolo)*
9. *Night Fever* by The Bee Gees *(Saturday Night Fever)*
10. *Unchained Melody* by The Righteous Brothers *(Ghost)*

10 FILM TITLE SONGS WHICH WENT TO NUMBER ONE

1. *A Hard Day's Night* (The Beatles, 1964)
2. *The One And Only* (Chesney Hawkes, 1991)
3. *Jailhouse Rock* (Elvis Presley, 1958)
4. *The Good, The Bad And The Ugly* (Hugh Montenegro And His Orchestra And Chorus, 1968)
5. *Stand By Me* (Ben E. King, 1987 - not recorded *for* the film but reached the top *because* of the film)
6. *Three Coins In The Fountain* (Frank Sinatra, 1954)
7. *Help!* (The Beatles, 1965)
8. *Who's That Girl* (Madonna, 1987)
9. *La Bamba* (Los Lobos, 1987)
10. *The Young Ones* (Cliff Richard And The Shadows, 1962)

10 FILMS WHICH HAVE DATES AS THEIR TITLES

1. *1776* (Director: Peter Hunt; Starred: William Daniels; 1972)
2. *1860* (Director: Alessandro Blasetti; Starred: Giuseppe Gulino; 1934)
3. *1871* (Director: Ken McMullen; Starred: Timothy Spall and John Lynch; 1990)
4. *1900* (Director: Bernardo Bertolucci; Starred: Burt Lancaster and Robert De Niro; 1976)
5. *1917* (Director: Stephen Weeks; Starred: Timothy Bateson; 1968)
6. *1918* (Director: Ken Harrison; Starred: William Converse-Roberts and Matthew Broderick; 1984)
7. *1941* (Director: Steven Spielberg; Starred: Dan Aykroyd and John Belushi; 1979)
8. *1969* (Director: Ernest Thompson; Starred: Robert Downey Jnr. and Kiefer Sutherland; 1988)
9. *1984* (Director: Michael Radford; Starred: John Hurt and Richard Burton; 1984)
10. *2010* (Director: Peter Hyams; Starred: Roy Scheider and Helen Mirren; 1984)

10 STARS WHOSE NAMES HAVE APPEARED IN THE TITLES OF FILMS

1. Greta Garbo: *Garbo Talks* (1984)
2. Brigitte Bardot: *Dear Brigitte* (1965)
3. Bela Lugosi: *Bela Lugosi Meets A Brooklyn Gorilla* (1952)
4. Douglas Fairbanks: *F As In Fairbanks* (1975)
5. Fred Astaire: *The Curse of Fred Astaire* (1984)
6. Ginger Rogers: *Ginger And Fred* (1986)
7. James Dean: *Come Back To The Five And Dime, Jimmy Dean, Jimmy Dean* (1982)
8. Humphrey Bogart: *The Man With Bogart's Face* (1980)
9. Clark Gable: *The Woman Who Married Clark Gable* (1985)
10. Errol Flynn: *In Like Flynn* (1985)

10 PEOPLE WHO APPEARED IN MOVIES AS THEMSELVES

1. Billy Graham (*Two A Penny* 1967)
2. Cliff Michelmore (*A Jolly Bad Fellow* 1964)
3. Mark Twain (*A Curious Dream* 1907)
4. Clarence Darrow (*From Dusk To Dawn* 1913)
5. Stirling Moss (*The Beauty Jungle* 1964)
6. Buzz Aldrin (*The Boy In The Plastic Bubble* 1976)
7. Michael Parkinson (*Madhouse* 1974)
8. A.J.P. Taylor (*Rockets Galore* 1958)
9. Jonathan Ross (*The Tall Guy* 1989)
10. Queen Alexandra (*Women Who Win* 1919)

10 THINGS WE KNOW ABOUT THE VIETNAM WAR FROM THE MOVIES

1. It was illegal to shoot without first shouting 'Motherf***er!'
2. Pop music was played continuously in the jungle
3. Vietcong soldiers had no feelings
4. American officers weren't required to do any actual fighting
5. Senior American officers were all barking mad
6. Ten times as many Americans died as Vietnamese
7. Uniform was optional
8. Drug-taking was compulsory
9. Saluting was banned
10. Very few Americans survived the war and those that did were bitter and twisted

10 ACTRESSES WHO SHED CLOTHES FOR MOVIES

1. Susan Sarandon. In *Pretty Baby* (1978), you can see her naked breasts when Keith Carradine is photographing her.

2. Jodie Foster. In *Backtrack* (1981), her naked breasts can be seen as she leans out of the shower to get her towel.

3. Ellen Barkin. In *Siesta* (1987), she appears briefly in a full frontal nudity long shot taking off her clothes before lying down fully naked.

4. Laura Dern. In *Wild At Heart* (1990), her naked breasts are visible at various times - particularly when she's putting on her top.

5. Melanie Griffith. In *Something Wild* (1986), she strips down to her naked breasts in bed with Jeff Daniels.

6. Nicole Kidman. In the Australian film, *Windrider* (1986), you can see her bum as she gets out of bed and puts on her dressing-gown.

7. Daryl Hannah. In *Reckless* (1984), you can see her breasts - albeit in a red light - while she's making love to her co-star.

8. Rosanna Arquette. In *The Executioner's Song* (1982), her naked breasts are visible in several scenes.

9. Glenn Close. In *Fatal Attraction* (1987), you can see her naked breasts when she's in bed with Michael Douglas.

10. Bridget Fonda. In *Aria* (1987), her naked breasts and bum are briefly visible.

10 ACTORS WHO SHED CLOTHES FOR MOVIES

1. Robert De Niro. In *1900* (1976), you can see his naked front when he's in bed with a girl.

2. John Malkovich. In *The Sheltering Sky* (1990), you can see his naked front when he gets out of bed to open the door.

3. Tom Cruise. In *All The Right Moves* (1983), you can very briefly see his naked front as he gets undressed with co-star Lea Thompson.

4. Robin Williams. In *The Fisher King*, you can see him dancing around in the nude in the park at night.

5. Pierce Brosnan. In *Live Wire* (1992), you can see his bum during a sex scene.

6. Sean Bean. In *Stormy Weather* (1988), you can see his bum while he's putting on his underwear during a scene with Melanie Griffith.

7. Harvey Keitel. In *The Piano* (1993), you can see his naked front when he pulls back the curtain to show himself to Holly Hunter.

8. Kevin Bacon. In *Pyratea* (1991), you can see his bum while he's fooling around in bed with co-star Kyra Sedgwick.

9. Patrick Swayze. In *Roadhouse* (1989), you can briefly see his bum when he gets out of bed.

10. Alec Baldwin. In *The Getaway* (1993), you can see his bum when he pulls down his pants.

10 MOVIES FEATURING MARINE LIFE

1. *Day of The Dolphin* (1973) George C. Scott and his wife (in real life) Trish Van Devere teach dolphins how to speak English. "Now say 'Oscar star in sex scandal'...."

2. *A Fish Called Wanda* (1988) Kevin Kline, as Otto, the psychopath, eats Michael Palin's goldfish - live. And he won a Best Supporting Oscar in the process.

3. *Boy On A Dolphin* (1957) Starring Sophia Loren and Alan Ladd, this is about a diver who finds a valuable Greek artefact in the sea. The dolphin got the best notices.

4. *Piranha* (1978) A crazy doctor keeps man-eating piranhas which are accidentally allowed to escape with predictable consequences.

5. *Killer Fish* (1979) Starring Marisa Berenson, Karen Black and Lee Majors, this was a film clearly developed in the wake of the *Jaws* series. It's alternative title was *Deadly Treasure of The Piranha* which tells you all you need to know about it.

6. *The Incredible Mr Limpet* (1964) This was about a clerk who becomes an animated dolphin and joins the Navy. Not suprisingly it (to coin a phrase) sank.

7. *Star Trek IV: The Voyage Home* (1986) Set in contemporary San Francisco, the film was all about Captain Kirk and Mr Spock trying to kidnap a pair of whales to return them to the sea to stop them becoming extinct.

8. *Island of The Blue Dolphins* (1964) Two orphans grow up on a Californian island with wild dogs and, yes, the eponymous dolphins for company.

9. *The Little Mermaid* (1989) Disney film which was set (almost entirely) under the sea ("under the sea, under the sea") and featured a talking flounder.

10. *The Big Blue* (1988) This French film starred Rosanna Arquette and Jean-Marc Barr as a pair of divers but the real stars were the dolphins and the rest of the marine life.

10 THINGS WHICH ALWAYS HAPPEN AT THE CINEMA

1. It always takes two people to tear your ticket.

2. The usherette will only show you to your seat if it is still light.

3. Any drink you leave on the floor will be spilt when you get out of your seat.

4. In a multi-screen cinema complex, the longest queue is always for the film you want to see.

5. If anyone in the cinema is eating popcorn from a bag (rather than a bucket) they will be sitting right next to you.

6. The people on the end of your row always want to watch right through the credits at the end of the film.

7. The film only starts precisely on time if you're late.

8. During the advertisements either you or your companion will say: "Do you remember those awful ads they used to do for minicabs and Indian restaurants?"

9. The person with the weakest bladder always sits in the middle of the row.

10. Three months after you see a film at the cinema it will be the only decent movie available at the video shop.

10 THINGS ROBERT DE NIRO HAS DONE TO 'FIND' HIS CHARACTERS FOR FILMS

1. *Raging Bull* (1980) For his Oscar-winning role as boxer Jake La Motta, De Niro learned how to box - training with La Motta for six months and breaking the caps on the ex-boxer's teeth. La Motta later said that if De Niro tired of acting he could earn a living as a boxer. For the film's later scenes where his character becomes much fatter, De Niro gained 60 pounds which - ever the man of discipline - he later shed.

2. *Taxi Driver* (1976) For this role, De Niro was obliged to <u>lose</u> weight - some two and a half stones. He also worked as a taxi-driver. Once he picked up a fare who, recognising him, said, "You're the actor, aren't you? Guess it's hard to find steady work".

3. *New York, New York* (1977) Most actors, when required to portray musicians, settle for a rough approximation of pretending to play their instruments. Not so De Niro. Cast as a saxophonist, he actually learned to play the saxophone. His playing was still dubbed over by a professional but his finger-placement earned him praise from the experts.

4. *Midnight Run* (1988) In this comedy-thriller, De Niro played a bounty hunter. To prepare for the role, he went out on the road with a real bounty hunter to see how the job is done. He also learned how to pick a lock for one scene but managed to do it so well that the scene had to be dropped for fear that it would instruct kids how to do it.

5. *The Deer Hunter* (1978) In this film, De Niro played a steelworker so, guess what?, De Niro went to live in a steelworking community for a few weeks before shooting to get a feel for his character. He also performed his own stunts for the film - including the one where he has to jump from a helicopter into the river. However, fortunately for his many fans, he *didn't* (practise or) play *real* Russian Roulette.

6. *The Mission* (1986) For his role as a former slave-trader living among South American Indians in the 18th century, De Niro was obliged to learn how to fence. As usual, he went the whole hog and, by the end of the film, he could fence to competition standard.

7. *The Godfather Part 2* (1974) It was for this role, as the young Vito Corleone, that De Niro won his first Oscar. And quite rightly too for, to get into his character and play the part with conviction, De Niro learned how to speak not just Italian but Sicilian Italian.

8. *The Untouchables* (1987) For his brief but brilliant portrayal of Al Capone, De Niro not only put on weight but he also put plugs up his nose to look and sound more like the infamous gangster. As if this weren't enough, he also wore silk underwear bought from the firm which had supplied Capone.

9. *True Confessions* (1981) One of De Niro's more forgettable movies. He played a priest who gets caught up in a murder case involving his policeman brother. Once again, De Niro learnt a language for a role - this time, Latin.

10. *A Bronx Tale* (1993) This was De Niro's first film as a director and he was determined that it would be absolutely accurate. He himself was playing a bus driver and so he trained to be a bus driver. He even took the New York bus drivers' exam, passing second time round.

THE LAST 10 ENGLISH-LANGUAGE FILMS TO WIN THE PALME D'OR FOR BEST FILM AT THE CANNES FILM FESTIVAL

1. *Secrets And Lies* (1996)
2. *Pulp Fiction* (1994)
3. *The Piano* (1993 sharing the Palme D'Or with the Hong Kong film *Farewell My Concubine*)
4. *Barton Fink* (1991)
5. *Wild At Heart* (1990)
6. *sex, lies, and videotape* (1989)
7. *The Mission* (1986)
8. *Paris, Texas* (1984)
9. *Missing* (1982 sharing the Palme D'Or with the Turkish film *Yol*)
10. *All That Jazz* (1980 sharing the Palme D'Or with the Japanese film *Kagemusha*)

10 PEOPLE NOMINATED FOR FOUR OR MORE OSCARS WITHOUT EVER WINNING

1. Richard Burton: 7 nominations
2. Peter O'Toole: 7 nominations
3. Deborah Kerr: 6 nominations
4. Alfred Hitchcock: 5 nominations
5. Arthur Kennedy: 5 nominations
6. Montgomery Clift: 4 nominations
7. Mickey Rooney: 4 nominations
8. Albert Finney: 4 nominations
9. Marsha Mason: 4 nominations
10. Glenn Close: 4 nominations

10 OSCAR 'ONLYS'

1. The **Only** actress to win four Oscars: Katharine Hepburn, for *Morning Glory* (1932-33), *Guess Who's Coming To Dinner?* (1967), *The Lion In Winter* (1968) and *On Golden Pond* (1981). The actor Walter Brennan holds the record for the most Oscars for an actor with three (all as Best Supporting Actor).
2. The **Only** actor to win an Oscar for less than ten minutes work: Anthony Quinn, who was on screen for only nine minutes in *Lust For Life* (1956).
3. The **Only** sequel to win an Oscar as Best Film: *The Godfather Part II* (1974).
4. The **Only** actress to win an Oscar for playing an Oscar nominee: Maggie Smith in *California Suite* (1978).
5. The **Only** Oscar which has been sold for more than half a million dollars: Vivien Leigh's for *Gone With The Wind* which fetched $510,000 at auction in 1994.
6. The **Only** actress to win a Best Supporting Actress Oscar for playing the <u>title</u> role in a film: Vanessa Redgrave for *Julia* (1977).
7. The **Only** Two Films In Which All The Members Of The Cast Have Been Nominated For Oscars: *Who's Afraid of Virginia Woolf?* (1966), which had a cast of four and *Sleuth* (1972) which had a cast of two.
8. The **Only** family in which three generations have won Oscars: The Hustons: Walter for *The Treasure of The Sierra Madre* (1948), John for *The Treasure of The Sierra Madre* and Anjelica for *Prizzi's Honor* (1985). Walter and John Huston are also the only father and son to win acting Oscars for the same film.
9. The **Only** mother and daughter to be nominated for Oscars in the same year: Diane Ladd and her daughter Laura Dern for *Rambling Rose* (1991).
10. The **Only** sisters to both win Best Actress Oscars: Joan Fontaine for *Suspicion* (1941) and Olivia de Havilland for *To Each His Own* (1946). And they didn't speak to each other!

10 LINES OF DIALOGUE WHICH HELP TO EXPLAIN MOVIE TITLES

1. "And on tonight's chat show we'll be meeting that wonderful raconteur, Sir Peter Ustinov and that hilarious comic, Jimmy Tarbuck"
   The Usual Suspects

2. "Calm down Steve, I think you *were* offside"
   Raging Bull

3. "...and this is the chamber of the House of Commons"
   Dirty Rotten Scoundrels

4. "Help! I suffer from a fear of crowds..."
   In Bed With Madonna

5. "So there's absolutely no chance of introducing a rave section in *Come Dancing?*"
   Strictly Ballroom

6. "Hello, I'm Victor Ki...aagh" *Death of a Salesman*

7. "Please welcome the Duchess of York's new media adviser"
   Mission: Impossible

8. "Hi, Ronnie, this is Brucie. Terry, Kenny and I were wondering whether you'd make up a four for golf"
   Get Shorty

9. "Claudia Schiffer, meet David Mellor"
   Beauty And The Beast

10. "Oooh, has someone been eating onions?"
    Backdraft

10 FORGOTTEN MOVIE STARS IN GREAT MOVIES – AND WHO WE REMEMBERED

1. Christopher Jones in *Ryan's Daughter* (Sarah Miles, Robert Mitchum)

2. Vivian Blaine in *Guys And Dolls* (Marlon Brando, Frank Sinatra, Jean Simmons)

3. Richard Beymer in *West Side Story* (Natalie Wood)

4. Jules Munshin in *On The Town* (Frank Sinatra, Gene Kelly)

5. Brad Dexter in *The Magnificent Seven* (Yul Brynner, Steve McQueen, Robert Vaughn, Charles Bronson, James Coburn, Horst Buchholz)

6. Betsy Blair in *Marty* (Ernest Borgnine)

7. Christopher Gable in *The Boyfriend* (Twiggy)

8. Paul Le Mat in *American Graffiti* (Ron Howard, Richard Dreyfuss)

9. Louise Fletcher in *One Flew Over The Cuckoo's Nest* (Jack Nicholson)

10. Karen Lynn Gorney in *Saturday Night Fever* (John Travolta)

10 FABULOUS PARTS ACTORS TURNED DOWN

1. Robert Preston's role in *The Music Man* - Cary Grant (who said that if they didn't give the role to Preston, he would even <u>watch</u> the film. They did and Preston duly won the Best Actor Oscar)

2. Dustin Hoffman's role in *The Graduate* - Robert Redford

3. George C. Scott's role in *Patton* - Lee Marvin

4. Eddie Murphy's role in *Beverly Hills Cop* - Sylvester Stallone

5. Al Pacino's role in *The Godfather* - Warren Beatty

6. Humphrey Bogart's role in *The Maltese Falcon* - George Raft

7. Robert Redford's role in *Butch Cassidy And The Sundance Kid* - Marlon Brando

8. Al Jolson's role in *The Jazz Singer* - Eddie Cantor

9. Peter Finch's role in *Network* - Henry Fonda

10. Kris Kristofferson's role in *A Star Is Born* - Elvis Presley

10 BRITISH ACTORS WHO WON AN OSCAR FOR BEST ACTOR

1. Ronald Colman *A Double Life* 1947
2. Laurence Olivier *Hamlet* 1948
3. Alec Guinness *Bridge On The River Kwai* 1957
4. David Niven *Separate Tables* 1958
5. Rex Harrison *My Fair Lady* 1964
6. Paul Scofield *A Man For All Seasons* 1966
7. Ben Kingsley *Gandhi* 1982
8. Daniel Day Lewis *My Left Foot* 1990
9. Jeremy Irons *Reversal Of Fortune* 1991
10. Anthony Hopkins *The Silence of The Lambs* 1992

10 ALTERNATIVE OSCARS

1. Best Actress For Getting Photographed Getting Out Of A Limousine: Sharon Stone
2. Best Actor For Pretending To Be Absolutely Humbled By The Honour Of It All: Sir Anthony Hopkins
3. Best Actress At Putting On A Brave Face When She's Lost: Glenn Close
4. Best Director At Putting On A Brave Face When He's Lost: Steven Spielberg
5. Best Actor At Being Silly With Interviewers: Robin Williams
6. Best Actress Reading Out An Award (Non-Giggling): Julia Roberts
7. Best Actress Reading Out An Award (Giggling): Goldie Hawn
8. Best Actor In A Tuxedo: George Hamilton
9. Best Actress At Looking As Though She Slept In Her Dress: Whoopi Goldberg
10. Best Director Who Won't Be There As He's Playing Jazz In A New York Bar: Woody Allen

10 ACTORS WHO NEVER WON AN OSCAR

1. Gene Kelly
2. Steve McQueen
3. Cary Grant
4. Glenn Ford
5. James Mason
6. Stewart Granger
7. Charles Boyer
8. Anthony Quayle
9. Montgomery Clift
10. Kirk Douglas

10 ACTRESSES WHO NEVER WON AN OSCAR

1. Greta Garbo
2. Agnes Moorehead
3. Carole Lombard
4. Barbara Stanwyck
5. Lana Turner
6. Judy Garland
7. Lee Remick
8. Natalie Wood
9. Rita Hayworth
10. Gloria Swanson

10 CLASSIC MOVIES WHICH DIDN'T WIN A SINGLE OSCAR

1. *The Big Sleep* (1946)
2. *The Caine Mutiny* (1954)
3. *The Maltese Falcon* (1941)
4. *Kind Hearts And Coronets* (1948)
5. *Lenny* (1974)
6. *Cat On A Hot Tin Roof* (1958)
7. *The Lady Vanishes* (1938)
8. *Oliver Twist* (1948)
9. *North By Northwest* (1959)
10. *Singin' In The Rain* (1952)

10 MODELS IN FILMS

1. Elle MacPherson: *Sirens*
2. Lauren Hutton: *The Gambler*
3. Jerry Hall: *Batman*
4. Jean Shrimpton: *Privilege*
5. Paulina Porizkova: *Her Alibi*
6. Twiggy: *The Boyfriend*
7. Margaux Hemingway: *Lipstick*
8. Isabella Rossellini: *Wild At Heart*
9. Shakira Caine: *The Man Who Would Be King*
10. Marie Helvin: *The Children*

THE 10 GREATEST FILMS OF ALL TIME – ACCORDING TO THE MEMBERS OF THE BRITISH FILM INSTITUTE

1. *Casablanca* 1942
2. *Les Enfants Du Paradis* 1944
3. *Citizen Kane* 1941
4. *Singin' in the Rain* 1952
5. *2001: A Space Odyssey* 1968
6. *Some Like It Hot* 1959
7. *Seven Samurai* 1954
8. *Gone With The Wind* 1939
9. *The Third Man* 1949
10. *One Flew Over the Cuckoo's Nest* 1975

10 LINES USED TO PROMOTE FILMS

1. "Only the rainbow can duplicate its brilliance!" *The Adventures of Robin Hood*
2. "Love is not a thing that grows only in the dark!" *All The Way Home*
3. "It's an ooh-la-lapalooza!" *Artists And Models Abroad*
4. "The two most gorgeous humans you've ever beheld - caressed by soft tropic winds - tossed by the tides of love!" *Bahama Passage*
5. "It's tremonstrous! The absolute apex of the super-shivery!" *The Black Cat*
6. "She insulted her soul!" *Dishonored Lady*
7. "First they moved (1895)! Then they talked (1927)! Now they smell!" *Scent of Mystery*
8. "Sing Judy! Dance Judy! The world is waiting for your sunshine!" *A Star Is Born*
9. "Meet the girls with the thermo-nuclear navels! The most titillating time bombs you've ever been tempted to trigger!" *Dr Goldfoot And The Girl Bombs*
10. "Where there's smoke, there must be someone smoking!" *Easy Living*

10 MOVIE STARS' FORMER JOBS

1. Jeremy Irons: Social Worker
2. Charlton Heston: Artists' model
3. Michele Pfeiffer: Supermarket Assistant
4. Sean Connery: French Polisher
5. Valerie Perrine: Stripper
6. Diana Rigg: Coffee Bar Assistant
7. Alan Alda: Taxi Driver
8. Julie Walters: Nurse
9. Burt Lancaster: Circus Acrobat
10. Malcolm McDowell: Coffee Salesman

THE 10 MOST SUCCESSFUL BOND THEMES

1. *A View To A Kill (A View To A Kill)* Duran Duran (reached Number 2)
2. *The Living Daylights (The Living Daylights)* A-Ha (5)
3. *Licence To Kill (Licence To Kill)* Gladys Knight (6)
4. *Nobody Does It Better (The Spy Who Loved Me)* Carly Simon (7)
5. *For Your Eyes Only (For Your Eyes Only)* Sheena Easton (8)
6. *Live And Let Die (Live And Let Die)* Wings (9)
7. *Goldeneye (Goldeneye)* Tina Turner (10)
8. *You Only Live Twice (You Only Live Twice)* Nancy Sinatra (11)
0. *James Bond Theme (Dr No)* John Barry (13)
10. *From Russia With Love (From Russia With Love)* Matt Monro (20)

10 THINGS BOND GIRLS ALWAYS SAY

1. "You fix the drinks and I'll slip into something more comfortable"
2. "Who's that man in our bathroom?"
3. "Oh Jems, I never knew it could be like this"
4. "I have the master tape here in my bikini"
5. "Do be careful, darling, I don't want you to get into any trouble"
6. "Have there been many other women?"
7. "He forced me to work for him and I was so frightened"
8. "Jems, watch out, there's a tarantula in our bed"
9. "And to think we've only known each other for one hour"
10. "You're the first real man I've ever met"

10 THINGS BOND VILLAINS ALWAYS SAY

1. "I should like to take you on a tour of my private island"
2. "You have no chance of escape, you understand"
3. "It's so nice to have some civilised company for a change"
4. "My sharks have not been fed for days"
5. "Do you approve of the wine?"
6. "You have been an irritant for too long"
7. "Unfortunately your predecessor cannot be with us tonight"
8. "Tell me, Meester Bond, how much does the British Secret Service pay you?"
9. "Shaken not stirred. Am I correct?"
10. "Before you die I will tell you my master plan to take over the world"

10 PEOPLE WHO PLAYED THE SAME CHARACTER IN MORE THAN ONE BOND FILM

1. Bernard Lee (M)
2. Geoffrey Keen (The Minister)
3. Sean Connery (James Bond)
4. Lois Maxwell (Miss Moneypenny)
5. Timothy Dalton (James Bond)
6. Richard Kiel (Jaws)
7. Desmond Llewellyn (Q)
8. Roger Moore (James Bond)
9. Robert Brown (M)
10. Caroline Bliss (Miss Moneypenny)

10 BOND GIRLS' NAMES

1. Honey Rider (Ursula Andress in *Dr No*)
2. Domino (Kim Basinger in *Never Say Never Again*)
3. Tiffany Case (Jill St John in *Diamonds Are Forever*)
4. Tatiana Romanova (Daniella Bianchi in *From Russia With Love*)
5. Holly Goodhead (Lois Chiles in *Moonraker*)
6. Pussy Galore (Honor Blackman in *Goldfinger*)
7. Mary Goodnight (Britt Ekland in *The Man With The Golden Gun*)
8. Kissy Suzuki (Mie Hama in *You Only Live Twice*)
9. Solitaire (Jane Seymour in *Live and Let Die*)
10. Octopussy (Maud Adams in *Octopussy*)

10 MOVIES WHICH BECAME TV SERIES

1. *The Third Man*
2. *Dixon of Dock Green*
3. *Doctor Kildare*
4. *Casablanca*
5. *In The Heat of The Night*
6. *Master of Lassie* (from *Lassie Come Home*)
7. *The Saint*
8. *The Prime of Miss Jean Brodie*
9. *Quiller* (from *The Quiller Memorandum*)
10. *Man at the Top* (from *Room at the Top*)

10 THINGS SAID ABOUT MOVIE STARS

1. "Bogart's a helluva nice guy till 10.30 p.m. After that he thinks he's Bogart" (David Chasen)
2. "I have stopped swearing: I now just say 'Zsa Zsa Gabor'" (Noel Coward)
3. "Working with her is like being bombarded with water melons" (Alan Ladd on Sophia Loren)
4. "He has a face that convinces you that God is a cartoonist" (Jack Kroll of Woody Allen)
5. "Elizabeth Taylor's so fat she puts mayonnaise on an aspirin" (Joan Rivers)
6. "He sounds like he has a mouth full of wet toilet paper" (Rex Reed of Marlon Brando)
7. "He had the acting talents of the average wardrobe" (Clyde Jeavons and Jeremy Pascall of Rudolph Valentino)
8. "She was good at being inarticulately abstracted for the same reason that midgets are good at being short" (Clive James of Marilyn Monroe)
9. "His hair is coordinated with his teeth" (Pauyline Kael on Robert Redford)
10. "Working with her is like being hit over the head with a Valentine's card" (Christopher Plummer of Julie Andrews)

10 FILMS WHICH BECAME SITCOMS

1. *M*A*S*H*
2. *Paper Moon*
3. *Alice Doesn't Live Here Any More* (as *Alice*)
4. *Father Of The Bride*
5. *Nine To Five*
6. *Barefoot In The Park*
7. *Mr Smith Goes To Washington*
8. *Bob & Carol & Ted & Alice*
9. *Mr Deeds Goes To Town*
10. *Adam's Rib*

10 THINGS WE LEARNED ABOUT DINOSAURS FROM *JURASSIC PARK*

1. They're easy to clone - even by people who can't make car door locks work
2. They only eat bad people
3. They move slower than American kids
4. They grow incredibly quickly
5. They can open kitchen doors
6. They blend into their surroundings so well that people only ever notice them when they're practically right on top of them
7. They sneeze just like human beings
8. They can live on an island off the coast of Costa Rica without being spotted by planes, helicopters or satellite cameras and without dinosaur experts being aware of their existence
9. Some of them can be stroked
10. Their ultimate role in the great scheme of things is to persuade cynical scientists that maybe kids aren't so bad after all

10 THINGS WE KNOW ABOUT AMERICAN TEENAGERS FROM THE MOVIES

1. They've all got cars
2. They only see their parents at meal-times
3. Ill-fitting jeans are illegal
4. They don't need sleep
5. None of them smoke
6. They all have telephones in their bedrooms
7. They're not obliged to wait at traffic-lights
8. Acne doesn't exist
9. School attendance is optional past the age of 12
10. Even the poor ones are fabulously wealthy

10 STAGES IN THE MAKING OF A MOVIE

1. Idea
2. Treatment
3. Lunch
4. Script
5. Pre-production
6. Filming
7. Post-production
8. Hype
9. Profit
10. Written off against tax as a flop

Chapter 13

Politics

10 MPs WHO CHANGED PARTIES

1. Winston Churchill (Conservative-Liberal-Conservative)
2. Alan Howarth (Conservative-Labour)
3. Reg Prentice (Labour-Conservative)
4. Sir Oswald Mosley (Conservative-Labour-Fascist)
5. Dr David Owen (Labour-SDP)
6. Christopher Mayhew (Labour-Liberal)
7. Emma Nicholson (Conservative-Liberal)
8. Sir Cyril Smith (Labour-Liberal)
9. Peter Hain (Liberal-Labour)
10. Enoch Powell (Conservative-Ulster Unionists)

10 PEOPLE WHO WERE PRESIDENT OF THE OXFORD UNION

1. Edward Heath 1939
2. Tony Benn 1947
3. Robin Day 1950
4. William Waldegrave 1968
5. Michael Heseltine 1954
6. Jeremy Isaacs 1955
7. Brian Walden 1957
8. Gyles Brandreth 1969
9. Jeremy Thorpe 1951
10. Benazir Bhutto 1977

10 PEOPLE WHO WERE PRESIDENT OF THE CAMBRIDGE UNION

1. Norman St. John Stevas 1950
2. Douglas Hurd 1952
3. Greville Janner 1952
4. John Nott 1959
5. Leon Brittan 1960
6. John Selwyn Gummer 1962
7. Michael Howard 1962
8. Kenneth Clarke 1963
9. Norman Lamont 1964
10. Arianna Stassinopoulos 1971

10 BOOKS WRITTEN BY POLITICIANS

1. David Mudd: *Cornwall in Uproar*
2. Harry Greenway: *Adventures in the Saddle*
3. Jack Aspinwall: *Kindly Sit Down!*
4. Gerald Kaufman: *My Life in the Silver Screen*
5. Douglas Hurd: *The Smile on the Face of the Tiger*
6. Chris Mullin: *A Very British Coup*
7. John Prescott: *Not Wanted on Voyage*
8. Kenneth Baker: *I Have No Gun But I Can Spit*
9. Jonathan Aitken: *The Young Meteors*
10. Michael Foot: *Another Heart and Other Pulses*

10 COMMANDMENTS FOR POLITICIANS

1. Thou shalt have no other Gods before Power, Greed and Naked Ambition
2. Thou shalt make unto thee any graven image-maker if thou intends to appear on TV
3. Thou shalt not take the name of thy party leader in vain
4. Remember the Sabbath day and use it to meet thy constituents lest thou be de-selected
5. Honour thy Chief Whip that thy days in Parliament may be long and free from nagging
6. Thou shalt not kill bills which thy front bench has put before the house
7. Thou shalt not commit adultery with anyone who knows the telephone number of the *News Of The World*
8. Thou shalt not steal thy colleague's constituency if thine is rendered less winnable by boundary changes
9. Thou shalt not bear false witness unless it is in the House of Commons where you can claim parliamentary privilege
10. Thou shalt not covet thy neighbour's appearance on *Newsnight* - yea, even unto his being interviewed by Jeremy Paxman

10 BUDGET TRADITIONS

1. The Chancellor poses for photos with his wife
2. The Chancellor poses for photos with his briefcase
3. There is wonderment at the fact that the Chancellor is actually allowed to drink alcohol on the floor of the House of Commons (as though the rest of the place isn't awash with the stuff the rest of the time)
4. TV crews are sent to pubs in the City to find out "what the man in the street *(sic)* thinks"
5. The opposition say "it's a bad budget for the economy/jobs"
6. The Liberal Democrats have no idea what they think
7. Financial journalists describe the Chancellor as "bold", "adventurous" and "unpredictable" because they all got their predictions completely wrong
8. TV studios are full of instant "experts" whose every word further obscures the implications of the Budget
9. The TV news has shots of people filling up at petrol stations in a pathetic attempt to save themselves a few pence
10. Cigarettes go up in price

A SIMPLE GUIDE TO THE U.S. PRESIDENTIAL ELECTION

1. State primary: All right then, "Primary"
2. Electoral college: Yup, there's nothing you can't study in America
3. Favourite son: A chance to throw your hat in the ring
4. Convention: A chance to throw your hat in the air
5. Spin doctor: The pen is mightier than the penicillin
6. Matching funds: One for you, one for me
7. Presidential debates: The clash of the speech writers
8. First Lady: The rest were just women
9. The polls: Not to be ignored in Chicago
10. Running mate: Quick, honey, they've spotted us

10 THINGS SAID ABOUT JOHN MAJOR

1. "No advert for a country that boasts Savile Row" (Geoffrey Aquilina-Ross)

2. "I'm absolutely fed up with hearing how 'nice' Mr. Major is. Nice is not necessarily an asset. In a politician, it's probably a menace" (Michael Winner)

3. "I do not accept the idea that all of a sudden Major is his own man... There isn't such a thing as Majorism" (Margaret Thatcher)

4. "He is a ditherer and a dodger, a ducker and weaver. (Neil Kinnock)

5. "Poor John Major. What can you say except he will always look grey like his Spitting Image puppet" (Peter Howarth)

6. "It's quite a change to have a prime minister who hasn't any political ideas at all" (Michael Foot)

7. "John Major is appalling; no excuses - Man from Austin Reed" (Peter Howarth)

8. "U-turn-ip" *(The Sun)*

9. "He is more like a ventriloquist's dummy than a prime minister" (Sir Nicholas Fairbairn)

10. "He delivers all his statements as though auditioning for the speaking clock" (Stephen Glover)

10 THINGS SAID ABOUT SIR EDWARD HEATH

1. "If only he had lost his temper in public the way he does in private, he would have become a more commanding and successful national leader" (William Davis, former editor of *Punch*)

2. "Receiving support from Ted Heath in a by-election is like being measured by an undertaker" (George Gardiner, senior Conservative MP)

3. "There is an element of stony rigidity in his make-up which tends to petrify his whole personality in a crisis" (Denis Healey, the former Deputy Leader of the Labour Party)

4. "Margaret Thatcher and Ted Heath both have a great vision. The difference is that Margaret Thatcher has a vision that Britain will one day be great again and Ted Heath has a vision that Ted Heath will one day be great again" (Robert Jones, political commentator)

5. "May I suggest he pursues his alternative career and conducts orchestras since he does not know how to conduct himself" (Nicholas Fairbairn, late, eccentric Conservative MP)

6. "...he has clearly sublimated the normal man's sex drive to the point of being uninterested in women without any suggestion of its having been diverted into any improper or irregular direction" (John Boyd-Carpenter, a former colleague)

7. "In any civilised country Heath would have been left hanging upside down on a petrol pump years ago" (Auberon Waugh, the acerbic columnist, writing in *Private Eye*)

8. "He has developed the worst kind of sulks since Achilles refused to leave his tent to fight the Trojans" (*The Sun* in 1985 when he was constantly moaning about Mrs Thatcher)

9. "We must kick Ted in the groin. We must be rough with him" (Harold Wilson, when he was Prime Minister and Heath was Leader of the Opposition)

10. "He never expected a good Press and was always wary of journalists" (James Margach, political writer)

10 THINGS SAID ABOUT MARGARET THATCHER

1. "She has the mouth of Marilyn Monroe and the eyes of Caligula" (François Mitterrand)

2. "She adds the diplomacy of Alf Garnett to the economics of Arthur Daley" (Denis Healey)

3. "She is democratic enough to talk down to anyone" (Austin Mitchell)

4. "I wouldn't say she was open-minded on the Middle East so much as empty-headed. She probably thinks that Sinai is the plural of sinus" (Jonathan Aitken)

5. "Attila the hen" (Sir Clement Freud)

6. "In ten years, she'll probably replace Guy Fawkes as an effigy" (Ken Livingstone)

7. "If I were married to her, I'd be sure to have dinner ready when she got home" (George Shultz)

8. "She's the best man in England" (Ronald Reagan)

9. "I cannot bring myself to vote for a woman who has been voice-trained to speak to me as though my dog has just died" (Keith Waterhouse)

10. "She sounded like the Book of Revelation read out over a railway public address system by a headmistress of a certain age wearing calico knickers" (Clive James)

10 THINGS SAID BY MARGARET THATCHER

1. "In politics, if you want anything said, ask a man. If you want anything done, ask a woman"

2. "Pennies do not come from heaven: they have to be earned here on earth"

3. "To wear your heart on your sleeve isn't a very good plan. You should wear it inside where it functions best"

4. "It wouldn't be Spring, would it, without the voice of the occasional cuckoo?" (referring to the Bishop of Durham in 1985)

5. "I don't mind how much my Ministers talk - as long as they do what I say"

6. "You and I come by road or rail but economists travel by infrastructure"

7. "I owe nothing to Women's Lib"

8. "They have a new colour. They call it gold. It looks like yellow to me" (of the Liberal Democrats)

9. "If you are guided by opinion polls, you are not practising leadership, you are practising followship"

10. "No woman in my time will be Prime Minister or Chancellor of the Exchequer or Foreign Secretary - not the top jobs. Anyway, I would not want to be Prime Minister: you have to give yourself 100%" (in 1969)

10 FACTS ABOUT U.S. PRESIDENTS

1. Jimmy Carter (1977-81) developed the knack of reading at speed and was once tested and found to have a 95% comprehension rate reading at 2,000 words a minute. Carter was also the first President to have been born in a hospital

2. Ronald Reagan (1981-89) was the first - and so far only - President to have been divorced

3. Richard Nixon's (1969-74) mother, who named her son after King Richard The Lionheart, originally wanted him to be a Quaker missionary

4. Calvin Coolidge (1923-29) was famous for being a man of few words. At a White House dinner, a gushing female guest told him that her father had bet her that she wouldn't be able to get more than two words out of the President. "You lose" were the only words he spoke to her

5. When Franklin D. Roosevelt (1933-45) was five years old, he visited the White House and was told by the then President, Grover Cleveland (1885-89), "My little man, I am making a strange wish for you: it is that you may never be President of the United States". It is also worth noting that Roosevelt's mother dressed him exclusively in dresses until the age of five

6. Another example of a President meeting a future President came in 1963 when Bill Clinton (1993-) shook hands with John F. Kennedy (1961-63) at a White House reception for members of Boys' Nation

7. George Washington (1789-97) had wooden false teeth

8. When he was young, Rutherford Hayes (1877-81) suffered from a strange phobia: the fear of going insane

9. James Garfield (1881) could simultaneously write in Greek with one hand whilst writing in Latin with the other

10. At up to 24 stones, William Taft (1909-13) was the heaviest President and once had the misfortune of getting stuck in the White House bath tub. At just over seven stones, James Madison (1809-17) was the lightest President

10 ACTORS WHO PLAYED U.S. PRESIDENTS

1. Frank Windsor: George Washington in *Revolution*

2. Henry Fonda: Abraham Lincoln in *Young Mr Lincoln*

3. Alexander Knox: Woodrow Wilson in *Wilson*

4. Ralph Bellamy: Franklin D Roosevelt in *Sunrise at Campobello*

5. James Whitmore: Harry Truman in *Give 'Em Hell, Harry!*

6. Cliff Robertson: John F Kennedy in *PT 109*

7. Charlton Heston: Andrew Jackson in *The President's Lady*

8. Jason Robards: Ulysses Grant in *The Legend of the Lone Ranger*

9. Brian Keith: Theodore Roosevelt in *The Wind and The Lion*

10. Burgess Meredith: James Madison in *The Magnificent Doll*

THE LAST TEN LOSING PRESIDENTIAL AND VICE-PRESIDENTIAL CANDIDATES

Presidential Candidate	Vice-Presidential Candidate
1. 1996 Robert Dole	Jack Kemp
2. 1992 George Bush	Dan Quayle
3. 1988 Michael Dukakis	Lloyd Bentsen
4. 1984 Walter Mondale	Geraldine Ferraro
5. 1980 Jimmy Carter	Walter Mondale
6. 1976 Gerald Ford	Robert Dole
7. 1972 George McGovern	Sargent Shriver
8. 1968 Hubert Humphrey	Edmund Muskie
9. 1964 Barry Goldwater	William Miller
10. 1960 Richard Nixon	Henry Cabot Lodge

10 AUTHORS WHO WERE ONCE MPs

1. John Buchan
2. Hilaire Belloc
3. Andrew Marvell
4. Samuel Pepys
5. Daniel Defoe
6. Sir Thomas More
7. Richard Brinsley Sheridan
8. A.P. Herbert
9. Edward Gibbon
10. Jeffrey Archer

10 MPs WHO RAN THE LONDON MARATHON

1. Dick Douglas (Labour, Dunfermline West)
2. Gary Waller (Conservative, Keighley)
3. Edward Leigh (Conservative, Gainsborough and Horncastle)
4. Dennis Canavan (Labour, Falkirk West)
5. Alistair Burt (Conservative, Bury North)
6. Rhodri Morgan (Labour, Cardiff West)
7. John McFall (Labour, Dumbarton)
8. David Heathcoat-Amory (Conservative, Wells)
9. Doug Henderson (Labour, Newcastle-Upon-Tyne North)
10. Jonathan Aitken (Conservative, Thanet East)

10 THINGS WHICH HAPPEN EVERY PRESIDENTIAL ELECTION YEAR

1. An awful lot of promises are made...
2. ...None of which are actually kept
3. An 'eccentric' multi-billionaire will briefly look like a real contender
4. Sales of sleeping pills will drop alarmingly during the televised presidential debates
5. Hollywood stars will attempt to prove that they have minds of their own by making speeches on behalf of candidates - and prove exactly the opposite
6. Everyone gets very frightened when the most right-wing Republican wins a minor primary
7. The candidate who is ahead in the polls in the summer will lose in November
8. Teddy Kennedy will be kept well out of sight until after the Democratic convention
9. A lot of grown men will shed tears as they talk of how much they "lurve" their country
10. Lots of British newspaper hacks will develop a sudden interest in American politics in order to spend three months touring round the States.

10 EXCERPTS FROM THE SCOTTISH DEVOLUTION BILL

ARTICLE 1. All men are created equal and shall respond to the name 'Jimmy' - especially in Glasgow on a Saturday night at closing time.

ARTICLE 2. Only Scottish people (aye an' Sassenachs acting in Bill Forsyth films) will be allowed to use such vernacular expressions as "hoots mon", "och aye the noo" and "wee" and, even then, only whilst in Scotland. In particular we will be keeping an eye on Billy Connolly, Lulu, John Sessions and Tom Conti (though we dinnae ken whit sort o' Scottish name *that* is) an' ithers who act and talk as though bluidy Maidenhead an' Hampstead huv Lothian post codes.

ARTICLE 3. Although Scotland will be a free country, the people will NOT be allowed to bear arms, except in two instances: i) if attending Old Firm games ii) if the bluidy English cross the border steamin' oot o' the'r heeds

ARTICLE 4. Freedom of speech and expression (though see Article 2) is guaranteed to all Scotsmen (the lassies will keep silent). No Scotsman shall be deprived of life, liberty or property nor shall he be obliged to answer any question except "Who yae gawking at?"

ARTICLE 5. All political parties shall have the right to organise and to stand for election through the due process. However, we the people will no' guarantee the safety of bluidy Conservatives eejits- especially as they don't have any bluidy MPs.

ARTICLE 6. Anyone calling themselves a Scotsman will be obliged to talk like one and to behave like one. The correct answer to "huv a dram wae me?" is "aye" and not "oh, gosh, I'll have a mineral water, I suppose".

ARTICLE 7. Scottish children will study a properly Scottish curriculum concentrating on our ain folk like Rabbie Burns, Robert The Bruce, Sean Connery, Slim Jim and Andy Stewart.

ARTICLE 8. Scottish people have the right to be taxed fairly. Although we will be full members of the EU (oor farmers huv nae problem in doon nae wuk) we will no' accept any taxes on whisky - unless the ithers want us to tax their bluidy Perrier water.

ARTICLE 9. The only King that we the Scottish people are prepared to acknowledge is Denis Law and we dinnae gi'e a stuff for the Royal Family. Aye, though but that Princess Anne lassie will always be welcome at Murrayfield.

ARTICLE 10. The oil is bluidy ours.

"DON'T TELL MY MOTHER I'M IN POLITICS: SHE THINKS I PLAY THE PIANO IN A WHOREHOUSE!" 10 THINGS SAID ABOUT POLITICS AND POLITICIANS

1. "Politics is a blood sport" (Aneurin Bevan)

2. "Now I know what a statesman is: he's a dead politician. We need more statesmen" (Bob Edwards)

3. "Politics is the art of looking for trouble, finding it everywhere, diagnosing it incorrectly and applying the wrong remedy" (Groucho Marx)

4. "A politician is a statesman who approaches every question with an open mouth" (Adlai Stevenson)

5. "Politicians are the same all over. They promise to build a bridge even where there's no river" (Nikita Khrushchev)

6. "The reason there are so few female politicians is that it is too much trouble to put make-up on two faces" (Maureen Murphy)

7. "The politician is an acrobat: he keeps his balance by saying the opposite of what he does" (Maurice Barrès)

8. "It rarely pays in politics to be wise before the event" (Chris Patten)

9. "Politics is a dog's life without a dog's devotion" (Rudyard Kipling)

10. "A politician is an arse upon which everyone has sat except a man" (e.e. cummings)

THE 10 NUMBER ONE RECORDS AT THE TIME OF THE LAST 10 GENERAL ELECTIONS

1. May 1 1997: *Blood On The Dance Floor* (Michael Jackson)

2. April 9 1992: *Stay* (Shakespears Sister)

3. June 11 1987: *I Wanna Dance With Somebody (Who Loves Me)* (Whitney Houston)

4. June 9 1983: *Every Breath You Take* (The Police)

5. May 3 1979: *Bright Eyes* (Art Garfunkel)

6. Oct 10 1974: *Kung Fu Fighting* (Carl Douglas)

7. Feb 28 1974: *Devil Gate Drive* (Suzi Quatro)

8. June 18 1970: *In The Summertime* (Mungo Jerry)

9. March 31 1966: *The Sun Ain't Gonna Shine Anymore* (The Walker Brothers)

10. Oct 15 1964: *Oh Pretty Woman* (Roy Orbison)

10 PEOPLE WHO (UNSUCCESSFULLY) STOOD FOR PARLIAMENT

1. Sir Robin Day (Liberal)

2. Ted Dexter (Conservative)

3. Jonathan King (Royalist)

4. Pamela Stephenson (Blancmange Thrower)

5. David Bellamy (Referendum)

6. Vanessa Redgrave (Workers' Revolutionary)

7. Dennis Potter (Labour)

8. Cynthia Payne (Payne And Pleasure)

9. John Arlott (Liberal)

10. Lindi St. Clair (Corrective)

Chapter 14

Food & Drink

10 FOODS WHICH ARE SAID TO BE APHRODISIACS

1. Oysters. These are high in calcium, iron and vitamin A - all of which help with the process of 'lurve'. In fact, all shell-fish - especially lobster - have aphrodisiac qualities. The truth is that if you're taken (or you're taking someone) out for a lobster supper, you're going to be pretty turned on anyway.

2. Sunflower seeds. Apparently, these have to be 'raw'. Is there any other way?

3. Cabbage. Now, I like cabbage - especially with Roast Beef - but I was as amazed to learn about its invigorating effect on nookie as I was to learn about carrots and turnips. Though in the case of turnips, it's only the tops which are of use.

4. Tomatoes. You always knew that salad was good for you, well now you can order double portions. And tomato isn't the only thing which will pep up your love life. While you're at it (or, indeed, before if you catch my drift) check out some avocado, cucumber, green pepper, watercress and lettuce.

5. Lemons. Maybe this explains why cocktail bars always give you a slice of lemon with your drink: they're trying to get you in the mood. In fact, all citrus fruit - including limes and oranges - are good to eat if you want a healthy sex life.

6. Honey. This simple spread apparently contains something called the 'gonadotropic hormone' which apparently helps to stimulate the, er, 'sex glands'. Careful with what you're giving your kids, mums.

7. Garlic. Now this poses an interesting dilemma: you eat garlic to make yourself sexier but, of course, the more you eat, the less fanciable you become. Hmm. The same problem also applies to that other great aphrodisiac, onions.

8. Radishes. This raises similar problems to garlic and onions but also the possibility of wind which is, let's face it, hardly the greatest turn-on.

9. Betel nut (if you chew it). If you remember South Pacific, you'll remember Bloody Mary, the brothel madam, 'chewing betel nut'.

10. Strawberries. Tastier than many of the above 'remedies', strawberries will put you in the mood for almost anything - though not tennis if British performances at Wimbledon are anything to go by.

THE 10 OLDEST CHOCOLATE BARS STILL ON SALE

1. Fry's *Chocolate Cream* (1875)
2. Cadbury's *Dairy Milk* (1905)
3. Cadbury's *Bournville* (1908)
4. Cadbury's *Flake* (1911)
5. Fry's *Turkish Delight* (1914)
6. Cadbury's *Fruit & Nut* (1921)
7. Terry's 1767 *Bitter Bar* (1922)
8. Cadbury's *Crunchie* (1929)
9. Cadbury's *Whole Nut* (1930)
10. Terry's *Waifa Bar* (1934)

10 SWEETS AND CHOCOLATES NO LONGER WITH US

1. Spangles
2. Five Boys
3. Amazin
4. Milk Tray Block
5. Aztec
6. Rumba
7. Nutty Bar
8. Country Style
9. Space Dust
10. Pacers

10 INTERNATIONAL FOODS

1. **Spanish** omelette
2. **Danish** pastry
3. **Brazil** nuts
4. **Welsh** rarebit
5. **Turkish** delight
6. **Russian** salad
7. **Scotch** eggs
8. **French** bread
9. **Chinese** cabbage
10. **Swiss** roll

IS YOUR LOCAL RESTAURANT TRENDY? 10 TELL-TALE SIGNS

1. The only tomatoes it serves are "sun-dried"
2. Vegetables are "roasted" not boiled
3. The waiters will tell you "what I've got for you today"
4. Salads are always "warm"
5. Any pasta will be served with "pesto"
6. The only mushrooms served are "wild"
7. You can't get lettuce but you can get "rocket"
8. A bottle of mineral water will cost more than a bottle of wine in the off-licence next door
9. The table-cloth is made out of paper and you're encouraged to draw on it
10. You can get goat's cheese but you can't get cheddar

GOING TO A RESTAURANT?

	IN HEAVEN	IN HELL
1. The food is	French	German
2. The head waiter is	German	Spanish
3. The waiters are	Italian	American
4. The waitresses are	Thai	French
5. The entertainment is	Brazilian	Polish
6. The hygiene inspector is	British	Turkish
7. The other diners are	Danish	German
8. The wine waiter is	Australian	Bulgarian
9. The person in charge of the dessert trolley is	Italian	Russian
10. The car at home is	Swedish	Czech

KELLOGG'S TOP 10 CEREALS

1. Corn Flakes (Not just the most popular Kellogg's cereal but also the most popular brand and type of cereal in Britain. Important cereal information for those who have forgotten how good they are).

2. Frosties (Corn Flakes for people who are - or so it would seem - too lazy to put the sugar on themselves).

3. Rice Krispies (Snap, crackle and, indeed, pop. Not just flavoursome, we are told, but also a significant source of iron, vitamins and something called 'complex carbohydrates').

4. Bran Flakes (Regularising flakes of bran which taste even better with sultanas added. Hence the sapient introduction of Sultana Bran).

5. Crunchy Nut Corn Flakes (Frosties for a whole new generation of cereal lovers who like their flakes of corn with sweet and, indeed, crunchy topping).

6. All-Bran (Absolutely-no-messing-about 'fibre provider'. Ideal for folk who don't have to share a bathroom).

7. Fruit 'N' Fibre (Fruitsome cereal which is also more than a little fibrous. Fine if you can forget the TV commercials).

8. Coco Pops (Chocolate 'flavoured' Rice Krispies which will just about do for chocoholics - without milk - when they've run out of chocolate).

9. Special K (A 'balanced' cereal which was embarrassingly promoted in the 1970s by actor John Slater as the 'healthy' breakfast until he died of a heart attack. Special K have a similar calorific value to Frosties. I know which I would rather have.)

10. Honey Nut Loops (Loops of cereal covered in, er, honey and um, nuts).

THE 10 BESTSELLING CHEESES IN BRITAIN

1. English cheddar
2. Processed cheese
3. Cottage cheese
4. Irish cheddar
5. Scottish cheddar
6. Red Leicester
7. Edam
8. Cheshire
9. New Zealand cheddar
10. Double Gloucester

10 PEOPLE WHO HAVE HAD FOOD AND DRINK NAMED AFTER THEM

1. Queen Mary I (Bloody Mary)
2. Alexander The Great (Brandy Alexander)
3. St. Benedictine of Nursia (Benedictine)
4. Dame Nellie Melba (Peach Melba, Melba Sauce and Melba Toast)
5. Dom Perignon (Dom Perignon Champagne)
6. Giuseppe Garibaldi (Garibaldi Biscuits)
7. Viscount François de Chateaubriand (Chateaubriand Steak)
8. James Logan (The Loganberry)
9. John Montague, 4th Earl of Sandwich (The Sandwich)
10. Sir William Gage (The Greengage)

10 DISHES FROM AROUND THE WORLD

1. Sun-dried Maggots (China). The larvae of flies are dried in the sun and then eaten as a side dish or as a snack. China is also the country where they serve up Bear's paw Stew and Fried Grasshoppers.

2. Fried Calf's Head (Hungary). The head is sliced open, breaded and then fried. You'd have to be very Hungary....

3. Pig's Face And Cabbage (Ireland). What it says. The face of a pig is seasoned and baked and served up with boiled cabbage.

4. Stuffed Calf's Eyes (France). After the lenses, corneas and irises have been taken away, the eyes are stuffed with mushrooms and cooked. France is also the country where gourmets can eat such dishes as Pork Testicles In Cream, Grilled Rat and Sea Urchin Gonad Sauce.

5. Broiled Sparrows (Japan). Sparrows are cut in two and marinated before being grilled.

6. Barbecued Cow Heart (Peru). The heart of a cow is chopped up and then seasoned with chili peppers before being barbecued.

7. Stuffed Bear Paw (Romania). A bear's paw is prepared and then stuffed with a mixture of herbs and spices. It sounds disgusting but is probably no more so than pig's trotters.

8. Baked Bat (Samoa). The bat is prepared for cooking and then fried or baked with onions, salt and pepper.

9. Coconut-Cream Marinated Dog (Indonesia). Bits of dog are marinated in a coconut cream before being grilled on skewers.

10. Roasted Caterpillars (Laos). The insects are first salted and then roasted before being served on a bed of rice.

10 CELEBRITY RESTAURANT OWNERS

1. Sylvester Stallone, Bruce Willis and Arnold Schwarzenegger: Planet Hollywood

2. Chris Kelly: Midsummer House

3. Viscount Linley and The Earl of Lichfield: Deals

4. Mariel Hemingway: Sam's Restaurant

5. Michael Caine: Langan's Brasserie

6. Mikhail Baryshnikov: Columbus

7. Robert De Niro, Bill Murray, Lou Diamond Phillips and Christopher Walken: TriBeCa Grill

8. Bill Wyman: Sticky Fingers

9. Dudley Moore: 72 Maple Street

10. Patrick Swayze: Mulholland Drive Café

10 (GENUINE) COCKTAILS

1. Bucking Bronco
2. One Exciting Night
3. Damn the Weather
4. Sex On The Beach
5. Blood Transfusion
6. Boomerang
7. Between The Sheets
8. Income Tax
9. Wedding Bells
10. Goodnight Ladies

IF YOU'VE EVER BEEN TO A CHINESE RESTAURANT, YOU MIGHT HAVE WONDERED WHY IT IS THAT...

1. There are hundreds of dishes on the menu?

2. Horrible green peppers crop up everywhere?

3. You order a greater quantity of dishes than you would in any other sort of restaurant and then share them?

4. By the time any prawn dish gets round to you, there are no prawns left?

5. A complete meal can be prepared in five minutes?

6. There are never enough prawn toasts in the mixed hors d'oeuvres but no one wants to know the spring rolls

7. Half a crispy duck is never as much food as two quarters of crispy duck - even though they cost the same?

8. They never serve enough cucumber or pancakes with the crispy duck?

9. You only stop eating when you're full to bursting?

10. You always feel hungry two hours later?

10 LAWS OF BARBECUES

1. The people who bring supermarket hamburgers always cook themselves steaks

2. If there aren't enough sausages the last one can always be guaranteed to fall through the grate

3. The barbecue only really gets hot once all the food has been cooked

4. The smoke from the barbecue can be guaranteed to waft into the garden of your least neighbourly neighbour

5. The more gaudy the apron worn by the man doing the barbecue, the less likely it is that the meat will be cooked through properly

6. Any barbecue to which you invite more than six people will be washed out by rain - even during a drought

7. The more lighter fuel you use to get the barbecue going, the more likely you are to run out of matches

8. It is impossible to toast hamburger buns on the barbecue without burning them

9. It's only when you've finished the meal that you wish you had some bananas to cook on the barbecue

10. It is invariably a man who cooks on the barbecue; It is invariably a woman who cleans up the barbecue

10 THINGS SAID ABOUT WINE

1. "For when the wine is in, the wit is out." (Thomas Bacon)

2. "A cocktail is to a glass of wine what rape is to love." (Paul Claudel)

3. "Frenchmen drink wine just like we used to drink water before prohibition." (Ring Lardner Jnr.)

4. "This wine is too good for toast-drinking, my dear. You don't want to mix emotions up with a wine like that. You lose the taste." (Ernest Hemingway)

5. "The Spanish wine, my God, it is foul, catpiss is champagne compared, this is the sulphurous urination of some aged horse." (D. H. Lawrence)

6. "A cask of wine works more miracles than a church full of saints." (Italian proverb)

7. "A good general rule is to state that the bouquet is better than the taste, and vice versa." (Stephen Potter)

8. "One of the disadvantages of wine is that it makes man mistake words for thoughts." (Samuel Johnson)

9. "Eat bread at pleasure, drink wine by measure." (Randle Cotgrave)

10. "The Germans are exceedingly fond of Rhine wine. One tells them from vinegar from the label." (Mark Twain)

Chapter 15

Religion

10 RELIGIOUS CONVERSIONS

1. The Duchess of Kent (Protestant to Catholic)
2. Felicity Kendal (Christian to Jewish)
3. Cat Stevens/Yusuf Islam (Christian to Muslim)
4. Edwina Currie (Jewish to Protestant)
5. Hayley Mills (Christian to Hare Krishna)
6. Chris Eubank (Christian to Muslim)
7. John Gummer (Protestant to Catholic)
8. Tina Turner (Christian to Buddhist)
9. Elizabeth Taylor (Christian to Jewish)
10. Bob Dylan (Jewish to Christian to Jewish)

10 MEN WHO MIGHT VERY WELL HAVE BEEN PRIESTS

1. Joseph Stalin
2. David Alton MP
3. Christopher Marlowe
4. Stephen Fry
5. Ben Vereen
6. Morten Harket
7. Alan Bennett
8. Charles Darwin
9. Kenny Everett
10. Mike McShane

10 BORN-AGAIN CHRISTIANS

1. Mandy Smith
2. Glenn Hoddle
3. Donna Summer
4. David Suchet
5. Bobby Ball
6. Samantha Fox
7. Bernhard Langer
8. Charlene Tilton
9. Alvin Stardust
10. Rosemary Conley

THE TEN COMMANDMENTS – UPDATED

1. Thou shalt not hog all the proceeds of thy numbers come up on the National Lottery
2. Honour thy father and thy mother by not sending videos of them making complete idiots of themselves to Jeremy Beadle
3. Thou shalt not steal lest thou wishes to be sent on a safari holiday
4. Thou shalt not kill time but spend it wisely in a leisure centre
5. Thou shalt not copy CDs on to cassettes lest the music industry goeth bankrupt
6. Thou shalt not covet thy neighbour's Jaguar XJS
7. Thou shalt keep the Sabbath sacred for visits to B&Q and Texas
8. Thou shalt have an opinion on the Grant brothers from *EastEnders*
9. Thou shalt not commit unsafe sex, yea even unto the petting stage
10. Thou shalt not grass up thy friends to the police lest thy kneecaps are permanently removed

10 NEW SONGS FOR THE CHURCH HYMNAL

1. *Pray:* MC Hammer
2. *Bless You:* Martha and the Vandellas
3. *Hands To Heaven:* Breathe
4. *Faith:* George Michael
5. *Hallelujah:* Milk And Honey
6. *Mary's Prayer:* Danny Wilson
7. *Hymn:* Ultravox
8. *I Believe:* Frankie Laine
9. *I Say A Little Prayer:* Aretha Franklin
10. *God Only Knows:* The Beach Boys

10 SLOGANS SEEN OUTSIDE CHURCHES

1. Come to Ch**ch. What is missing?
2. Seven prayer-less days make one spiritually weak
3. Come in for a faith-lift
4. Bank on God for a higher rate of interest
5. It's impossible to lose your footing on your knees
6. Come to Church in September and avoid the Christmas rush
7. Danger! Live Church!
8. Sing a hymn for Him
9. Fight truth decay - brush up your Bible every day
10. Run to Church and keep spiritually fit

10 RELIGIOUS SECTS

1. The Moonies
2. The Living Word
3. Khumara
4. The Teachers
5. Up The People
6. The Raelians
7. The Living Word
8. The Church of Scientology
9. The Children of God
10. The Fellowship of The Army

10 PEOPLE WHO WERE BORN JEWISH

1. Burt Bacharach
2. Helen Reddy
3. Oliver Stone
4. Goldie Hawn
5. Harvey Keitel
6. William Shatner (Leonard Nimoy, his *Star Trek* co-star, is also Jewish)
7. Harrison Ford
8. Ruth Prawer Jhabvala
9. Dame Alicia Markova
10. Barbara Walters

Chapter 16

Words

10 PEOPLE WHOSE NAMES ARE USED AS RHYMING SLANG

1. Lionel Blair (Flares)
2. Franz Liszt (as in "Brahms and Liszt")
3. Jack Jones (On One's Own)
4. Nobby Stiles (Piles)
5. Emma Freud (Haemorrhoids)
6. Chas 'n' Dave (Shave)
7. Vera Lynn (Gin)
8. Ruby Murray (Curry)
9. Brian Clough (Rough)
10. Hank B. Marvin (Starvin')

10 SPOONERISMS

1. "Kinquering congs their titles take"
2. "Let us drink to the queer old dean"
3. "As you grow older, the weight of rages presses harder on the employer"
4. "The Lord is a shoving leopard"
5. "That is just a half-warmed fish"
6. "The cat popped on its drawers"
7. "Is the bean dizzy?"
8. "Please sew me to another sheet"
9. "Her husband was eaten by missionaries"
10. "You will leave by the next town drain"

10 EXPLANATIONS FOR BRAND NAMES

1. BABYCHAM: An abbreviation of "baby chamois" which is the goat-like antelope used in the TV commercials
2. VIM: From the Latin word meaning "with strength"
3. QUINK: From the words "quick drying ink"
4. HARPIC: From the first three letters of the first name and surname of the man who developed it: Harry Pickup
5. RYVITA: From the word "rye" and the Latin word for life "vita"
6. FINDUS: From the words "fruit industries" (i.e. F & Indus)
7. 7-UP: Named by the inventor who had already rejected six names for his product
8. MAZDA: Named after the Persian god of light
9. HOVIS: Derives its name from the Latin words "hominis vis" meaning "man's strength"
10. LEGO: From the Danish words "leg godt" meaning "play well"

10 PEOPLE WHO GAVE THEIR NAMES TO THINGS

1. Samuel Plimsoll. Plimsoll was a coal merchant and, later, an MP. He was extremely concerned about safety on board ships and the welfare of seamen. He invented the Plimsoll Line, which limited the amount of cargo a ship could carry. He also gave his name to the canvas shoes worn by sailors: plimsolls.

2. Sir George Everest. Sir George was Surveyor-general of India from 1830-43 and gave his name to that country's (and the world's) highest mountain. I suppose we - and leading mountaineers - can count ourselves lucky that, for an eminent Victorian, he was relatively modestly monickered. Mount Ponsonby-fforbes-Smythe would have been a challenge only to social climbers.

3. James Thomas Brudenell, 7th Earl of Cardigan. Cardigan, who led the Charge of The Light Brigade at the Battle of Balaclava in 1854, named the long-sleeved woollen waistcoat he wore under his coat a Cardigan. The name stuck.

4. Hugh Cecil Lowther, 5th Earl of Lonsdale. Lonsdale was another earl whose name lives on after his death. He was a huge boxing fan and the belt, which is given to any British boxer who wins the same title three times, is named after him. Lonsdale, who died in 1944 at the age of 87, was also - unlike that other noble boxing patron, the Marquis of Queensberry – a fine boxer himself and sparred with world champion John L. Sullivan.

5. Samuel Morse. Morse, an American artist who exhibited at our own Royal Academy, developed the Morse Code for use on the new electric telegraph. The Code, which was first used in 1838, eventually brought its inventor great fame and fortune.

6. Philip Dormer Stanhope, 4th Earl of Chesterfield. If you've ever sat on a well-padded, high-backed - perhaps leather - sofa, then you'll know what a Chesterfield is. Often very valuable, Chesterfields are named after the Earl who was an 18th-century politician. He also gave his name to an overcoat but this is now largely forgotten.

7. Peter Nissen. Nissen, a Canadian who fought for the British in World War I, invented the Nissen hut, a corrugated iron construction with a curved roof, as a shelter for men and equipment on the Western Front.

8. Charles Macintosh. Macintosh (there isn't a 'k' in his name), an 18th century Scottish industrial chemist, patented his Mackintosh waterproof coat in 1823. He actually made his discovery by accident while he was trying to find something to do with a manufacturing by-product.

9. Louis Braille. Braille, a Frenchman who went blind as a child, invented his system of raised type when he was a teacher of the blind. In 1829, when he was just 20, he published his first book in braille. Sadly, he died in his early forties.

10. Jean Nicot. Not the greatest way to go down in history but a form of immortality nevertheless. Nicot was the French ambassador to Portugal from 1559-1561. There he tried tobacco and took some back with him to France where the tobacco plant Nicotiana was named after him. From Nicotiana, of course, we get the word Nicotine.

THE 10 LONGEST UNHYPHENATED WORDS IN THE OXFORD ENGLISH DICTIONARY

1. Pneumonoultramicroscopicsilicovolcanoconiosis (45 letters)
2. Supercalifragilisticexpialidocious (34 letters)
3. Pseudopseudohypoparathyroidism (30 letters)
4. Floccinaucinihilipilification (29 letters)
5. Triethylsulphonemethylmethane (29 letters)
6. Antidisestablishmentarianism (28 letters)
7. Octamethylcyclotetrasiloxane (28 letters)
8. Tetrachlorodibenzoparadioxin (28 letters)
9. Hepaticocholangiogastronomy (27 letters)
10. Radioimmunoelectrophoresis (26 letters)

10 PUNSOMELY NAMED FISH & CHIP SHOPS

1. The Frying Squad (Bournemouth)
2. The Cod Father (Billericay)
3. The Little Chip (Gateshead)
4. Mr Chips (Inverness)
5. Codswallop (Frome)
6. Fryer Tuck (Margate)
7. Flash In The Pan (County Antrim)
8. Our Plaice (Broadstairs)
9. Rock & Sole (Richmond)
10. Cutty Shark (Durham)

10 PUNSOMELY NAMED HAIRDRESSERS' SALONS

1. Hairport
2. Fringe Benefits
3. Head Office
4. Cutting Time
5. The Clip Joint
6. Short & Curlers
7. Hairloom
8. Power Cuts
9. Hairs & Graces
10. Millionhairs

10 (GENUINE) EUROPEAN PRODUCTS

1. Plopp (Swedish toffee bar)
2. Grand Dick (French red wine)
3. Nora Knackers (Norwegian biscuits)
4. Moron (Italian wine)
5. Mukki (Italian yoghurt)
6. Cock (French deodorant)
7. Krapp (Scandinavian toilet paper)
8. Bum (Turkish biscuits)
9. Sor Bits (Danish mints)
10. Donkee Basterd Suker (Dutch sugar)

10 FRAGRANCES TRANSLATED

1. Ma Griffe: My Signature
2. Eau Sauvage: Savage Water
3. N'Aimez Que Moi: Love Only Me
4. Vent Vert: Green Wind
5. Jardin de Bagatelle: Garden Of Trifle
6. Adieu Sagesse: Bye Bye Wisdom
7. L'Interdit: The Forbidden
8. Eau Dynamisante: Very Dynamic Water
9. Calèche: Four-wheeled carriage
10. Rive Gauche: Left Bank

10 INTELLECTUAL WORDS EXPLAINED

1. Auteur: Artist who hogs all the credit
2. Jejune: Not a lot
3. Zeitgeist: What's hot and what's not
4. Angst: Posh nerves
5. Weltanschauung: Points of view
6. Leitmotiv: Here we go again
7. Recherché: Not for the like of you and me
8. Weltschmerz: Global bleeding heart
9. Soi disant: Blowing one's own trumpet
10. Rococo: Gaudy

10 PEOPLE WHO NAMED THEIR CHILDREN AFTER FAMOUS PEOPLE

1. Neneh Cherry: Named daughter Tyson, after Mike Tyson
2. Nicky Henson: Named son Keaton, after Buster Keaton
3. Gyles Brandreth: Named daughter Aphra, after Aphra Behn
4. Woody Allen: Named his son Satchel, after Louis 'Satchmo' Armstrong
5. Paul Young: Named daughter Levi, after Levi Stubbs (Four Tops)
6. Demi Moore and Bruce Willis: Named daughter Rumer, after the author Rumer Godden
7. Ricky Schroder: Named son Holden, after William Holden
8. Dave Stewart and Siobhan Fahey: Named son Django, after Django Reinhardt
9. Mickey Stewart: Named his son Alec, after Alec Bedser
10. Bryan Ferry: Named son Otis, after Otis Redding

10 WORDS RARELY USED IN THE SINGULAR

1. Assizes (Assize)
2. Paparazzi (Paparazzo)
3. Trivia (Trivium)
4. Auspices (Auspice)
5. Timpani (Timpano)
6. Minutiae (Minutia)
7. Graffiti (Graffito)
8. Scampi (Scampo)
9. Scruples (Scruple)
10. Measles (Measle)

10 WORDS RARELY USED IN THE POSITIVE

1. Kempt (Unkempt)
2. Corrigible (Incorrigible)
3. Maculate (Immaculate)
4. Placable (Implacable)
5. Effable (Ineffable)
6. Nocuous (Innocuous)
7. Pervious (Impervious)
8. Expurgated (Unexpurgated)
9. Peccable (Impeccable)
10. Evitable (Inevitable)

10 WORDS IN ESPERANTO

1. War = Milito
2. Conflict = Konflicto
3. Battle = Batalo
4. Disagreement = Mala
5. Anger = Kolero
6. Argument = Argumento
7. Attack = Atako
8. Tension = Tensio
9. Dispute = Disputo
10. Pre-emptive strike = Anticipita trafo

10 PEOPLE WHO USED THEIR MOTHERS' MAIDEN NAMES RATHER THAN THEIR FATHERS' SURNAMES

1. Diane Keaton (Hall)
2. Marilyn Monroe (Mortensen)
3. Ryan Giggs (Wilson)
4. Simone Signoret (Kaminker)
5. Pablo Picasso (Ruiz)
6. Shelley Winters (Schrift)
7. Rita Hayworth (Cansino)
8. John Standing (Leon)
9. Jean Harlow (Carpenter)
10. Leslie Howard (Stanier)

10 PEOPLE WHO HAD WEAPONS NAMED AFTER THEM

1. Mikhail Kalashnikov (The Kalashnikov Rifle)
2. Sir William Mills (The Mills Bomb)
3. Wilhelm & Peter Mauser (The Mauser Magazine Rifle)
4. Jim Bowie (The Bowie Knife)
5. Samuel Colt (The Colt Revolver)
6. Sir William Congreve (The Congreve Rocket)
7. Oliver Winchester (The Winchester Rifle)
8. Vyacheslav Molotov (The Molotov Cocktail)
9. Bertha Krupp (Big Bertha Mortar)
10. Henry Shrapnel (The Shrapnel Shell)

10 OMNIPRESENT WORDS WHICH WE NEVER ACTUALLY USE

1. Dwelling
2. Receptacle
3. Beverage
4. Affix
5. Remittance
6. Alight
7. Garment
8. Patrons
9. Infants
10. Gratuities

10 MEN WITH WOMEN'S NAMES

1. Dana Andrews (actor)
2. Gay Byrne (TV presenter)
3. Kerry Packer (media mogul)
4. Val Kilmer (actor)
5. Evelyn Waugh (author)
6. Shirley Crabtree (original name of the wrestler Big Daddy)
7. Mandy Patinkin (actor)
8. Gert Frobe (actor)
9. Kay Kyser (bandleader)
10. Marion Morrison (original name of the actor John Wayne)

10 WOMEN WITH MEN'S NAMES

1. Leslie Ash (actress)
2. Sean Young (actress)
3. Billie Whitelaw (actress)
4. George Eliot (novelist)
5. Gene Tierney (actress)
6. Glenn Close (actress)
7. Jerry Hall (model)
8. Teddy Beverley (singer)
9. Drew Barrymore (actress)
10. Daryl Hannah (actress)

10 COLLECTIVE NAMES

1. A skulk of foxes
2. A digest of laws
3. A murder of crows
4. A bench of bishops
5. A charm of goldfinches
6. A muster of peacocks
7. A shower of blessings
8. An unkindness of ravens
9. A dray of squirrels
10. A lodge of beavers

10 NAMES FOR BEARDS

1. Forked
2. Needle
3. Bodkin
4. Ducktail
5. Breakwater
6. Cathedral
7. Old Dutch
8. Anchor
9. Needle
10. Vandyke

10 PAIRS OF PEOPLE WHO BELONG TOGETHER

1. Katie RABETT & Frank WARREN
2. Sandy GALL & Pauline STONE
3. Alan ROUGH & Anne DIAMOND
4. David BRYANT & Peter MAY
5. Sir James SAVILE & Ramon Subba ROW
6. James LAST & Charles DANCE
7. Chris OLD & Rob BAILEY
8. Steve SHERWOOD & Frederic FORREST
9. John BIRD & Nicolas CAGE
10. Ronnie BARKER & Anita DOBSON

10 NAMES FOR FLOWERS AND PLANTS

1. None So Pretty
2. Old Man's Beard
3. Jack-Go-To-Bed-At-Noon
4. Dog's-Tooth-Grass
5. Morning Glory
6. Witches'-Butter
7. Gill-Over-The-Ground
8. Love-In-Idleness
9. Devil's Snuffbox
10. Elephant's Ears

10 THINGS WHICH ARE ACTUALLY BRAND NAMES

1. Li-Lo
2. Jiffy Bags
3. Optic
4. Catseyes
5. Rawlplug
6. Spam
7. Perspex
8. Calor Gas
9. Formica
10. Yo-Yo

10 PANGRAMS (SENTENCES WHICH USE ALL 26 LETTERS OF THE ALPHABET)

1. The quick brown fox jumps over a lazy dog
2. Xylophone wizard begets quick jive form
3. Wet squid's inky haze veils sex of jumping crab
4. Jackdaws love my big sphinx of quartz
5. Pack my box with five dozen liquor jugs
6. The five boxing wizards jump quickly
7. Quick wafting zephyrs vex bold Jim
8. Mr Jock, TV quiz PhD, bags few lynx
9. Six plump boys guzzled cheap raw vodka quite joyfully
10. XV quick nymphs beg fjord waltz

THE 10 MOST POPULAR NAMES FOR PUBS

1. The Red Lion
2. The Crown
3. The Royal Oak
4. The White Hart
5. The King's Head
6. The Bull
7. The Coach And Horses
8. The George
9. The Plough
10. The Swan

10 NAMES FOR RED LIPSTICKS

1. Wild Cherry
2. Radicchio
3. Scandale
4. Amour
5. Firecracker
6. Kashmir
7. Holly Berry
8. Censored
9. Strawberry Fair
10. Corsaire

10 UNUSUAL PUB NAMES

1. Bleeding Heart
2. Cardinal's Error
3. The Case is Altered
4. Rampant Cat
5. Naked Man
6. Pig and Whistle
7. Man with a Load of Mischief
8. Labour in Vain
9. Goat in Boots
10. Flying Horse

10 WORDS WHICH ARE ACTUALLY ALLOWABLE IN A GAME OF SCRABBLE

1. Bimbo
2. Fax
3. Hoover
4. Qwerty
5. Jacuzzi
6. Yuppie
7. Mars
8. Ciggies
9. Aspirin
10. Perrier

10 FANCY NAMES FOR JOBS

1. Baking Operative (Baker)
2. Utensil Sanitiser (Dish-washer)
3. Domestic Scientist (Cookery Teacher)
4. Rodent Strategist (Rat-catcher)
5. Financial Adviser (Insurance Salesman)
6. Household Technician (Charwoman)
7. Refuse Collector (Dustman)
8. Legal Executive (Solicitor's Clerk)
9. Tonsorial Analyst (Hairdresser)
10. Access Controller (Doorman)

10 PAINT NAMES AND THE COLOURS THEY CONCEAL

1. Portia (Peach)
2. Reverie (Light Peach)
3. Candesse (Lighter Peach)
4. Panache (Light Green)
5. Serenity (Pale Blue)
6. Melody (Lilac)
7. Meditation (Pale Lilac)
8. Cameo (Dark Beige)
9. Country Clover (Pink)
10. Satin Romance (Pale Pink)

THE 10 MOST VALUABLE WORDS YOU CAN MAKE AT SCRABBLE

Word	Meaning	Score (+ a bonus of 50 for using all 7 letters)
1. QUIZZIFY*	To cause to look odd	31

(N.B. If this were stretched across two triple word scores, it would total 419 points - including the 50 point bonus and the double letter bonus for the Z)

2. WHIPJACK	A whining beggar who pretends to be a sailor	29
3. HIGHJACK	Alternative spelling of Hijack	28
4. JUMBOIZE	To enlarge a ship by adding a prefabricated section	28
5. BEZIQUES	Plural of card game	28
6. CAZIQUES	West Indian chiefs	28
7. QUIZZERY*	Collection of quizzes or information pertaining to quizzes	28
8. TZADDIQS	In Judaism, leaders or persons of extraordinary piety	28
9. VIZCACHA	S. American burrowing rodent of heavy build	27
10. ZAMBUCKS	New Zealand or Australian colloquial term for members of St John's Ambulance Brigade	27

* indicates that the second Z is a blank.

10 ACRONYMOUS GROUPS

1. Dinky (Double Income No Kids Yet)
2. Orchid (One Recent Child - Heavily In Debt)
3. Triffid (Three Recent Infants Falling Further Into Debt)
4. Plants (Parents Looking After Numerous Toddlers)
5. Toads (Three Offspring - All Dependent Still)
6. Pofaced (Parents Of Four Active Children - Endless Debts)
7. Pots (Parents Of Teenagers)
8. Kitbag (Kids In Teens - Bankrupt And Grey)
9. Tulip (Two Used Leftover Insolvent Parents)
10. Cocoon (Cheap Old Childminder Operating On Nothing)

Chapter 17

Television

10 THINGS WE KNOW ABOUT THE POLICE FROM WATCHING *THE BILL*

1. They never stop motorists
2. Policemen are not allowed to work in CID until they're over 35
3. Suspects are always called "sir" or "madam"
4. Policemen never have affairs with policewomen
5. There is no such thing as "a bent copper"
6. Policemen never swear
7. If people hit them, they don't retaliate
8. They know the first name of everyone in "the community"
9. Racism just doesn't exist
10. They only work for three half-hours a week

10 PEOPLE WHO APPEARED IN *THE AVENGERS*

1. Peter Bowles
2. Penelope Keith
3. John Cleese
4. Kate O'Mara
5. Donald Sutherland
6. Warren Mitchell
7. John Thaw
8. Charlotte Rampling
9. Ronnie Barker
10. Christopher Lee

THE 10 WORST *BLIND DATE* TRIPS TO WIN

1. Jellied eel eating on Canvey Island
2. Going to the Norwegian Broadcasting Corporation to help them select their *Song For Europe*
3. Panhandling on New York's Lower East Side
4. Participating in a morris dancing festival in Lincoln
5. Touring a coathanger factory in Dusseldorf
6. Visiting a farm machinery factory in Gdansk
7. Attending a chiropody teaching workshop in Boulogne
8. Swimming off Blackpool beach
9. Going to a Bergman retrospective in Stockholm
10. Mail sorting in Bracknell

10 LAWS OF *BLIND DATE*

1. Men are not allowed to wear single-breasted suits

2. Everyone has to respond to questions by saying "Well…"

3. The girl who gives the sauciest replies to the questions always gets picked to go on the date

4. The man who gives the sauciest replies to the questions never gets chosen to go on the date

5. Anyone who lives North of Watford will be greeted by Cilla as "Our Kevin/Trevor/Gary"

6. If two out of three male contestants are wearing hair gel, the one who isn't wins

7. The audience is obliged to cheer if a contestant comes from anywhere but London

8. The audience is obliged to laugh when a contestant reveals his or her occupation

9. Cilla coos each time she sees a girl prettier than herself (Cilla does an awful lot of cooing)

10. Only air kisses are permitted

10 PEOPLE WHO WERE ON *THIS IS YOUR LIFE* BEFORE THE AGE OF 30

1. Twiggy (Aged 20)
2. Bonnie Langford (21)
3. Stephen Hendry (21)
4. Robin Cousins (22)
5. John Conteh (23)
6. George Best (25)
7. Ian Botham (25)
8. Kevin Keegan (27)
9. Elaine Paige (27)
10. Jim Davidson (29)

CREATE YOUR OWN DAYTIME TV PROGRAMME — 10 IDEAS YOU'LL NEED

1. Celebrity gardening spot with Penelope Keith
2. The Nolans perform their latest single
3. Exclusive in-depth interview with Paula Hamilton
4. Princess Michael of Kent attends a Gilbert and Sullivan operetta at a youth centre
5. Celebrity cookery spot with Derek Nimmo
6. A comic interlude with Stan Boardman
7. Leslie Thomas talks to us about his latest book
8. Susan Hampshire tells us about a new project to help dyslexics
9. Coffee on the sofa with Russell Grant
10. Nanette Newman shows us her collection of children's poems

10 PEOPLE WHO HAVE BEEN ON *THIS IS YOUR LIFE* TWICE

1. Sir Andrew Lloyd Webber
2. Frankie Vaughan
3. Richard Briers
4. Sir Jimmy Savile
5. Honor Blackman
6. Shirley Bassey
7. Edward Woodward
8. Sir Harry Secombe
9. Dame Vera Lynn
10. Sir Peter Ustinov

10 CODENAMES FOR *THIS IS YOUR LIFE* TARGETS

1. Frank Carson: Cracker
2. Phil Collins: Jacket
3. William Shatner: Beam
4. Nigel Kennedy: Bow
5. Jean Boht: Yeast
6. Trevor McDonald: Burger
7. Keith Barron: Knight
8. Patrick Mower: Lawn
9. Sandy Gall: Beach
10. Stephanie Beacham: Powder

THE FIRST 10 PEOPLE ON *THIS IS YOUR LIFE* (1955)

1. Eamonn Andrews (Broadcaster who became the show's presenter after the first show)
2. Yvonne Bailey (French Resistance heroine)
3. Ted Ray (Comedian)
4. Reverend James Butterworth (Worked with underprivileged children)
5. C.B. Fry (Sportsman)
6. Johanna Harris (British Red Cross)
7. Donald Campbell (Speed king)
8. Joe Brannelly (Music publisher)
9. Stanley Matthews (Footballer)
10. Henry Starling (Porter at Billingsgate Market)

10 THINGS WE KNOW ABOUT THE NHS FROM WATCHING *CASUALTY*

1. There are as many male nurses as there are female nurses
2. Nurses can always find the time to join you for a cup of tea
3. Ambulances arrive on the scene in seconds
4. Nurses are addressed by their surnames
5. Hospital consultants are addressed by their first names
6. Hospital porters are incredibly obliging
7. There are rarely queues in Accident & Emergency
8. Hospital loos are absolutely spotless
9. There's always a social worker available to discuss problems
10. One in four people who come into Accident & Emergency discover that they have previously undiagnosed brain tumours

10 ACTS WHICH APPEARED ON *OPPORTUNITY KNOCKS*

1. Les Dawson
2. Paper Lace
3. Tom O'Connor
4. Peters And Lee
5. Mary Hopkin
6. Mud
7. Engelbert Humperdinck
8. Bobby Crush
9. Bonnie Langford
10. Freddie Starr

10 SITCOMS WHICH BECAME FILMS

1. *Till Death Us Do Part* (1968)
2. *Please Sir* (1971)
3. *George And Mildred* (1980)
4. *Rising Damp* (1980)
5. *Steptoe And Son* (1972)
6. *Dad's Army* (1971)
7. *The Likely Lads* (1976)
8. *Are You Being Served?* (1977)
9. *The Addams Family* (1991)
10. *Porridge* (1979)

10 HOLLYWOOD STARS WHO PLAYED *BATMAN* BADDIES IN THE ORIGINAL TV SERIES

1. George Sanders (Mr Freeze). Sanders only appeared in one episode but he holds the distinction of being the only Batman baddie to have been married to another Batman baddie (Zsa Zsa Gabor who played Minerva)

2. Roddy McDowall (The Bookworm). All The Bookworm's crimes revolved around - guess? - books

3. Art Carney (The Archer). The Archer was a Robin Hood character: he stole from the rich (e.g. millionaire Bruce Wayne) and gave the money to the people of Gotham City

4. Joan Collins (The Siren). The Siren's trick was to stop people in their tracks with a voice that had a seven-octave range (a bit like Cleo Laine with attitude)

5. Shelley Winters (Ma Parker). Ma Parker spiked the Batmobile with a bomb which would make the car explode when the speed hit sixty

6. Zsa Zsa Gabor (Minerva). Zsa Zsa played a villainess who owned a beauty salon which was...wait for it...equipped with huge hairdryers which could read the minds of her wealthy clients. This was the last ever episode of *Batman* (so it was *her* fault)

7. Vincent Price (Egghead). Egghead was the bald be-domed super-intelligent super-criminal

8. Liberace (Chandell). The be-jewelled maestro played two roles: a nice guy pianist named Harry and his nasty twin brother, Chandell, who wanted to marry Bruce Wayne's Aunt Harriet to get his hands on her fortune

9. Cliff Robertson (Shame). Shame was a rogue cowboy who captured our heroes and placed them in the path of a cattle stampede

10. Eartha Kitt (Catwoman). Eartha was purr-fect for the feline role but was, in fact, one of three actresses who played the role (Julie Newmar and Lee Meriwether were the others while Michelle Pfeiffer played Catwoman in the 1992 film *Batman Returns*). Bob Kane, the inventor of Batman, modelled the original Catwoman on the 1930s actress Jean Harlow

WANT TO BE A TV NEWSREADER? HERE ARE 10 THINGS YOU'LL HAVE TO BE ABLE TO DO

1. Play with a computer terminal as the title music fades
2. Sound as though you've actually written the script yourself
3. Avoid eating baked beans and pickled onions or drinking fizzy drinks
4. Fold your hands in front of you
5. Resist calling politicians 'liars'
6. Turn to look at your co-presenter when he or she starts to speak
7. Pretend to write things
8. Pronounce silly words like 'Uranus' without giggling
9. Smile nauseatingly before mentioning any elderly member of the Royal Family
10. Appear as a guest on a TV game show

10 THINGS WE KNOW ABOUT AMERICAN LIFESAVERS FROM WATCHING *BAYWATCH*

1. Lifeguard duties include reuniting wayward teenagers with their parents...

2. ...and apprehending drug smugglers

3. Female lifeguards go to work in full make-up

4. Skimpy swimsuits help you run faster

5. Male lifeguards would rather help their sons with their homework than fool around with female lifeguards

6. The kiss of life requires the application of lip-gloss

7. Silicone is a vital buoyancy aid

8. Salt-water does wonders for hair

9. The oldest male lifeguard is always likely to be the fastest runner

10. There's no such thing as an ugly lifeguard

10 PEOPLE WHO APPEARED ON *UNIVERSITY CHALLENGE* AS COMPETITORS

1. David Mellor (Christ's College, Cambridge)

2. Clive James (Pembroke College, Cambridge)

3. Sebastian Faulks (Emmanuel College, Cambridge)

4. Miriam Margolyes (Magdalene College, Cambridge)

5. Alastair Little (Downing College, Cambridge)

6. John Simpson (Magdalene College, Cambridge)

7. Stephen Fry (Queens' College, Cambridge)

8. Dr George Davidson - the 1994 overall champion of *Mastermind* (Jesus College, Oxford)

9. Andrew Morton (Sussex)

10. Malcolm Rifkind (Edinburgh)

10 STAGES IN THE DEVELOPMENT OF THE TV GAME SHOW

1. 940 B.C.: King Solomon gives away a baby in the first ever quiz show

2. 1170: In an end game, King Henry II asks "Who will rid me of this turbulent priest". All four contestants get the right answer

3. 1192: Richard the Lionheart plays *Name That Tune* whilst imprisoned in Germany

4. 1215: King John signs the Magna Carta. No provision is made for game shows.

5. 1216: King John dies during the resulting civil war with the barons

6. 1415: King Henry V leads his team to an *It's A Knockout* win at Agincourt

7. 1620: The Pilgrim Fathers set sail for America where there will one day be more game shows on the schedules

8. 1763: At the conclusion of the Seven Years' War, carriage clocks are given away as consolation prizes for the losers

9. 1815: Napoleon wins a six-year holiday on St. Helena

10. 1928: Bob Monkhouse is born

THE 10 LAWS OF TV GAME SHOWS

1. Contestants are not allowed to giggle when the Lada is described as "a luxury car"

2. For presenters, knowledge of adverbs is optional but golf club membership is compulsory

3. The harder the questions, the cheaper the prize

4. Hostesses must be stupid enough to laugh at the presenter's jokes

5. Holidays are always "fabulous"

6. Contestants who work for the Inland Revenue must expect to be booed by the audience; contestants who work as nurses must expect a round of applause

7. When the presenter refers to "the computer", he actually means "the producer"

8. The geography of the British Isles is always rearranged into TV regions - as in "So you live in Granadaland"

9. The more programmes recorded per day, the more the more the presenter will refer to "today's show"

10. If the presenter puts his arm around a male contestant, he is obliged to apologise lest anyone think him a homosexual

10 UNANSWERED TV QUESTIONS

1. Why does one person play against two on *Blockbusters*?

2. Why do we never see the upstairs of the houses in *Coronation Street*?

3. Are there first names on the driving licences of Lovejoy and Inspector Morse?

4. Why do the presenters on holiday programmes never miss their flights or turn up at half-finished hotels?

5. Why don't people ever buy crisps in The Rover's Return?

6. Did Chris Evans used to be in *Thunderbirds*?

7. Why doesn't anyone fight back against Emu?

8. Why were there never any raves in Pop Larkin's fields?

9. What do BBC weathermen do with their clothing allowance?

10. Why are there no ugly children in *Neighbours* and *Home And Away*?

10 GUEST APPEARANCES IN SIT. COMS.

1. Linda McCartney (*Bread*)

2. John Cleese (*Cheers*)

3. Vincent Hanna (*Blackadder The Third*)

4. Roy Hattersley (*Chef*)

5. Lulu (*Absolutely Fabulous*)

6. Kylie Minogue (*The Vicar of Dibley*)

7. George Hamilton (*Birds of A Feather*)

8. Larry King (*Spin City*)

9. Midge Ure (*Filthy, Rich & Catflap*)

10. Noel Edmonds (*The Detectives*)

10 MOVIE STARS WHO STARTED OFF IN SITCOMS

1. Richard Dreyfuss: *Karen* (1964)
2. Michael J Fox: *Family Ties* (1982-9)
3. Jamie Lee Curtis: *Operation Petticoat* (1977-78)
4. Sally Field: *Gidget* (1965-66)
5. Warren Beatty: *The Many Loves Of Dobie Gillis* (1955-59)
6. Anne Archer: *Bob & Carol & Ted & Alice* (1973-74)
7. Beau Bridges: *Ensign O'Toole* (1962-63)
8. Robin Williams: *Mork And Mindy* (1978-82)
9. Steve Guttenberg: *Billy* (1978-79)
10. Danny De Vito: *Taxi* (1978-83)

10 IMPRESSIONS A FOREIGNER WOULD HAVE ABOUT THE BRITISH AFTER WATCHING OUR TV SIT COMS

1. We're all middle-class...
2. ...unless we're lovable Cockney rogues
3. Families always eat breakfast together
4. Whenever men return home from work they always say, "hello, darling, I'm home"
5. Any *au pair* girl will be beautiful and have long blonde hair and a large bust
6. Vicars invariably pop round just when the man of the house is innocently helping the *au pair* girl remove a stain from her T-shirt
7. The walls of British houses wobble when doors are shut
8. The English language contains no swear words
9. No matter what happens, everything always turns out fine within half-an-hour
10. British people are very easily entertained

10 SITCOMS WHICH WERE SPIN-OFFS FROM OTHER SITCOMS

1. *George and Mildred (Man About the House)*
2. *Frasier (Cheers)*
3. *Going Straight (Porridge)*
4. *Empty Nest (The Golden Girls)*
5. *In Sickness And In Health (Till Death Us Do Part)*
6. *Laverne And Shirley (Happy Days)*
7. *Grace And Favour (Are You Being Served?)*
8. *Rhoda (The Mary Tyler Moore Show)*
9. *The Fenn Street Gang (Please Sir)*
10. *Tabitha (Bewitched)*

10 UPDATED SIT. COMS.

1. *Please Serve Yourself*
2. *Dad's United Nation Peace Keeping Forces*
3. *The Unrestructured Chauvinistic Lads*
4. *Doctor In The Is-There-Any-Chance-You-Could-Make-It-Down-To-The-Surgery*
5. *Terry And December*
6. *It Ain't Half Hot Without The Ozone Layer, Mum*
7. *First Of The Autumn Alka Seltzer*
8. *Man About The Housing Trust Accomodation*
9. *Waiting For The Buses*
10. *Men Behaving*

10 CHARACTERS FOR THE ULTIMATE SIT COM CAST

1. Eccentric but lovable husband in chunky jumper . . . . .Richard Briers

2. His elegant long-suffering wife . . . . .Hannah Gordon

3. Eccentric but lovable husband's even longer-suffering elder sister . . . . .Wendy Craig

4. Wife's snooty best friend . . . . .Penelope Keith

5. The burglar who injures himself whilst breaking in . . . . .Karl Howman

6. The doctor who treats the burglar . . . . . . .Geoffrey Palmer

7. Over-excited shop girl who hands elegant wife the wrong bag containing thousands of pounds of uncut diamonds . .Su Pollard

8. Plausible conman who persuades the elegant wife to hand it back . . . . .Peter Bowles

9. Attractive next door neighbour with whom the eccentric but lovable husband in chunky jumper is caught in a potentially compromising position . . . . . .Felicity Kendal

10. Vicar who catches eccentric but lovable husband in chunky jumper with attractive next door neighbour in a potentially compromising position . . . . .Derek Nimmo

10 PEOPLE WHO HAVE PRESENTED POINTS OF VIEW

1. Robert Robinson
2. Kenneth Robinson
3. Anne Robinson
4. Tony Robinson
5. Barry Took
6. Alan Bennett
7. Tim Rice
8. Nanette Newman
9. Miles Kington
10. Andrew Sachs

TEN THINGS WE KNOW ABOUT WORLD WAR II FROM WATCHING TV MINI SERIES

1. The War began in 1941

2. The Americans and Russians weren't really Allies

3. Britain's sole role in the war was to provide quaint locations for American servicemen

4. No officer was so important that he couldn't be spared to sort out his love life

5. Senior naval officers were all over seventy

6. Wherever people went they always bumped into people they knew

7. 99% off all Allied casualties were American

8. No-one died in the London Blitz

9. Women were not allowed to drive generals unless they slept with them

10. White American privates happily took orders from black American sergeants

10 ACTORS IN PROGRAMMES BEFORE THEY BECAME FAMOUS

1. Anthony Andrews: *The Pallisers*
2. Johnny Briggs: *No Hiding Place*
3. Paul Eddington: *The Adventures Of Robin Hood*
4. Tony Anholt: *The Protectors*
5. Anthony Valentine: *Billy Bunter*
6. Jan Harvey: *Sam*
7. Leonard Rossiter: *Z Cars*
8. Keith Barron: *A Family At War*
9. Peter Dean: *Big Deal*
10. Jill Gascoine: *Within These Walls*

APART FROM BOTHAM & BEAUMONT, PARROTT & McCOIST – 10 PEOPLE WHO CAPTAINED TEAMS ON *A QUESTION OF SPORT*

1. Cliff Morgan
2. Henry Cooper
3. Freddie Trueman
4. Brendan Foster
5. Bobby Moore
6. Mary Rand
7. Gareth Edwards
8. Willie Carson
9. Emlyn Hughes
10. John Barnes

10 PEOPLE WHO APPEARED IN *CORONATION STREET*

1. Joanna Lumley (Elaine Perkins)
2. Peter Noone (Stanley Fairclough)
3. Gorden Kaye (Bernard Butler)
4. Paula Wilcox (Janice Langton)
5. Mollie Sugden (Nellie Harvey)
6. Richard Beckinsale (P.C. Willcocks)
7. Michael Ball (Malcolm Nuttall)
8. Prunella Scales (Eileen Hughes)
9. Davy Jones (Colin Lomax)
10. Martin Shaw (Robert Croft)

10 PEOPLE AND THE SOAPS THEY ACTED IN

1. Derek Nimmo: *Neighbours*
2. Jenny Hanley: *Emmerdale*
3. Clive James: *Neighbours*
4. Joanne Whalley-Kilmer: *Coronation Street*
5. Peter Purves (*EastEnders*)
6. Angela Thorne: *Emmerdale*
7. David Jason: *Crossroads*
8. Malcolm McDowell (*Crossroads*)
9. Frederick Jaeger: *Take The High Road*
10. Diane Keen: *Crossroads*

10 PEOPLE WHO HAVE GUESTED ON U.S. TV SHOWS

1. Richard Branson: *Baywatch*
2. Leonard Cohen: *Miami Vice*
3. Ray Charles: *Moonlighting*
4. Norman Beaton: *The Cosby Show*
5. Peter Noone: *My Two Dads*
6. Phil Collins: *Miami Vice*
7. Dionne Warwick: *The Rockford Files*
8. Carly Simon: *thirtysomething*
9. Boy George: *The A-Team*
10. Davy Jones: *My Two Dads*

10 THINGS SOAP STARS DID BEFORE

1. William Roache (Ken Barlow, *Coronation Street*) was an army captain who once served in Arabia living among Bedouins (none of whom spoke English)

2. Dean Sullivan (Jimmy Corkhill, *Brookside*) was a primary school teacher

3. Pam St. Clement (Pat Butcher, *EastEnders*) was a journalist

4. Sheila Mercier (Annie Sugden, *Emmerdale*) was in the WAAF and worked with RAF fighter command during World War II

5. Ian Smith (Harold Bishop, *Neighbours*) used to write scripts for *Prisoner Cell Block H.*

6. Stefan Dennis (Paul Robinson, *Neighbours*) trained as a chef

7. Norman Bowler (Frank Tate, *Emmerdale*) was a deckboy on an oil tanker

8. Bill Treacher (Arthur Fowler, *EastEnders*) was a steward with the P&O

9. Sue Nicholls (Audrey Roberts, *Coronation Street*) is actually the Hon. Sue Nicholls and the daughter of a former Tory M.P.

10. Elizabeth Dawn (Vera Duckworth, *Coronation Street*) worked in Woolworth's

10 PEOPLE WHO APPEARED IN SOAPS AS THEMSELVES

1. Loyd Grossman (*Brookside*)

2. Freddie Trueman (*Emmerdale*)

3. Bernard Manning (*Coronation Street*)

4. Russell Grant (*Brookside*)

5. Princess Margaret (*The Archers*)

6. Chris Lowe of The Pet Shop Boys (*Neighbours*)

7. Harold Macmillan (*The Archers*)

8. Martin Offiah (*Emmerdale*)

9. Bruce Grobbelaar (*Brookside*)

10. Paula Yates (*Brookside*)

10 THINGS A FOREIGNER WOULD KNOW ABOUT LONDON FROM WATCHING EASTENDERS

1. Everybody knows everybody else

2. Children never make any noise

3. Only heterosexuals contract AIDS

4. Women are only attractive under the age of 20

5. No one eats McDonald's

6. There is no such thing as racism

7. Hardly anyone ever watches TV

8. Smiling is proscribed by law

9. People only have friends who live within walking distance

10. Swearing is forbidden

10 SONGS BY EASTENDERS STARS

1. Anita Dobson: *Anyone Can Fall In Love*

2. Nick Berry: *Every Loser Wins*

3. Letitia Dean & Paul J. Medford: *Something Outta Nothing*

4. Peter Dean: *Can't Get A Ticket For The World Cup*

5. Sophie Lawrence: *Love's Unkind*

6. Jan Graveson: *Anyone Who Had A Heart*

7. Wendy Richard (With Mike Sarne): *Come Outside*

8. Michelle Gayle: *Sweetness*

9. June Brown: *Little Donkey*

10. The Cast of *EastEnders*: *Roll Out The Barrel*

10 EXPRESSIONS HEARD ON *EASTENDERS*

1. "Trust me"
2. "Sorted"
3. "Out of order"
4. "<u>Well</u> out of order"
5. "Let's go dahn the Vic"
6. "Leave it aht"
7. "You're my bruvver" (exclusive to the Mitchell brothers)
8. "Let's have a nice cuppa tea"
9. "What you 'aving?"
10. "Did you 'ear about the fire?"

10 ISSUES COVERED BY *EASTENDERS*

1. Alzheimer's Disease (Mo Butcher)
2. Gay love (Colin & Barry)
3. Mental illness (Arthur Fowler and Joe Wicks)
4. Alcoholism & Attempted suicide (Angie Watts)
5. Lesbianism (Della & Binny)
6. Schoolgirl pregnancy (Michelle)
7. HIV/AIDS (Mark & Gill Fowler)
8. Insurance Fiddles (Grant & Phil Mitchell)
9. Rape (Kathy & Willmott-Brown)
10. Drink-driving (Pat Butcher)

10 MYSTERIES OF *EASTENDERS*

1. Where does Dr Legg go for months on end?
2. Why does Pauline's son, Martin, talk so little?
3. Why is Albert Square so free from racism?
4. Why does hardly anyone smoke?
5. Why does hardly anyone smile?
6. Given that there are railway bridges in Albert Square, why does no one ever talk about taking the *train* "up west" rather than the bus?
7. Why are Pauline Fowler's nails so beautifully manicured - given that she works in a laundrette?
8. Why haven't Grant and Phil noticed that their mum's changed into a *Carry On* star?
9. Why does Walford Town FC's season only last for three weeks?
10. Why don't the inhabitants of Albert Square ever watch *EastEnders* - or, for that matter, *Coronation Street*?

10 THINGS WE KNOW ABOUT AUSTRALIA FROM WATCHING SOAP OPERAS

1. There are only thirty people in the whole country and they all know each other
2. Australians aren't interested in cricket or rugby
3. Weekly barbecues are compulsory by law
4. There are no milkmen in Melbourne
5. There are no Aborigines in Australia
6. Back doors can't be locked
7. All males under the age of 18 are obliged to ride skateboards (unless they're surfing)
8. Relatives only exist when they are actually present
9. Smoking is illegal
10. No one talks about soap operas

10 PEOPLE WHO PRESENTED THE FIRST EDITION OF...

1. *Jackanory:* Lee Montague 1964
2. *A Question of Sport:* David Vine 1970
3. *Blue Peter:* Leila Williams, Christopher Trace 1958
4. *Top Of The Pops:* Jimmy Savile 1964
5. *The Golden Shot:* Jackie Rae 1967
6. *Come Dancing:* Sylvia Peters 1950
7. *News At Ten:* Alastair Burnet 1967
8. *Panorama:* Patrick Murphy 1953
9. *Tomorrow's World:* Raymond Baxter 1965
10. *Newsnight:* Peter Snow, Peter Hobday 1980

10 TV SOAPS WHICH ARE NO LONGER WITH US

1. *Albion Market*
2. *The Grove Family*
3. *Eldorado*
4. *Crossroads*
5. *Sixpenny Corner*
6. *General Hospital*
7. *The Newcomers*
8. *United*
9. *Emergency - Ward 10*
10. *Compact*

10 BRITISH PROGRAMMES WHICH WON THE GOLDEN ROSE OF MONTREUX

1. *Black And White Minstrel Show* 1961
2. *Frost Over England* 1967
3. *Monty Python's Flying Circus* (Silver Rose, 1971; Honorary Golden Rose, 1995)
4. *The Paul Daniels Magic Easter Show* 1985
5. *The Comic Strip Presents...The Strike* 1988
6. *Hale & Pace* 1989
7. *Mr Bean* 1990
8. *A Night Out On Mount Edna: The Dame Edna Everage Christmas Special* 1991
9. *Don't Forget Your Toothbrush* 1995
10. *Cold Feet* 1997

THE FIRST 10 PROGRAMMES BROADCAST ON ITV

1. Opening Ceremony
2. *Channel Nine* (variety show)
3. Drama
4. Professional Boxing
5. News
6. Gala Night
7. Star Cabaret
8. Preview
9. *Sixpenny Corner* (soap opera)
10. Hands About The House

THE FIRST TEN PROGRAMMES SHOWN ON BBC 2 (Tuesday 21st April 1964)

1. 11.00 Play School Closedown
2. 19.15 *Zero Minus Five* (Introductory Programme)
3. 19.20 *Line-Up* (Arts Programme)
4. 19.30 *The Alberts' Channel Too* (Variety Show)
5. 20.00 *Kiss Me Kate* (Musical starring Howard Keel and Millicent Martin)
6. 21.35 *Arkady Raikin* (Soviet comedian)
7. 22.20 *Off With A Bang* (Fireworks from Southend Pier)
8. 22.35 *Newsroom* (News)
9. 23.02 *Jazz 625* (Duke Ellington In Concert) Closedown
10. 11.00 *Play School* (The next day)

THE 10 MOST COMMON ITEMS SUBMITTED TO *THE ANTIQUES ROADSHOW*

1. 20th-century pottery
2. Prints and reproductions
3. Violins
4. Dinky Toys
5. Pocket watches
6. Wedding rings
7. Electro-plated silver
8. Dolls and teddies
9. Travel souvenirs
10. Japanese egg-shell tea sets

THE 10 MOST UNUSUAL ITEMS SUBMITTED TO *THE ANTIQUES ROADSHOW*

1. A 19th-century portable shower
2. A tennis ball cleaner
3. Japanese erotica
4. The personal diary of a 19th century sea captain on his way to Australia
5. A gold plaque
6. An owl slip-wear cup - worth £20,000
7. Salt cellars - thought by the owner to be made of bronze - which turned out to be early 19th-century gold salt cellars, and later sold for £56,000
8. A picture of a volcano - used as a dart board for several years - which turned out to be very rare and worth £10,000
9. A painting - found rolled up in an attic - which later sold for £100,000
10. A typewriter dating back to the turn of the century

10 TV CHARACTERS AND THE TEAMS THEY SUPPORTED

1. Alf Garnett *(Till Death Us Do Part):* West Ham
2. Robin Tripp *(Man About The House):* Southampton
3. Loadsamoney *(Friday Night Live):* Spurs
4. Norman Stanley Fletcher *(Going Straight):* Leyton Orient (N.B. in *Porridge*, there was a suspicion that he was a Spurs supporter)
5. Terry McCann *(Minder):* Fulham
6. Yosser Hughes *(Boys From The Blackstuff):* Liverpool
7. Stavros *(Friday Night Live):* Arsenal
8. Bob Ferris *(The Likely Lads):* Newcastle United
9. Simon Wicks *(EastEnders):* West Ham United
10. Robbie Box *(Big Deal):* Fulham

10 TV SERIES WHICH BECAME MOVIES

1. *The Flintstones*
2. *The Addams Family*
3. *The Fugitive*
4. *Batman*
5. *Dragnet*
6. *The Sweeney*
7. *The Beverly Hillbillies*
8. *Mission: Impossible*
9. *The Untouchables*
10. *Tom And Jerry*

A TOP 10 OF TV PROGRAMMES

1. ONE Man And His Dog
2. The TWO Ronnies
3. THREE Of A Kind
4. 4 What It's Worth
5. Police 5
6. The 6 O'Clock Show
7. SEVEN Days
8. EIGHT Is Enough
9. Not The NINE O'Clock News
10. News At TEN

10 GROUPS OF PEOPLE YET TO HAVE THEIR OWN DRAMA SERIES

1. Casual Tees (Occasional golfers)
2. The Gentle Hutch (Rabbit owners)
3. Taking Out (Fast-food restaurant owners)
4. Roots (Dentists)
5. Forever Preen (Male models)
6. Wides (Cricket umpires)
7. Rings (Computer dating agencies)
8. The Till (Supermarket checkout girls)
9. L.A. Jaw (Californian psychotherapists)
10. Triangles (Maths teachers)

10 TV PRESENTERS WHOSE CHILDREN FOLLOWED IN THEIR FOOTSTEPS

1. Cliff Michelmore (son, Guy)
2. Paul Daniels (son, Martin)
3. Gloria Hunniford (daughter, Caron Keating)
4. Richard Dimbleby (sons, David and Jonathan)
5. Nanette Newman (daughter, Emma Forbes)
6. Jess Yates (daughter, Paula)
7. Harry Corbett (son, Matthew)
8. Barry Norman (daughter, Samantha)
9. Magnus Magnusson (daughter, Sally)
10. Sir Clement Freud (daughter, Emma)

10 PEOPLE WHO PRESENTED JACKANORY

1. Rik Mayall
2. Joanna Lumley
3. Sean Hughes
4. Paul Merton
5. Mike McShane
6. Tony Slattery
7. Dawn French
8. Richard Briers
9. Helena Bonham-Carter
10. Victoria Wood

Chapter 18

The Media

THE FIRST 10 CASTAWAYS ON *DESERT ISLAND DISCS* (Starting January 29th 1942

1. Vic Oliver (comedian)
2. James Agate (critic)
3. Commander Campbell (mariner and Explorer)
4. C.B. Cochran (showman)
5. Pat Kirkwood (actress)
6. Jack Hylton (bandleader)
7. Captain Dingle (explorer)
8. Joan Jay (glamour girl)
9. The Reverend Canon W.H. Elliott (Precentor of the Chapels Royal)
10. Arthur Askey (comedian)

10 PEOPLE WHO CHOSE DICKENS NOVELS ON *DESERT ISLAND DISCS*

1. Ernie Wise: *The Mystery Of Edwin Drood*
2. Frankie Howerd: *David Copperfield*
3. Eric Clapton: *Barnaby Rudge*
4. Robert Robinson: *The Pickwick Papers*
5. Julian Symons: *Bleak House*
6. Jack Warner: *A Tale Of Two Cities* (in English and French)
7. Jonathon Porritt: *Bleak House*
8. Dick Emery: *A Christmas Carol*
9. Sir Learie Constantine: *The Old Curiosity Shop*
10. Tom Courtenay: *Great Expectations*

10 BOOKS CHOSEN ON *DESERT ISLAND DISCS*

1. Cilla Black: *Aesop's Fables*
2. Bob Hoskins: *Catch 22* by Joseph Heller
3. David Essex: *The Guinness Book of Records*
4. Joan Collins: *The Complete Works Of Oscar Wilde*
5. Roger Moore: *Noble House* by James Clavell
6. Gary Glitter: *The Times Concise Atlas*
7. Michael Gambon: *Republican Party Reptile* by P.J. O'Rourke
8. Anita Roddick: *Prince of Tides* by Pat Conroy
9. Salman Rushdie: *Arabian Nights*
10. Jane Asher: *Tess of The D'Urbervilles* by Thomas Hardy

THE 10 MOST POPULAR LUXURIES ON *DESERT ISLAND DISCS*

1. Piano
2. Writing materials
3. Bed
4. Guitar
5. Typewriter
6. Radio receiver
7. Golf club and golf balls
8. Painting materials
9. Wine
10. Perfume

10 LUXURIES CHOSEN BY CASTAWAYS ON *DESERT ISLAND DISCS*

1. A life-sized papier mâché model of Margaret Thatcher and a baseball bat (John Cleese)
2. Having *The Sporting Life* delivered daily (Des O'Connor)
3. Basil Brush films and a projector (Dame Judi Dench)
4. An inflatable rubber woman (Oliver Reed)
5. An inflatable woman and a puncture repair kit (Michael Crawford)
6. A deckchair (Eric Morecambe); a deckchair ticket machine (Ernie Wise)
7. A television set that does not work (Sir Robert Mark)
8. A motorway service station (Noel Edmonds)
9. Nelson's Column (Lionel Bart)
10. A self-operated nuclear strike force for defence (John Bird)

10 PEOPLE WHO CHOSE ELTON JOHN SONGS ON *DESERT ISLAND DISCS*

1. Jeffrey Archer: *Candle In The Wind*
2. Ian Botham: *I'm Still Standing*
3. Trevor Brooking: *Don't Let The Sun Go Down On Me*
4. David Hemmings: *Love Song*
5. Billy Connolly: *Sorry Seems To Be The Hardest Word*
6. John Conteh: *Bennie And The Jets*
7. Andrew Lloyd Webber: *Mona Lisas And Mad Hatters*
8. Marti Caine: *Tonight*
9. Mark McCormack: *Candle In The Wind*
10. Robin Cousins: *Sorry Seems To Be The Hardest Word*

10 PEOPLE WHO CHOSE THEIR OWN RECORDS ON *DESERT ISLAND DISCS*

1. Cilla Black (*Anyone Who Had A Heart*)
2. Hylda Baker (*Give Us A Kiss*)
3. Sir David Frost (Excerpt from *The Frost Report On Everything*)
4. Tony Bennett (*Smile*)
5. Gary Glitter (*Rock And Roll I Gave You The Best Years Of My Life*)
6. Dame Edna Everage (*My Bridesmaid And I*)
7. Alan Price (*House Of The Rising Sun*)
8. Mel Brooks (*Springtime For Hitler*)
9. Clive Dunn (*Grandad*)
10. Dudley Moore (*Little Miss Britten*)

10 PEOPLE WHO CHOSE BEATLES' RECORDS ON *DESERT ISLAND DISCS*

1. Lord King: *She's Leaving Home*
2. Dr David Owen: *Lucy In The Sky With Diamonds*
3. Robin Knox-Johnston: *She Loves You*
4. H.R.H. The Duchess of Kent: *Maxwell's Silver Hammer*
5. Keith Floyd: *Hey Jude*
6. Tony Blair: *In My Life*
7. Ian Botham: *Yesterday*
8. Mark McCormack: *And I Love Her*
9. Barbara Castle: *Love Me Do*
10. Anita Dobson: *Please Please Me*

10 PEOPLE WHO CHOSE PAUL SIMON SONGS ON *DESERT ISLAND DISCS*

1. Frederick Forsyth: *The Sound Of Silence*
2. James Bolam: *Silent Night - Seven O'Clock News*
3. Gareth Edwards: *Bridge Over Troubled Water*
4. Douglas Adams: *Hearts And Bones*
5. Rowan Atkinson: *Still Crazy After All These Years*
6. Val Doonican: *Scarborough Fair*
7. Colin Welland: *Bridge Over Troubled Water*
8. Isabel Allende: *El Condor Pasa*
9. Delia Smith: *The Sound of Silence*
10. Marti Webb: *Bridge Over Troubled Water*

10 PEOPLE WHO CHOSE ROLLING STONES' RECORDS ON *DESERT ISLAND DISCS*

1. Sir Andrew Lloyd Webber: *(I Can't Get No) Satisfaction*
2. Dr Desmond Morris: *It's Not Easy*
3. Zoe Wanamaker: *Sympathy For The Devil*
4. Katharine Hamnett: *You Can't Always Get What You Want*
5. Bob Champion: *(I Can't Get No) Satisfaction*
6. Paul Smith: *Sympathy For The Devil*
7. Bob Hoskins: *Honky Tonk Women*
8. Ian Botham: *Get Off Of My Cloud*
9. David Wilkie: *Hot Stuff*
10. Salman Rushdie: *Sympathy For The Devil*

10 PEOPLE WHO CHOSE BOB DYLAN RECORDS ON *DESERT ISLAND DISCS*

1. James Fox: *I Believe In You*
2. Lord Lichfield: *Just Like A Woman*
3. General Norman Schwarzkopf: *Times They Are A-Changin'*
4. Brian Glover: *Like A Rolling Stone*
5. Sir Edmund Hillary: *Blowin' In The Wind*
6. Robert Powell: *Don't Think Twice, It's Alright*
7. Jenny Agutter: *I Want You*
8. Joan Bakewell: *Mr Tambourine Man*
9. Natalie Wood: *Just Like A Woman*
10. Juliet Stevenson: *Shelter From The Storm*

10 SONGS THEY REALLY SHOULD REQUEST ON DESERT ISLAND DISCS

1. *All By Myself* (Eric Carmen)
2. *Rescue Me* (Fontella Bass)
3. *Sandy* (John Travolta)
4. *Message In A Bottle* (The Police)
5. *Out Of Touch* (Daryl Hall And John Oates)
6. *Ain't Got No - I Got Life* (Nina Simone)
7. *I Talk To The Trees* (Clint Eastwood)
8. *Solitaire* (Andy Williams)
9. *Living On An Island* (Status Quo)
10. *Life On Your Own* (The Human League)

10 PEOPLE WHO'VE GUESTED AS BBC DISC JOCKEYS

1. Nanette Newman (for Judith Chalmers)
2. Jools Holland (for Andy Kershaw)
3. Phil Collins (for Simon Bates)
4. Whitney Houston (for Simon Bates)
5. Michael Ball (for David Jacobs)
6. Dame Barbara Cartland (for a Special)
7. Lenny Henry (for a Special)
8. Denis Healey (for Richard Baker)
9. Billy Bragg (for Janice Long)
10. Moira Stewart (for Steve Race)

10 CHARACTERS FROM THE GOON SHOW

1. Hercules Grytpype-Thynne
2. Major Bloodnok
3. Little Jim
4. Minnie Bannister
5. Count Moriarty
6. Bluebottle
7. The Red Bladder
8. Neddy Seagoon
9. Eccles
10. Henry Crunn

10 THINGS SAID BY RADIO DJs – AND WHAT THEY REALLY MEAN

1. "Hi, tonight I'm sitting in for John Peel" = When *is* he going to retire?
2. "We've got a whole bunch of great goodies for you" = I will be playing some music
3. "Hey, Sandra, Oldham sounds like a great place" = I wouldn't be seen dead there
4. "Oh yeah, Cliff's a great guy" = When's he going to invite me to play tennis with him?
5. "So what kind of music do you like, Mike?" = Not that I could give a damn but it doesn't hurt to be democratic
6. "I don't like to talk about it but I do a lot of work for charity" = Who's this Harry Enfield then?
7. "We've had tons of requests" = One letter and two phone calls
8. "I was at the Oasis concert the other day" = I may be old but I can still hack it
9. "You know, being a DJ is the greatest job on earth" = How else would I get £2,000 just to open a supermarket?
10. "And don't forget you'll get the chance to meet me at our Summer Roadshow" = I'll be the fat balding midget with the squint

THE FIRST 10 RECORDS EVER PLAYED ON RADIO 1

1. *Flowers In The Rain* (The Move)
2. *Massachusetts* (The Bee Gees)
3. *Even The Bad Times Are Good* (The Tremeloes)
4. *Fakin' It* (Simon & Garfunkel)
5. *The Day I Met Marie* (Cliff Richard)
6. *You Can't Hurry Love* (The Supremes)
7. *The Last Waltz* (Engelbert Humperdinck)
8. *Baby Now That I've Found You* (The Foundations)
9. *Good Times* (Eric Burdon And The Animals)
10. *A Banda* (Herb Alpert And The Tijuana Brass)

10 PEOPLE WHO STOOD IN FOR JIMMY YOUNG

1. Edwina Currie
2. Julian Pettifer
3. Esther Rantzen
4. Frank Bough
5. Rosie Barnes
6. Harry Carpenter
7. Ken Livingstone
8. David Frost
9. Glenys Kinnock
10. Alan Whicker

10 FORMER JOURNALISTS

1. Frederick Forsyth
2. Chrissie Hynde
3. Vanessa Feltz
4. Evelyn Waugh
5. Ali MacGraw
6. Jilly Cooper
7. Mark Knopfler
8. Janet Street-Porter
9. Neil Tennant
10. Steve Harley

10 PEOPLE WHO WERE EDITORS

1. Michael Foot *The Evening Standard*
2. Nina Myskow *Jackie*
3. John Freeman *New Statesman*
4. Libby Purves *Tatler*
5. Nigel Lawson *The Spectator*
6. Sally Beaumann *Queen*
7. Anthony Holden *Sunday Today*
8. Richard Branson *Student*
9. Julian Critchley *Town*
10. Sir Alastair Burnet *The Daily Express*

10 PEOPLE WHO WERE *TIME* MAGAZINE'S 'MAN OF THE YEAR'

1. Mahatma Gandhi (1931)
2. Mrs Wallis Simpson (1937)
3. Adolf Hitler (1939)
4. Joseph Stalin (1940)
5. Queen Elizabeth II (1953)
6. Martin Luther King (1964)
7. Ayatollah Khomeini (1980)
8. Newt Gingrich (1995)
9. Cory Aquino (1987)
10. Ted Turner (1991)

10 PEOPLE WHO SUCCESSFULLY SUED *PRIVATE EYE*

1. Sir James Goldsmith
2. Randolph Churchill
3. Nora Beloff
4. Desmond Wilcox
5. Jeremy Thorpe
6. Armand Hammer
7. Lord Bethell
8. Nigel Dempster
9. Ken Livingstone
10. Gerald Howarth

10 THINGS SAID ABOUT JOURNALISM

1. "The secret of successful journalism is to make your readers so angry they will write half your paper for you" (C.E.M. Joad)

2. "Journalism is organised gossip" (Edward Egglestone)

3. "Newspapers are unable, seemingly, to discriminate between a bicycle accident and the collapse of civilisation" (George Bernard Shaw)

4. "When a journalist enters the room, your privacy ends and his begins" (Warren Beatty)

5. "Good taste is, of course, an utterly dispensable part of any journalist's equipment" (Michael Hogg)

6. "An investigating journalist is one who can think up plausible scandals" (Lambert Jeffries)

7. "Take off the dateline and one day's paper is the same as the next" (Marshall McLuhan)

8. "Facing the press is more difficult than bathing a leper" (Mother Teresa)

9. "Journalists write because they have nothing to say, and have something to say because they write" (Karl Kraus)

10. "A reporter is a man who has renounced everything in life but the world, the flesh and the devil" (David Murray)

10 PHOTOS WE SEE EVERY YEAR

1. Photographers taking photos of starlet at the Cannes Film Festival

2. The leading members of the Government and the Opposition exchanging pleasantries as they file off to the House of Lords for the Queen's Speech

3. London Marathon runner collapsing on the line

4. The summer bank holiday traffic jam

5. The snowless roof of the London Weather Centre on Christmas Day

6. Deserted (except for one person) ground during a county cricket match

7. Someone asleep at a party conference

8. London bobby dancing with an extremely fat black woman at the Notting Hill Carnival

9. Child licking an ice-cream to stay cool during heatwave

10. A street full of estate agents' For Sale boards to illustrate either a) the boom or b) the recession

WANT TO LAUNCH A WOMEN'S MAGAZINE? HERE ARE 10 ARTICLES TO GET YOU GOING

1. Signed letter from the editor which starts with the word Hi! and ends with the words Happy Reading!

2. Sue Lawley: What _Should_ She Do Next?

3. Holding Back The Tears: We Meet The Survivors

4. Super Cindy! We Get The Low-Down On Richard Gere's Pretty Woman!

5. Want To Become An Aromatherapist? We Show You How!

6. Maureen Lipman: Why I Feel Guilty About Not Being With My Kids

7. Jane Asher's Fabulous Party Cakes. How _Does_ She Do It!

8. Having It All? Meet The Women Who Juggle

9. Jane Seymour: This Time It's For Real

10. How To Turn Your Man Into A New Man And Make Him Fall In Love With You All Over Again!

10 (UNINTENTIONALLY) HILARIOUS HEADLINES

1. SHOT OFF WOMAN'S LEG HELPS NICKLAUS TO 66
2. SQUAD HELPS DOG BITE VICTIM
3. DRUNK GETS NINE MONTHS IN VIOLIN CASE
4. DOCTOR TESTIFIES IN HORSE SUIT
5. THUGS EAT THEN ROB PROPRIETOR
6. CITY MAY IMPOSE MANDATORY TIME FOR PROSTITUTION
7. ENRAGED COW INJURES FARMER WITH AXE
8. GRANDMOTHER OF EIGHT MAKES HOLE IN ONE
9. FARMER BILL DIES IN HOUSE
10. DEFENDANT'S SPEECH ENDS IN LONG SENTENCE

10 SHAREHOLDERS – PAST AND PRESENT – OF PRIVATE EYE

1. Peter Cook
2. Jane Asher
3. Sir Dirk Bogarde
4. Bernard Braden
5. Peter Sellers
6. Barry Fantoni
7. Oscar Lewenstein (who he? Ed)
8. Er...
9. ...that's...
10. ...it

10 GENUINE MAGAZINE TITLES (PAST AND PRESENT)

1. *Vending Today*
2. *Fur Weekly News*
3. *Cranes Today*
4. *The Embalmer*
5. *Civil Service Whip*
6. *Commercial Rabbit*
7. *Flying Saucer Review*
8. *Bee World*
9. *Fancy Fowl*
10. *The Tea Club Magazine*

10 ENTRIES FROM PRIVATE EYE'S COLEMANBALLS COLUMN

1. "It's been a wet month just about everywhere, but surprisingly not everywhere" (Weatherman Michael Fish putting his fin in it)
2. "Yes, the Great Fire of London. It started in a baker's shop in Pudding Lane in 1666. I wonder if it's still there?" (Dave Lee Travis)
3. "What's your name, Kate?" (Simon Bates)
4. "I must apologise to the deaf for the loss of subtitles" (Angela Rippon)
5. "And don't forget, on Sunday you can hear the two-minute silence on Radio One" (DJ Steve Wright)
6. "If we can just get young people to do as their fathers did, that is wear condoms." (Richard Branson, talking about his Mates)
7. "Dudley Moore without a piano is like chalk without cheese" (Nick Owen)
8. "I see my mum as often as I like - which is not as often as I'd like." (Leo Sayer or, rather, Say er...)
9. "Did you write the words or the lyrics?" (Bruce Forsyth)
10. "And that's a self-portrait of himself, by himself" (Richard Madeley)

10 JOURNALISTS WHO APPEARED IN FILMS

1. Clive James: *Barry McKenzie Holds His Own*
2. Michael Parkinson: *Madhouse*
3. Malcolm Muggeridge: *Heavens Above*
4. Andrew Neil: *Dirty Weekend*
5. Bernard Levin: *Nothing But The Best*
6. Godfrey Winn: *Billy Liar*
7. David Robinson: *If...*
8. Sir David Frost: *The VIPs*
9. Richard Dimbleby: *Libel*
10. Joan Bakewell: *The Touchables*

10 STAGES IN A RELATIONSHIP AS REPORTED IN *HELLO!*

1. So Happy: Janet And John Reveal Their Whirlwind Romance
2. John Talks For The First Time About His Love For Janet As They Announce Their Engagement
3. Sunshine And Smiles: Exclusive Photographs Of Janet And John's Star-studded Wedding
4. Janet And John Invite Us In To Their Sumptuous Home And Tell Us How Their Love Has Grown From Strength To Strength In The Past Six Weeks
5. Janet Talks To Us Of Her Joy At The Thought Of Becoming A Mother For The First Time
6. Janet And John Introduce Us To Their Four-day Old Son, Tarquin
7. On Holiday With Janet And John As They Dismiss Rumours Of Marital Difficulties
8. The Sad Story Behind The Break-up Of Janet And John
9. John Tells Us Of His Sorrow As He Loses Battle To Keep His Children
10. Janet Introduces Us To David And Tells Us How She's Found Happiness At Last

10 PEOPLE MONSTERED BY *VIZ*

1. The Duchess of York ("Fergie's video sex romp")
2. Jim Bowen ("I still use public lavatories")
3. Wendy James ("Wobbly Wendy could weigh in at 21 stone - fears Doc")
4. Ben Elton ("Ben laughs to hide the tears")
5. Christopher Biggins ("Biggins says 'big uns' are best")
6. Rodney Bewes ("Bewes sets target for walnut industry")
7. Jim Morrison ("My Paris hotel bath death tragedy was all a big mix-up")
8. Cliff Richard ("Cliff's nuts set to blow")
9. Jimmy Nail ("'I'm scared of dinosaurs' says TV's Spender")
10. Brian May ("My nits hell!")

10 NEWSPAPER COLUMNIST SPEAK

1. "I was reading in the paper the other day" (Don't think I don't do any research)
2. "As any mother will tell you" (Or, indeed, the children's nanny)
3. "I was talking to this taxi-driver" (I still have contact with working people)
4. "Something must be done" (But not, of course, by me)
5. "I'm all for freedom of speech..." (Don't be silly)
6. "He should try working for a living" (Just look at me: five three-hour lunches a week and I still manage to write a thousand words)
7. "What really concerns me..." (...and my editor and proprietor)
8. "It makes you think, doesn't it" (Well it took me an extra five minutes to write the column this week)
9. "The solution is simple" (Regular readers will have guessed as much)
10. "It came as no surprise to learn" (Thank God for hindsight)

Chapter 19

Advertising

10 EXPRESSIONS USED IN TOY ADVERTISEMENTS . . . AND WHAT THEY REALLY MEAN

1. "As seen on TV" (er, *Watchdog*)
2. "Fun for all the family!" (The family that plays together, slays together)
3. "Traditional toy made by craftsmen" (Boring as hell)
4. "Educational" (Buy it or your kid's going to grow up disadvantaged)
5. "Educational & Fun" (. . . and they'll blame you for it)
6. "Guaranteed unbreakable" (But not in the hands of a child)
7. "Ideal for anyone from 8 to 80" (Or anyone else you know with a mentality of an 8-year old)
8. "Toys at unbelievable prices!" (Cheap and nasty)
9. "Toys at pocket-money prices" (Very cheap and nasty)
10. ". . . And there's a whole series to collect!" (It's time to take out a second mortgage)

10 PEOPLE WHO HAVE ADVERTISED AMERICAN EXPRESS

1. Roger Daltrey
2. Dame Judi Dench
3. Neil Simon
4. Ella Fitzgerald
5. Pauline Collins
6. Seve Ballesteros
7. Christian Lacroix
8. Ray Charles
9. Catherine Deneuve
10. John Cleese

10 PEOPLE WHO DON'T DO COMMERCIALS

1. The Queen
2. Bob Dylan
3. The Pope
4. Daniel Day-Lewis
5. Neil Young
6. Bruce Springsteen
7. Paul McCartney
8. Prince Charles
9. Ben Elton
10. Ian Hislop

10 CHARACTERS IN TV COMMERCIALS

1. Sid (British Gas)
2. Fred (Homepride)
3. Arthur (Kattomeat)
4. Cyril (Wonderloaf)
5. Beattie (British Telecom)
6. Norman (Sun Alliance)
7. Ben (Bird's Eye Beefburgers)
8. Malcolm (Vicks Sinex)
9. Katie (Oxo)
10. Humphrey (Milk Marketing Board)

10 PEOPLE WHO PROVIDED VOICES FOR THE PG TIPS CHIMPS

1. Peter Sellers (recorded the voices for the very first ad for which he received £25)
2. Stanley Baxter
3. Arthur Lowe
4. Bruce Forsyth
5. Pat Coombs
6. Kenneth Connor
7. Irene Handl
8. Bob Monkhouse
9. Kenneth Williams
10. Miriam Margolyes

WHAT P.R. COMPANIES SAY TO PROSPECTIVE CLIENTS . . . AND WHAT THEY ACTUALLY MEAN

1. "We can do a lot for your company's image"
   (You can do a lot for our company's bank account)
2. "We have extensive experience in this field"
   (We've been fired by every one of your competitors)
3. "You have to consider long-term strategy"
   (Please don't get rid of us after six months)
4. "We often place our clients in *The Times)*
   (That's *The Brentford Times)*
5. "We're a young firm and so we have to try that little bit harder"
   (Unfortunately, I'm also the tea-boy)
6. "We intend to rationalise your company's profile on our computer"
   (We are going to blind you with science)
7. "We will need to charge you for necessary expenses"
   (I've already reserved a regular table at The Savoy)
8. "Remember, you have to get the right marketing mix"
   (Don't blame us - blame the advertising agency)
9. "We don't have expensive offices"
   (Well not until we bank your first cheque)
10. "I just know we're going to do some wonderful things together"
    (Wimbledon, Lord's, Glyndebourne . . . I can't wait)

PEOPLE WHO WORKED IN ADVERTISING

1. Hugh Grant (as an account executive)
2. Ridley Scott (as a director - e.g. on Hovis)
3. Fay Weldon (as a copywriter - e.g. 'Go To Work On An Egg')
4. Salman Rushdie (as a copywriter - e.g. 'Cream Cakes: Naughty But Nice')
5. Murray Walker (as an account director. For most of his commentating career, Murray's day job was in advertising. He worked on the 'Mars A Day' campaign.)
6. James Herbert (as a copywriter)
7. Sir Alec Guinness (as a copywriter)
8. Sir David Puttnam (as an account director)
9. Irma Kurtz (as a copywriter)
10. Len Deighton (as a copywriter)

THE FIRST 10 COMMERCIALS BROADCAST ON ITV

1. Gibbs SR toothpaste
2. Cadbury's drinking chocolate
3. Kraft cheese
4. Dunlop tyres
5. *Woman* magazine
6. Surf washing powder
7. National Benzole petrol
8. Lux soap
9. Ford cars
10. Guinness

10 THINGS SAID ABOUT ADVERTISING

1. "Advertising agency: eighty-five per cent confusion and fifteen per cent commission." (Fred Allen)
2. "Advertising is legalised lying." (H. G. Wells)
3. "Time spent in the advertising business seems to create a permanent deformity like the Chinese habit of foot-binding." (Dean Acheson)
4. "Advertising is a racket. Its constructive contribution to humanity is exactly zero." (F. Scott Fitzgerald)
5. "TV commercials are the yak in a box." (Shelby Friedman)
6. "Promise, large promise, is the soul of an advertisement." (Samuel Johnson)
7. "Advertising is the art of making whole lies out of half truths." (Edgar A. Shoaff)
8. "Advertising is the rattling of a stick inside a swill bucket." (George Orwell)
9. "Advertising may be described as the science of arresting the human intelligence long enough to get money from it." (Stephen Leacock)
10. "Half the money I spend on advertising is wasted, and the trouble is, I don't know which half." (Lord Leverhulme)

10 PEOPLE WHO ADVERTISED CLEANING PRODUCTS

1. Alan Freeman: Omo
2. Liza Goddard: Lenor
3. Fanny and Johnny Cradock: Fairy Soap
4. Jimmy Young: Flash
5. Betty Driver: Oxydol
6. Craig Douglas: Fairy Snow
7. Christine Truman: Daz
8. Frank Windsor: Tide
9. Tony Blackburn: Fairy Liquid
10. Val Doonican: Dreft

10 PEOPLE WHO ADVERTISED COCA-COLA

1. Marvin Gaye
2. James Brown
3. The Troggs
4. Roy Orbison
5. The Beach Boys
6. The Bee Gees
7. The Supremes
8. Aretha Franklin
9. The Everly Brothers
10. The Four Tops

10 PEOPLE WHO ADVERTISED PEPSI

1. Michael Jackson
2. Tina Turner
3. David Bowie
4. Gloria Estefan
5. Cindy Crawford
6. Madonna
7. The Spice Girls
8. Hammer
9. Robert Palmer
10. Lionel Richie

Chapter 20

The World

THE 10 WEALTHIEST COUNTRIES IN THE WORLD

1. U.S.
2. Japan
3. Germany
4. France
5. U.K.
6. Brazil
7. Canada
8. China
9. Spain
10. South Korea

10 INDISPENSABLE THINGS INVENTED OR DISCOVERED IN THE 19TH CENTURY

1. The vacuum flask (1892)
2. The car (1884)
3. The telephone (1876)
4. Aspirin (1889)
5. The can opener (1860)
6. The x-ray (1895)
7. The record player (1877)
8. The cylinder lock (1860)
9. Elastic (1820)
10. The facsimile machine (1843)

THE 10 MOST POPULAR NAMES FOR GOLDFISH IN BRITAIN

1. Jaws
2. Goldie
3. Fred
4. Tom
5. Bubbles
6. George
7. Flipper
8. Ben
9. Jerry
10. Sam

THE 10 OLDEST SURVIVING BUSINESSES IN THE U.K.

1. Aberdeen Harbour Board (Founded in 1136)
2. Cambridge University Press (1534)
3. Oxford University Press (1586)
4. Durtnell Ltd. (Builders - 1591)
5. Old Bushmills Distillery Company Ltd (Whisky distillers - 1608)
6. Post Office (1635)
7. Alldays, Peacock & Company Ltd (Manufacturers of fans - 1650)
8. Hays Ltd (Office services - 1651)
9. Vandome & Hart Ltd (Manufacturers of weighing machines - 1660)
10. James Gibbons Ltd (Locksmiths - 1670)

10 COUNTRIES WHERE THERE ARE MORE WOMEN THAN MEN

1. Monaco
2. Russia
3. Portugal
4. Austria
5. Germany
6. U.K.
7. Jamaica
8. Hungary
9. Cayman Islands
10. Italy

10 COUNTRIES WHERE THERE ARE MORE MEN THAN WOMEN

1. Vatican City
2. The Falkland Islands
3. Kuwait
4. Libya
5. Pakistan
6. Sri Lanka
7. Greenland
8. Singapore
9. Albania
10. Cuba

10 'ILLEGAL' THINGS THAT MOST OF US DO

1. Exceed the speed limit
2. Sample the unwrapped sweets in confectionery shops
3. Use the phone at work for personal calls
4. Put CDs and records on to cassette
5. Fail to declare things bought on holiday at customs
6. Steal soap from hotels
7. Ask people working on your car or your home if they'll "take off the VAT for cash"
8. Listen to pirate radio stations
9. Park on double yellow lines
10. Watch or play football (which is, believe it or not, still technically illegal!)

10 SCIENTIFIC ADVANCES AND WHEN THEY TOOK PLACE

1. The first heart pacemaker (external) was fitted in 1952. The first internal pacemaker was fitted in 1958.
   The first successful heart operation had been carried out in 1896 by Louis Rehn in Frankfurt, Germany.
2. The earliest process of colour photography - using three colours - was patented (by William Morgan-Brown) in 1876.
3. The duplicating machine was patented by James Watt as long ago as 1780.
   The photocopier was invented in 1938 by Chester Carlson of New York.
4. Linoleum, the floor covering used in many kitchens, was patented in 1863 by Frederick Walton of London.
5. The world's first scheduled passenger air service started in Florida in 1914.
6. The first British telephone directory was published by the London Telephone Company in 1880. It listed in excess of 250 names and numbers.
7. The first electric burglar alarm was installed in 1858 by one Edwin T. Holmes of Boston, Massachusetts. It is not recorded whether it actually worked or not.
8. The London Undergound system was inaugurated in 1863.
9. The first commercially successful escalator was patented in 1892 by Jesse Reno of New York.
10. The typewriter was patented by Henry Mill in 1714 although he never managed to market his

10 EXTRAORDINARY HAPPENINGS

1. BABY LUCK. Some coincidences are just <u>too</u> extraordinary to believe. Try this one: in 1975 in Detroit, a baby fell out of a building 14 storeys up. Fortunately, it landed on a man named Joseph Figlock and so survived. A year later, another baby fell from the same building and survived by falling on...Joseph Figlock.

2. LIVE MUSHROOMS. A nun at a convent in Clwyd tried but failed to grow mushrooms in the convent grounds. Following her death at the age of 79 in 1986, a decent crop of mushrooms has grown on her grave every autumn. Nowhere else in the convent do mushrooms grow.

3. SPONTANEOUS COMBUSTION. In 1938, Phyllis Newcombe, 22, combusted spontaneously at a dance hall during a waltz Many people witnessed this unexplained phenomenon which has parallels with the combustion of a British pensioner, Euphemia Johnson, who died when she suddenly burst into fire while she was enjoying her afternoon tea.

4. A GOLDEN SHEEP. In 1984, a Greek Orthodox priest was cooking a sheep's head when he discovered that the sheep had a jaw composed of 14-carat gold (worth some £4,000). The sheep had come from a herd owned by the priest's own brother-in-law and he couldn't come up with any plausible explanation - and nor could the Greek Ministry of Agriculture when they looked into the case.

5. ABRAHAM LINCOLN'S GHOST. The ghost of the assassinated U.S. President is said to haunt the White House. Among those who have 'seen' Abe's ghost are a maid who was in the room with First Lady Eleanor Roosevelt and Queen Wilhelmina of the Netherlands. Similarly, Anne Boleyn's ghost is said to revisit her childhood 'haunt', Blickling Hall in Norfolk, on May 19, the date in 1536 on which she was executed.

6. DOUBLE PROOF. A pair of identical American twin boys were separated at birth in 1940 and adopted by different people who didn't know each other. Each boy was named James, each boy married a woman named Linda, had a son named James Alan, and was then divorced. When they eventually met up at the age of 39, they found that their hobbies, experiences and tastes had been and were remarkably similar.

7. LET IT RAIN. In 1986, American Judge Samuel King was annoyed that some jurors were absent from his Californian court because of heavy rain. So he issued a decree: "I hereby order that it cease raining by Tuesday". California suffered a five-year drought. So in 1991, the judge decreed, "Rain shall fall in California beginning February 27". Later that day, California had its heaviest rainfall in a decade.

8. DEAD AGAIN. In Bermuda, two brothers were killed precisely one year apart at the age of 17 by the same taxi driver carrying the same passenger on the same street. The two boys had each been riding the same moped.

9. FISHY FACT. In 1969, a Finnish farmer was cutting wood when, in the middle of an aspen log, he found a dried fish. There was no way that the fish could have got there and yet there it was.

10. A TIME TO DIE: It is often said that when a person dies, their spouse often dies soon afterwards but this is exceptional. Charles Davies died at 3.00 in the morning at his sister's house in Leicester. When she phoned his home in Leeds to tell his wife, she discovered that Charles's wife had also just died...at 3.00 in the morning.

10 SEX LAWS FROM AROUND THE WORLD

1. In Riga, Latvia, married couples are not allowed to have sex while arguing.

2. In Kuwait, it is illegal for a married man to look at another woman "in a sensual manner". Nor can any man look lustfully at a statue of a woman or a female animal.

3. In Matagalpa, Nicaragua, men <u>must</u> divorce their wives if they catch them committing adultery but women are not allowed to divorce their husbands if they catch them.

4. In Bhutan, younger brothers are not allowed to get married - or even lose their virginity - before their older brothers do.

5. In Tallin, Estonia, couples are not allowed to play chess in bed while making love.

6. If a couple rent a hotel bedroom in Sioux Falls, South Dakota, U.S. for just <u>one</u> night, the twin beds have to be a minimum of two feet apart.

7. In Costa Rica, single women are banned from "any kind of lewd activities or behaviour" with a man.

8. In Oblong, Illinois, U.S., it is against the law to make love while fishing or hunting on your wedding day.

9. In Jordan, husbands are legally obliged to make love to wives "at least once every four months".

10. In Valencia, Venezuela, single men and women are not allowed to have sex with anyone who is deformed or who is a known 'idiot'.

10 EXAMPLES OF HOW THE VALUES IN A GAME OF MONOPOLY COMPARE TO REAL LIFE

1. 'DRUNK IN CHARGE' FINE £20 Someone found drunk in charge of a vehicle could expect a fine in the region of £350 - as well as a year's disqualification.

2. YOU HAVE WON SECOND PRIZE IN A BEAUTY CONTEST COLLECT £10 The runner-up in the Miss UK beauty contest gets £1,000.

3. PAY HOSPITAL £100 At London's Cromwell Hospital, a basic operation like a hip replacement costs £6850.

4. SPEEDING FINE £15 The fine for speeding is now between £70 and £100.

5. PICCADILLY £280 A single site in Piccadilly - the London Pavilion - was bought by the Burford Group for £13 million.

6. DOCTOR'S FEE PAY £50   A Harley Street doctor will typically charge £75 for an initial consultation

7. MAYFAIR In Monopoly, a house costs £200. A 4-bedroom house in Mayfair would today cost a minimum of £900,000.

8. YOU HAVE WON A CROSSWORD COMPETITION COLLECT £100 The first prize in the *Daily Mail* crossword competition is £20.

9. MAKE GENERAL REPAIRS ON ALL OF YOUR HOUSES. FOR EACH HOUSE PAY £25, FOR EACH HOTEL PAY £100 According to the Building Cost Information Service, to make general repairs on a house - and assuming three men working for a week - would cost about £1,000; to make general repairs on a hotel - and assuming twelve men working for four weeks - would cost about £16,000.

10. PAY SCHOOL FEES OF £150 According to ISIS (Independent Schools Information Service), fees for a day school range between £2,100 and £8,700 a year.

THE 10 MOST LANDED UPON MONOPOLY SQUARES

1. Trafalgar Square
2. Go
3. Marylebone Station
4. Free Parking
5. Marlborough Street
6. Vine Street
7. Kings Cross Station
8. Bow Street
9. Water Works
10. Fenchurch Street Station

10 MODERN PARADOXES

1. As cars are built to travel faster so the roads become more congested
2. By the time you're wealthy enough to afford a family-sized house, your children are old enough to have left home
3. As phone dialling becomes quicker, so dialling codes become longer
4. As English soccer players are paid increasingly more, so the English international team has become increasingly unsuccessful
5. As the birth rate falls, so class sizes get bigger
6. As information about safe sex intensifies, so too does the rate of sexually transmitted diseases
7. As police methods of capturing criminals improve (e.g. with scientific advances like DNA), so the crime rate increases
8. In restaurants, the biggest mark-ups are made on wine - which is, of course, the one thing that restaurants don't actually have to cook or prepare
9. The more money the BBC makes from selling videos, books and programmes, the more it pleads poverty
10. The more students across the country pass GCSEs and A Levels with higher grades, the more we are told that each successive generation is getting thicker

10 COUNTRIES AND THEIR PREDICTED POPULATION FOR THE YEARS 2000 AND 2050 (AS PREDICTED BY WORLD POPULATION PROSPECTS)

Country	2000	2050
1. United Kingdom	57.3 million	51.2 million
2. United States	268 million	299.2 million
3. France	57.9 million	52.3 million
4. China	1,212 million	1,554.9 million
5. India	1,013 million	1,591.2 million
6. Pakistan	145.3 million	423.8 million
7. Australia	18.7 million	23.9 million
8. Brazil	179.5 million	368 million
9. Iran	73.9 million	251.8 million
10. Japan	130 million	115 million

THE 10 MOST POPULAR SUMMER HOLIDAY DESTINATIONS FOR BRITISH TOURISTS

1. Balearic Islands
2. Mainland Spain
3. Greek islands
4. The U.S.A.
5. Turkey *(Midnight Express? Thank you, that'll do nicely)*
6. The Canary Islands
7. Cyprus
8. The Caribbean
9. Portugal
10. Italy

10 APRIL FOOLS' DAY PRANKS

1. Probably the most famous British April Fools' Day prank was the Spaghetti Harvest on BBC TV's *Panorama* in 1957. Its presenter was the venerable Richard Dimbleby, definitely not a prankster. So millions of people were taken in when he told them about the spaghetti harvest and 'showed' them the spaghetti 'growing' and being 'dried' in the sun.

2. In 1976, Patrick Moore told radio listeners that while Pluto passed behind Jupiter, there would be a decrease in gravitational pull. He said that if people were to jump in the air they would feel as though they were floating. This was of course just a prank but several people rang up to say that they had enjoyed doing just that.

3. In 1994, Mars took out full page advertisements in newspapers announcing their 'New Biggest Ever Mars Bar'. The 'Emperor'-sized Mars Bar was 32lbs of 'thick chocolate, glucose and milk'. Understandably, it was only 'on sale' for one day. April 1.

4. In 1977, the normally po-faced *Guardian* produced a whole supplement on the island of San Seriffe - which of course didn't exist. Many readers were taken in by the authentic nature of the words and pictures. In fact, it was a fine spoof with plenty of clues - mostly relating to printing terms - for sharper minds.

5. In 1979, London's Capital Radio announced that because of all the constant changing between British Summertime and Greenwich Mean Time, we had gained an extra 48 hours which would have to be lost by the cancellation of April 5 and April 12. Readers phoned in wondering what would happen to birthdays, anniversaries and other such things.

6. Not to be outdone, in 1980, the BBC World Service told its listeners that Big Ben's clock-face would be replaced by a digital face. Since the World Service is treated with a lot of reverence, many people were taken in - only to be relieved by discovering the truth.

7. In 1992, some joker fitted a huge sign on the roof of the stand at the Hollywood Park racetrack which read 'WELCOME TO CHICAGO'. This was visible to all passengers on flights coming into Los Angeles and caused no little consternation.

8. When Ken Livingstone was leader of London's GLC in the 1980s, he took part in a radio spoof which told people that London would be starting an experiment of driving on the right instead of the left. He said that he wanted to hasten Britain's integration with the rest of the E.C. Needless to say, although some people were initially fooled, no one actually switched sides!

9. The German car firm, BMW, often perpetrate the funniest April Fools' pranks. In 1983, they ran a full-page ad for "The first open-top car to keep out the rain even when it's stationary" (supposedly something to do with 'artificial airstreams'). Other years have produced gems such as 'A BMW you need never wash again', 'WARNING: are you driving a genuine BMW' and, in 1993, a TV commercial introducing an 'anti-tracking device for secret lovers everywhere'.

10. In 1973, a Dr Ronald Clothier gave a serious sounding lecture on Radio 3 about Dutch Elm Disease in which he 'revealed' that rats which had been exposed to the disease had developed a resistance to the human cold. This was of course nonsense and it was eventually revealed that Dr Clothier was, in fact, none other than Spike Milligan!

10 OF BARRY HUMPHRIES' GREATEST STUNTS

1. In Training: Humphries' greatest stunt was performed while he was a university student. He took his seat on a Melbourne commuter train. At the first stop, one of his pals boarded the train and served him a grapefruit. At the next stop, another pal took away the grapefruit and brought him cornflakes. And so on - through the eggs and bacon and the coffee - until he had been served a full breakfast. What really made the stunt, however, was that not a word was exchanged between Humphries and his friends throughout the charade.

2. Going Underground: In a similar, less elaborate stunt, regularly done when he was performing in a play at Stratford East, Humphries would travel on the London Underground and bewilder fellow travellers by asking them if they could direct him to the buffet car.

3. It's legal! One of his favourite tricks was to get a female co-conspirator to dress up as a schoolgirl. The two of them would start kissing and when a policeman showed up to ask him what he was doing with a 'minor', he would flourish her birth certificate proving that she was, in fact, over 18.

4. Cruel To Be Unkind: One particularly unpleasant stunt was performed - like many of his others - on a train. His friend would board a train pretending to be blind with his leg in plaster and wearing a neck brace. Humphries would then get on board pretending to be a German and then start abusing, physically and verbally, his friend. Humphries was never challenged by other passengers. Meanwhile, after he got off, his friend would sit there saying, "forgive him, forgive him".

5. Rubbish! For this stunt, Humphries would fill a public dustbin with rubbish and then just before it reached the top, he would put in some really expensive food - smoked salmon, cooked chicken etc. - and champagne and then he would cover all this fare with a layer of rubbish. Then when some people arrived, Humphries, dressed as a tramp, would astonish them by rummaging in the bin and pulling out fabulous delicacies.

6. Movie Movie: In 1968, when the cinema was infested with a plague of ludicrous *avant-garde* films, Humphries invented a 'film director' named Martin Agrippa, who had supposedly been working with the Blind Man's Cinema and who had made a film which had won the 'Bronze Scrotum' in Helsinki. Together with the (genuine) film director Bruce Beresford, he made a spoof film which was subsequently exhibited at several Festivals of Underground Cinema where it was taken entirely seriously.

7. Good clean fun: with a group of friends, Humphries used to go to a shop every day at the same time and pay for a bar of Lux soap but would always decline to take the soap away with them. They would sometimes get strangers to do the same thing. Each time, the shopkeeper would say "you've forgotten your soap" to which Humphries & Co. would respond "I don't want the soap, I just want to buy it!". Eventually, Humphries took the soap out of the shop but returned saying "I'm sorry, I forgot to leave the soap". The poor shop-keeper eventually moved to another part of town - and who could blame him?

8. Pass the sick-bag: On his frequent flights between Australia and Britain, Humphries would pass the time by surreptitiously putting some Russian (or vegetable) salad in a sick-bag and then, when other passengers were watching, he would pretend to throw up into the sick-bag. He would then proceed to eat the contents of the sick-bag. Yeuggh!

9. On the streets: Humphries didn't just restrict this 'gag' to aeroplanes but also performed it to a wider public. He would put some Russian salad on the pavement and then return to it later and eat it with a spoon. Once, in Fleet Street in the 1960s, a policeman approached him but found himself so sickened that he started retching. Humphries took the opportunity to disappear.

10. Keeping In Character: Perhaps Humphries' greatest stunt was the invention of the Melbourne housewife, Edna Everage, who later metamorphosed into the superstar, Dame Edna Everage (inevitably attended by her bridesmaid, the perennial spinster Madge Allsop). So skilful has this ongoing stunt been that there are many people who genuinely believe in 'her'. Perhaps 'his' greatest coup came when he appeared on *Desert Island Discs* as Dame Edna and chose eight records which were all, appropriately enough, recorded by real dames.

10 'LANDS'

1. Land of The Free (U.S.)
2. Land of My Fathers (Wales)
3. Land of The Long White Cloud (New Zealand)
4. Land of Enchantment (Mexico)
5. Land of The Rising Sun (Japan)
6. Land of Dance (Cuba)
7. Land of Mystery (India)
8. Land of The People (China)
9. Land of Opportunity (Canada)
10. Land of Hope And Glory (England)

10 COUNTRIES WHICH HAD THEIR NAMES CHANGED

1. Rhodesia (to Zimbabwe)
2. Abyssinia (to Ethiopia)
3. Belgian Congo (to Zaire)
4. Dahomey (to Benin)
5. Siam (to Thailand)
6. Persia (to Iran)
7. Basutoland (to Lesotho)
8. Ceylon (to Sri Lanka)
9. British Honduras (to Belize)
10. Gold Coast (to Ghana)

THE 10 LARGEST ISLANDS IN THE WORLD

1. Greenland
2. New Guinea
3. Borneo
4. Madagascar
5. Baffin Island
6. Sumatra
7. Great Britain
8. Honshu, Japan
9. Ellesmere Island
10. Victoria Island

THE FIRST 10 MEN IN SPACE

1. Yuri Gagarin (USSR)
2. Alan B. Shepard (USA)
3. Virgil ('Gus') Grissom (USA)
4. Gherman Titov (USSR)
5. John Glenn (USA)
6. Malcolm Scott Carpenter (USA)
7. Andrian Nikolayev (USSR)
8. Pavel Popovich (USSR)
9. Walter Schirra (US)
10. Leroy Gordon Cooper (US)

10 CITIES/TOWNS WHICH HAD THEIR NAMES CHANGED

1. Constantinople (Istanbul)
2. Saigon (Ho Chi Minh City)
3. Tenochtitlàn (Mexico City)
4. Peking (Beijing)
5. Danzig (Gdansk)
6. Edo (Tokyo)
7. Salisbury (Harare)
8. Leningrad (St. Petersburg)
9. New Amsterdam (New York)
10. Christiana (Oslo)

10 CAPITAL CITIES – AND WHAT THE NAMES ACTUALLY MEAN

1. Khartoum (Sudan) - 'elephant's trunk'
2. Bangkok (Thailand) - 'wild-plumb village'
3. Buenos Aires (Argentina) - 'good winds'
4. Montevideo (Uruguay) - 'I saw the mountain'
5. Kuala Lumpur (Malaysia) - 'mud-yellow estuary'
6. Brussels (Belgium) - 'buildings on a marsh'
7. Freetown (Sierra Leone) - 'town for liberated slaves'
8. Rangoon (Burma) - 'end of strife'
9. Sofia (Bulgaria) - 'wisdom'
10. Tehran (Iran) - 'warm place'

10 COUNTRIES WHICH HAD DRIVING TESTS BEFORE WE DID (In 1935)

1. Italy
2. Spain
3. Portugal
4. Norway
5. Holland
6. France
7. Germany
8. Turkey
9. Denmark
10. Sweden

10 1960s DANCES

1. The Gravy
2. The Hully Gully
3. The Stomp
4. The Jerk
5. The Frug
6. The Watusi
7. The Locomotion
8. The Monkey
9. The Mashed Potato
10. The Shag

10 ITEMS OF FOOTWEAR FROM THE DIM AND DISTANT PAST

1. Brothel Creepers
2. Baseball Boots
3. Jellies
4. Chelsea Boots
5. Jesus Sandals
6. Pixie Boots
7. Monkey Boots
8. Platform Shoes
9. Kinky Boots
10. Winkle Pickers

10 DISTINCTIVE HAIRSTYLES

1. Flat-Top
2. Argentine Ducktail
3. Crewcut
4. Quiff
5. Elephant's Trunk
6. Conk
7. Beehive
8. Spike-Top
9. Suedehead
10. Flop

THE TOP 10 DESTINATIONS FOR BRITISH COUPLES MARRYING ABROAD

1. St Lucia
2. Kenya
3. Jamaica
4. Barbados
5. Antigua
6. The Seychelles
7. Mauritius
8. Florida
9. Bali
10. Fiji

10 THINGS WHICH SIMPLY DISAPPEARED

1. Deelybobbers
2. Space Hoppers
3. Pet Rocks
4. Clackers
5. Hai Karate After-Shave
6. Cabbage Patch Dolls
7. Broomball
8. Lava Lamps
9. Gonks
10. Paper Knickers

WHAT A 10-STONE PERSON WOULD WEIGH ELSEWHERE

1. Pluto - 7 lbs
2. The Moon - 1st 10 lbs
3 Mercury - 3 st 11 lbs
4 Mars - 3 st 11 lbs
5. Uranus - 9 st 1 lbs
6. Venus - 9 st 11 lbs
7. Saturn - 10 st 11 lbs
8. Neptune - 11 st 12 lbs
9. Jupiter - 25 st 5 lbs
10. The Sun - 280 st

10 ARMY RANKS AND HOW THEY CORRESPOND IN THE NAVY AND AIR FORCE

ARMY	NAVY	RAF
1. Field Marshal	Admiral of the Fleet	Marshal of the RAF
2. General	Admiral	Air Chief Marshal
3. Lieutenant-General	Vice Admiral	Air Marshal
4. Major-General	Rear Admiral	Air Vice-Marshal
5. Brigadier	Commodore	Air Commodore
6. Colonel	Captain	Group Captain
7. Lieutenant-Colonel	Commander	Wing Commander
8. Major	Lieutenant-Commander	Squadron Leader
9. Captain	Lieutenant	Flight Lieutenant
10. Lieutenant	Sub-Lieutenant	Flying Officer

THE 10 CAR COLOURS WITH THE WORST RATE OF ACCIDENTS

1. Black (17.9 accidents per 1,000 cars)
2. White (16)
3. Red (15.7)
4. Blue (14.9)
5. Grey (14.7)
6. Gold (14.5)
7. Silver (14.2)
8. Beige (13.7)
9. Green (13.4)
10. Yellow (13.3)
10. Brown (13.3)

THE TOP 10 TYPES OF EMPLOYMENT IN BRITAIN

1. Manufacturing Industries
2. Banking, Finance And Insurance
3. Shops And Retail Distribution
4. Public Administration
5. Education
6. Health And Veterinary Services
7. Wholesale Distribution And Repairs
8. Hotels And Catering
9. Construction
10. Transport

10 COUNTRIES BRITAIN'S FOUGHT BATTLES OR WARS AGAINST

1. Holland (1652)
2. China (1856)
3. Turkey (1827)
4. Sweden (1756)
5. Spain (1588)
6. U.S.A. (1812)
7. Egypt (1827)
8. France (1337)
9. Russia (1854)
10. Austria (1756)

THE 10 BRITISH PLACES WITH THE LONGEST NAMES

1. Gorsafawddachaidraigddanheddogleddollônpenrhyn-areurdraethceredigion (Gwynedd: 67 letters)
2. Llanfairpwllgwyngyllgogerychwyrndrobwllllantysiliogog-ogoch (Gwynedd: 58 letters)
3. Sutton-Under-Whitestonecliffe (North Yorkshire: 27 letters)
4. Llanfihangel-Yng-Ngwynfa (Powys: 22 letters)
5. Llanfihangel-Y-Crouddyn (Dyfed: 21 letters)
6. Llanfihangel-Y-Traethau (Gwynedd: 21 letters)
7. Cottonshopeburnfoot (Northumberland: 19 letters)
8. Blakehopeburnhaugh (Northumberland: 18 letters)
9. Coignafeuinternich (Inverness: 18 letters)
10. Claddochbaleshare/Claddochknockline (Outer Hebrides: 17 letters)

10 MODERN INVENTIONS (HOW DID WE EVER LIVE WITHOUT THEM?)

1. Round tea bags
2. Personal stereos
3. Mineral water
4. Camcorders
5. Fabric softeners
6. Computerised organisers
7. 0891 numbers
8. Pump-up trainers
9. Jug kettles
10. Combined shampoo and conditioner

10 COUNTRIES WITH MORE SHEEP THAN PEOPLE

1. Australia
2. Bolivia
3. Argentina
4. South Africa
5. Uruguay
6. Ireland
7. The Falkland Islands
8. Lesotho
9. New Zealand
10. Iceland

THE 10 EUROPEAN CITIES WITH THE WORST TRAFFIC CONGESTION

1. Lisbon (Average speed of traffic: 5.8 mph)
2. Paris (8.5 mph)
3. London (10.4 mph)
4. Istanbul (11.2 mph)
5. Athens (12.4 mph)
6. Madrid (14.9 mph)
7. Budapest (16.5 mph)
8. Berlin (18.2 mph)
9. Rome (22.4 mph)
10. Warsaw (23 mph)

10 COUNTRIES WHICH STILL DRIVE ON THE LEFT-HAND SIDE OF THE ROAD

1. Cyprus
2. Pakistan
3. Australia
4. Uganda
5. South Africa
6. Indonesia
7. Sri Lanka
8. Kenya
9. Japan
10. India

Chapter 21

...At the End

YOU KNOW YOU'RE IN PARADISE WHEN...

1. The traffic-lights turn green just as you approach them all the way home

2. You hear yourself being quoted approvingly

3. You find yourself living next door to a reclusive millionairess who doesn't have any living relatives, has just one month to live and has taken a shine to you

4. The only noise you can hear when you step out of your front door is birdsong

5. You open a brown envelope and an Inland Revenue tax rebate flutters out

6. All the wine gums left in the packet are black

7. You hear the clink of ice on glass as you read your novel by a deserted swimming-pool on a hot - but not humid - afternoon when everyone else is at work

8. The local authority announces an amnesty on parking fines

9. The train you are travelling on arrives early

10. You read in the paper that your favourite food is, contrary to received medical opinion, actually extremely good for you

10 NEW SINS

1. Watching a telethon without pledging any money

2. Deliberately ripping new jeans to look trendy

3. Booking a table at a restaurant and not showing up

4. Taking coat-hangers from hotels

5. Writing to a newspaper agony aunt for advice

6. Not clearing away your tray at McDonald's

7. Moving on to the bottom layer of a box of chocolates before finishing the top one

8. Drinking a can of drink in the street

9. Leaving a theatre before the actors have finished their curtain calls

10. Sounding a horn when collecting someone rather than getting out of the car

10 UNDISCOVERED GREEK ISLANDS

1. Domestos
2. Gigolos
3. Biros
4. Desperados
5. Asbestos
6. Peccadillos
7. Kudos
8. Giros
9. Mosquitos
10. Mossbros

10 WAYS TO KNOW THAT A HOUSE HAS KIDS

1. The fridge is covered in school notes held in place by tacky novelty magnets

2. The lock on the bathroom door doesn't work

3. The first thing you hear when you walk through the door is horrible music played far too loudly

4. You have to strain your neck to look at valuable ornaments in the living-room

5. There are no beers in the fridge

6. There are clothes drying on all the radiators

7. The hallway wallpaper is lighter at the top than it is at the bottom

8. There is a cupboard full of unwanted miniature packets of Corn Flakes from Kellogg's Variety Packs

9. There are at least three broken radios on a shelf in the kitchen

10. The newspapers are unopened

YOU KNOW THE HOLIDAY'S OVER WHEN...

1. The pilot says the weather on the ground at Gatwick is overcast

2. W.H. Smith are advertising their 'Back To School Specials'

3. The only people wearing shorts are boys and joggers

4. People you meet are already talking about next summer

5. Beach hats are marked down to half-price

6. You find yourself saying "Oh well, let's hope it's an Indian Summer"

7. The TV companies replace boring repeats with boring new programmes

8. You don't bother buying another bottle when the suntan oil runs out

9. Sales of diet books go down

10. Ice cream parlours no longer put seats outside

IS IT A POSH RESTAURANT? 10 TELL-TALE SIGNS

1. Not only are there no 'chips', there aren't even any french fried potatoes

2. You have to fight back the temptation to ask the waiter to take back the dish and have it cooked properly

3. You have to wait half an hour before you can even sit at the table

4. The mushrooms and the rice will always be wild

5. You are the only person you don't recognise in the restaurant

6. No charge is made for mineral water

7. There isn't a single main course that doesn't incorporate offal into its list of ingredients

8. The pasta and vegetables are so al dente you wonder why they bothered to cook them in the first place

9. If the food is Chinese, there are no numbers on the menu

10. The restaurant chef is seated at the next table being interviewed for a Sunday newspaper supplement

10 JOBS THAT AREN'T AS HARD AS THEY'RE CRACKED UP TO BE

1. TV scheduler
2. Member of Parliament
3. Film director
4. Rural vicar
5. Model
6. Orchestra conductor
7. Interior decorator
8. G.P.
9. Judge
10. TV newsreader

10 WAYS TO KNOW YOU'VE MADE IT

1. TV impressionists 'do' you
2. *Hello!* sends a photographer to your 'sumptuous' home
3. No-one says "Who's that?" when you take off your mystery guest mask on a TV game show
4. Just the mention of your name gets a laugh on *Have I Got News For You?*
5. You're always stopped at customs
6. You're invited back to the school from which you were expelled to present the prizes on Speech Day
7. You're invited to become a director of your local football club
8. The police *don't* let you off with a caution when you're caught speeding
9. Jeffrey Archer invites you round to eat shepherd's pie and drink champagne
10. Estate agents use your name to increase the price of your former home

10 TRIUMPHS FOR OPTIMISM OVER EXPERIENCE

1. Elizabeth Taylor getting married again
2. Buying a hot dog from the kiosk in the cinema foyer
3. Turning up late for a Mike Tyson fight
4. Attempting to win at the hoop-la at the fair
5. Cilla expressing excitement at the prospect of finding out whether a couple hit it off on their Blind Date
6. Staying for the second half of an amateur dramatic pantomime
7. Jane Seymour telling *Hello!* magazine that she's at last found true happiness
8. Planning a picnic for a bank holiday
9. Buying a box of dates at Christmas
10. Picking Graeme Hick for England

10 ARMY KNIVES

1. The ITALIAN army knife has...an ice cream scoop
2. The DUTCH army knife has a...spare bicycle spoke
3. The FRENCH army knife has a...garlic crusher
4. The JAPANESE army knife has a...mini ritual sword
5. The IRISH army knife has a....knife sharpener
6. The BELGIAN army knife has a...chip-fork
7. The SWEDISH army knife has a...razor-blade
8. The KOREAN army knife has a...dog whistle
9. The GREEK army knife has a...kebab skewer
10. The NORWEGIAN army knife has a...torch

10 LAWS OF CRUISING

1. However many clothes you pack you never have the ones you need

2. The swimming pool is always smaller than the one in the brochure

3. The better the food, the choppier the sea

4. Very few of the officers sound like gentlemen

5. The average age of the passengers is somewhere between 80 and deceased

6. You are always the most interesting person on your table

7. All the most exciting foods on the open air buffet are always gone before you get there

8. By the time the air conditioning in your cabin is fixed you've already been to all the hot countries

9. Whichever excursion you choose, you will always be on the oldest coach

10. However much you tip your steward they always look as though they expected

10 ENTRIES FROM THE BUSINESSMAN'S BOOK OF QUOTES

1. To lose one account may be regarded as a misfortune, to lose two looks like carelessness

2. Time and temporary secretaries wait for no man

3. I have nothing to declare except my dividend

4. In the company of the blind, the one-eyed man is managing director

5. There are lies, damned lies and expense accounts

6. Give us the cheque and we'll finish the job

7. From each according to his abilities, to each according to his abilities

8. A man who is tired of lunch is tired of life

9. He who can, does. He who cannot is made redundant

10. There's no such thing as a free Vauxhall Cavalier

10 GREAT MODERN TRUTHS

1. Anything worth having is either immoral, illegal or fattening

2. You never find something you've lost until you replace it

3. In order to get a bank loan, you must first prove that you don't need one

4. Beauty is only skin-deep but ugliness goes right to the bone

5. Computers do what you tell them to do - not what you *want* them to do

6. When you dial a wrong number, it's never engaged

7. If you really want to make an enemy, do someone a favour

8. It takes longer to lose weight than it did to put it on

9. Stamps which don't stick when you want them to will stick to other things when you do want them to

10. If, on any given evening, there are only two TV programmes worth watching, they'll be on at the same time

10 BORING THINGS SAID BY NON-SMOKERS

1. "I'm all for personal freedoms but..."

2. "Each cigarette takes ten minutes off your life"

3. "Whenever I go to a party where people are smoking my clothes always reek of smoke the next day"

4. "I don't mind you smoking if you don't mind me breaking wind"

5. "Smoking-related diseases cost the NHS billions of pounds every year"

6. "Kissing a smoker is like kissing an old ashtray"

7. "I don't know if you saw that documentary the other night"

8. "It's got to the point now where we just won't allow smoking in our house"

9. "Nicotine's a poison, you know"

10. "I'm sorry but it does state quite clearly that this is a No Smoking area"

10 BORING THINGS SAID BY SMOKERS

1. "It's a free world, isn't it?"

2. "I know this bloke who died of lung cancer and he never smoked a single cigarette in all his life"

3. "Everything in moderation"

4. "I could stop today and be run over by a bus tomorrow"

5. "It's the tax on cigarettes that keeps the country on its feet"

6. "I gave up but I put on so much weight that I started again"

7. "We're a persecuted minority"

8. "My grandfather smoked 60 a day and he lived to be 93"

9. "I need something to do with my hands"

10. "No one ever died as a result of *smoking and driving*"

VISITING DISNEYLAND EUROPE? 10 THINGS YOU'D EXPECT TO SEE

1. The Enchanted Butter Mountain

2. Mickey and Minnie duetting on *Je T'Aime...Moi Non Plus*

3. The Seven Dwarfs chain-smoking Gitanes

4. Computerised all-singing all-dancing models of Johnny Halliday and Jacques Brel

5. Snow White with hairy armpits

6. The Magical Wine Lake

7. Donald Duck and his abnormally large liver

8. Cinderella in couture rags

9. Some old men in berets grunting and playing boules

10. Twice daily (except Sundays): English lamb burning

10 NURSERY RHYMES UPDATED

1. Height-Challenged Jack Horner
2. Ride An Awayday Supersaver To Banbury Cross
3. Differently-Abled Simon
4. Little Ms Muffet
5. Baa Baa Non-Caucasian Sheep
6. Mary, Mary, Quite Entitled To Exercise A Woman's Right To Change Her Mind
7. London Bridge Has Broken Down - Because Of A Lack Of Investment In The Infrastructure
8. See This Chainsaw, Margery Daw
9. One, Two, Lace Up A Trainer
10. Tom, Tom, The Subject Of A Social Worker's Case Conference

10 THINGS PARENTS DO TO EMBARRASS THEIR CHILDREN

1. Call children's friends by their nicknames
2. Insist on dancing at their children's parties
3. Persist in calling the weekly allowance 'pocket money' - especially in company
4. Stand at the door and wave at them as they go off on a date
5. Refuse to take part in the parents' race on sports day
6. Take part in the parents' race on sports day
7. Ask if they've finished their homework as they're about to go out with their friends
8. Kiss them effusively in public
9. Show their children's boyfriends/girlfriends baby pictures
10. Make references to the fact that they (the parents) are still sexually active

10 THINGS CHILDREN DO TO EMBARRASS THEIR PARENTS

1. Reveal Mum and Dad's pet names for each other
2. Lead the chorus of laughter when their parents attempt to do anything sporty
3. Refuse to wear clothes suitable for a formal occasion
4. Swear in front of elderly relatives
5. Repeat parental rows verbatim to third parties
6. Refuse to introduce them to their friends
7. Pick their nose at the dinner table in front of guests
8. Dye their hair a disgusting colour and wear earrings anywhere but their ears
9. Remind them what they <u>really</u> think of someone in front of that person
10. Say 'Mum and Dad say we're too poor to have a holiday this year' just as their parents are trying to impress someone

10 THINGS FOR SALE – GUARANTEED UNUSED

1. Bob Geldof's razor
2. John Major's bottle of Grecian 2000
3. Claire Rayner's supply of Slimfast
4. Margaret Beckett's hand-mirror
5. Francis Rossi's Dictionary of Guitar Chords
6. Chrissie Hynde's McDonald's gift vouchers
7. Ronnie Biggs's tickets for the next Policeman's Ball
8. Kenneth Clarke's trainers
9. Clint Eastwood's tin of drinking chocolate
10. Bruce Forsyth's bottle of Wash 'N' Go

ARE YOU POLITICALLY CORRECT? 10 TELL-TALE SIGNS

1. The only F-word in your vocabulary is fibre
2. You don't see why colleagues have to address each other by their first names
3. You think that a hamburger is an inhabitant of Northern Germany
4. You carry consent forms as well as condoms
5. You haven't missed a benefit concert in the past three years
6. You wish the *Guardian* weren't so right-wing
7. You would resign as a matter of principle if a colleague put up some mistletoe at the firm's Christmas party
8. You don't think Nicaraguan coffe tastes as good as it used to
9. You go to cricket matches with Harold Pinter
10. The worst thing you can imagine being accused of is heterosexism

10 LAWS OF MOVING HOUSE

1. The home you are moving to will always have fewer lightbulbs left in it than the home you sold
2. Removal men are forbidden by their union to refuse cups of tea
3. The new front door is always narrower than the old one
4. Any item needed in an emergency can always be located at the bottom of the most inaccessible tea-chest
5. Problems will always arise within ten minutes of someone saying "Things seem to be running pretty smoothly"
6. Whenever new furniture and old wallpaper come into contact the new furniture will lose
7. Whenever old furniture and new wallpaper come into contact the new wallpaper will lose
8. The people you are selling to always want to move in before the people you're buying from want to move out
9. No move can be so nightmarish that the presence of children can't make it any worse
10. Removal men get up earlier than solicitors

THE FAMILY THAT...

1. The family that plays together stays together
2. The family that drinks together sinks together
3. The family that bops together stops together
4. The family that sails together wails together
5. The family that clicks together sticks together
6. The family that flies together dies together
7. The family that smokes together chokes together
8. The family that sews together grows together
9. The family that shops together drops together
10. The family that weeds together bleeds together

10 EURO LAWS WE'RE AWAITING

1. All pint – sorry, 'litre' – glasses must have lids on them
2. All maps will be redrawn to show Brussels in the centre of Europe
3. The singing of 'Erewego, erewego, erewego' at football matches will be prohibited but the selling of firecrackers will be permitted
4. Sausages must measure at least 10cm in length and 8cm in circumference
5. All political parties will be made to incorporate the word 'Democrats' into their title
6. It will be strictly forbidden to sell razors to women
7. Every 100gms of cooked food must contain at least 2gms of garlic
8. The month of August will be made a public holiday
9. Onions must be worn whilst riding bicycles
10. All British farmers will be made to cease work so that Luxembourg farmers have a chance to catch up with their production quotas

10 WHO ON EARTH THOUGHT OF...?

1. Making geese livers explode to make pâté de foie gras
2. Putting feet into brown paper bags to avoid air sickness
3. Ventriloquism
4. Bungee jumping
5. Eating sturgeons' eggs
6. Putting corks on a hat in Australia
7. Chewing gum
8. Putting worms into tequila bottles
9. Prairie oysters
10. Egg and spoon races

10 THINGS WE DON'T WANT TO HEAR ABOUT ANY MORE

1. Elizabeth Taylor's illnesses
2. Gazza's marriage
3. Posh Spice's love life
4. Paula Yates's children
5. Sting's concern for the Planet
6. The Prince of Wales's views on architecture
7. Maureen Lipman's guilt about not spending more time with her kids
8. Peter Mandleson's influence over the Prime Minister
9. Oprah Winfrey's diets
10. Sir James Savile's charity work

DO YOU NEED TO GO ON AN ASSERTIVENESS TRAINING COURSE? 10 TELL-TALE SIGNS

1. You pull in to let milk floats overtake you
2. You don't sit down on the bus in case anyone else needs the seat
3. You allow Jehovah's Witnesses to come into your home
4. You leave tips in McDonalds
5. Your spare room is stuffed to the gills with encyclopedias, dusters and aerial photos of your house
6. Geese say 'Boo' to you
7. When your rubbish isn't collected you phone to apologise to the council
8. All three political parties have you down as a certainty
9. You don't correct people when they get your name wrong
10. You never leave a clothes shop without buying something

10 LAWS OF WEDDINGS

1. The bride and groom will always argue about whether ex-boyfriends and girlfriends should be invited
2. The bride will never be slimmer than on her wedding day
3. The bridesmaids' dresses never fit all of them properly
4. The bridegroom never knows what to do with the gloves that come with the morning suit
5. The bride will either trip up or tear the train of her wedding dress when she steps out of the bridal car
6. During the service the person sitting next to you will remind you that one in three marriages end in divorce
7. The photographer will always be the worst-dressed male present
8. The duller the bride's father, the longer his speech will be
9. The bride's mother will always wear a fixed smile during the best man's speech
10. The second cheapest item on the wedding list will always be the first to go

THE WORLD'S 10 OLDEST PUNCHLINES

1. No, she went of her own accord
2. Doctor Who!
3. No, constable, I was driving too fast to see it
4. Yeth, and I'm only thixteen
5. To get to the other side
6. Why, are you coming apart?
7. There's nothing queer about Carruthers
8. Be quiet, sir, or they'll all want one
9. You hum it and I'll play it
10. No, its just the way I walk

10 WAYS TO SOUND LIKE LAW-YEED GRO-OWSMAN (Loyd Grossman)

1. EAUVER (Over) as in "David, its eauver to you"
2. ORPULENT (Opulent) as in "And as we enter the orpulent drawing-room"
3. KOOSE KOOSE (Cous cous) as in "And in the red kitchen the koose koose is being prepared"
4. THESS (This) as in "Thess is really delicious"
5. MORNEGTOOW (Mange-tout) as in "And in the yellow kitchen, the mornegtoow and ginger salad looks divine"
6. GAURTHIC (Gothic) as in "Here in the Gaurthic dining room"
7. PASTOR (Pasta) as in "Mmm.. this pastor machine is a really useful kitchen tool"
8. CHALKLET (Chocolate) as in "Yah, the chalklet roulade really is superb"
9. MORSTER (Master) as in "The morster bedroom has a rustic, masculine feel to it"
10. FLAWMBAY (Flambé) as in "Mmm... I love to flawmbay a few wild mushrooms with raspberry vinaigrette"

10 THINGS WHICH ARE MIGHTILY REASSURING

1. The clink of ice cubes in a glass
2. The smell of cakes cooking
3. Natural history programmes
4. The crackle of a log fire
5. *It's A Wonderful Life*
6. Country pubs
7. Sergeant Bob Cryer in *The Bill*
8. Alan Freeman still being on the radio
9. Sweet shops still selling penny chews
10. The sound of willow on leather

10 DANGERS OF A FEDERAL EUROPE

1. Germans getting to *our* beaches first
2. Johnny Halliday records on Radio 2
3. Dubbed soap operas at peak-time
4. Pro-celebrity *pétanque* on all five channels
5. Applying to Luxembourg for car tax
6. The links will stop breaking down on the Eurovision Song Contest
7. Pit bull terriers - with rabies
8. Chips are called french fries and are only served with mayonnaise
9. A wait of half an hour for the TV weatherman to get round to your region
10. Borussia Moenchengladbach's results given prominence over Northampton Town's

A MAN WHO IS TIRED OF LONDON IS TIRED OF...

1. Apologies for delays on the Underground system
2. Bicyclists wearing personal stereos
3. Being asked the way to 'Lychester Square'
4. Hearing friends say "Why don't you move to the country?"
5. Waiting to have wheel clamps removed
6. Having his car windscreen washed at traffic-lights
7. Not being able to get in to see the latest West End show because of all the visitors
8. Deciding what to do with the London Weighting Allowance
9. Free local newspapers
10. Hearing taxi-drivers' views on capital punishment

10 EXAMPLES OF THIRD WORLD SPEAK

1. Developing (Under-developed)
2. Loans (Aid)
3. Aid (Exploitation)
4. Free election (The results are freely available before the votes have been cast)
5. Emergency relief (Yup, it's another pop concert)
6. Helping people to help themselves (Selling beads to tourists)
7. Indigenous culture (*Starsky and Hutch* dubbed in the local dialect)
8. Western surpluses (Dumping of high tar cigarettes)
9. Political amnesties (Bodies released from jail for burial)
10. Post-colonialism (Dictators rule in the name of the Queen)

10 WAYS TO BE PREPARED FOR LIFE'S TRIALS

1. Take a pen with you to the bank
2. Carry a large novel when waiting for a train
3. Wear a vest when going on a daytrip to the seaside
4. Smuggle in a pillow to any amateur dramatic performance of Shakespeare
5. Keep a personal alarm by the telephone for when kitchen telesales people ring up
6. Take a doggie bag to a carvery
7. Wear earplugs if within five miles of the vicinity of a heavy metal concert
8. Purchase a sizeable amount of 'Sorry it's late' birthday cards
9. Buy Alka Seltzer when getting an Indian takeaway
10. Rent a video on any given Saturday night

10 THINGS WE'RE ALL GOING TO HAVE TO DO ONE DAY

1. Write scripts for *The Bill*
2. Start the National Lottery
3. Go on a local radio phone-in
4. Have our names romantically linked with Madonna
5. Appear as contestants on *Fifteen-To-One*
6. Bare our souls to Oprah
7. Be interviewed for an opinion poll
8. Go out for a drink with Oliver Reed
9. Send in a photo to and/or appear in a Readers' Wives magazine
10. Recognise someone we know on *Crimewatch UK*

10 THINGS WHICH ARE DUE TO MAKE A COMEBACK

1. Cabbage Patch dolls
2. Identity bracelets
3. Psychedelia
4. Ouija boards
5. Dance marathons
6. Maxi-skirts
7. CB Radio
8. Pinball
9. Bell-bottoms
10. Strikes

THE 10 LAWS OF GARDENING

1. Your most expensive plants never come through. However, the weeds will.
2. If a flower only blooms for two weeks, you can guarantee that it will start doing so on the day you go on holiday
3. As soon as you water the garden, it rains
4. The only way to guarantee colour in your garden all year round is to buy a gnome
5. No matter how threadbare your lawn is, you'll always get grass in the cracks between the paving stones
6. You always get the most of what you want the least
7. Whichever garden tool you need is always at the very back of the shed
8. Nothing ever looks the way it did on the seed packet
9. Other people's garden tools only ever work in other people's gardens
10. Weeds will always grow faster than you can pull them out - no matter how much time you spend weeding - unless you're trying to cultivate a wild garden

10 THINGS WHICH CAN BE FOUND IN EVERYONE'S GARDEN SHED

1. Any number of broken plant pots
2. An empty calor gas container
3. A wheelbarrow with only one wheel
4. Three tins of paint with lids which can't be opened
5. Half a dozen jam jars containing mould
6. A bicycle tyre
7. A broken manual lawnmower
8. A stained and ripped lawnmower manual
9. A pile of dog ends
10. A completely inaccessible work-bench

10 MOVIES FOR GARDENERS

1. *Bulb Fiction*
2. *Seed Of Love*
3. *A Fistful of Dahlias*
4. *Remains Of The Daisy*
5. *Wayne's Weed*
6. *Shears Gotta Have It*
7. *Hoe's That Girl?*
8. *Empire of The Sunflower*
9. *Rake It Or Leave It*
10. *The Lawnmower Man*

10 THINGS WHICH JUST DON'T RESPOND TO CHARM

1. Speeding cameras
2. Fitness
3. Hanging wallpaper (unless you can charm someone else into doing it for you)
4. Cashpoint machines which have rejected your card
5. Quitting smoking
6. The Inland Revenue (only joking, guys)
7. An engaged phone
8. Buzzing flies (especially at night)
9. Broken videos
10. Dieting

10 UTTERLY DAFT THINGS PARENTS SAY

1. "Would you *like* a smack?"
2. "I'll teach you to be disobedient"
3. "Those who ask don't get"
4. "Wait till your father gets home"
5. "You don't hear me talking to my parents like you talk to me"
6. "And what time do you call this?"
7. "You'll be the death of me"
8. "You're asking to be punished"
9. "Stand still while I'm smacking you!"
10. "We never had electronic toys"

10 MODERN DILEMMAS

1. Wine or mineral water
2. Jokey or serious answering-machine message
3. Breakfast TV or radio
4. Letter or fax
5. Y-fronts or boxer shorts
6. Natural birth or pain relief
7. Credit card or cheque
8. Public transport or traffic jam
9. Sex or celibacy
10. Pager or portable telephone

10 THINGS THE AMERICANS DO BETTER THAN US

1. Tell other countries what they're doing wrong
2. Invade other countries when they don't listen to what they've been told
3. Play baseball
4. Watch very bad television programmes
5. Call their mothers 'mom'
6. Daft fads like 'political correctness'
7. Persecute indigenous minorities
8. Guzzle gas
9. Guzzle hamburgers
10. Murder each other

10 TOY ACCESSORIES WE'RE WAITING FOR

1. Lego: Abbatoir
2. Scalextric: Sponsorship agents
3. Turtle Transformers: Portillo
4. Barbie Doll: Home pregnancy kit
5. Hornby: Surly buffet-car salesman
6. Power Rangers: Steroid testing kit
7. Scrabble: Dyslexic version
8. My Little Pony: Manure shovel
9. Action Man: The un-neutered version
10. Subbuteo: Gobbing footballers

10 WAYS TO KNOW IF YOU SURVIVED NEW YEAR'S EVE

1. Your blood is less than 30% proof
2. The minicab driver didn't have to clean out the back of his car afterwards
3. You don't have to go around asking your friends how to address a magistrate
4. People don't compliment you on your new black eyeliner when you're not wearing any
5. You know the names of everyone you kissed last night
6. You're fit enough to fight your way through the January sales
7. You weren't knocked unconscious during the *Auld Lang Syne* crush
8. You're using matchsticks to light cigarettes rather than to keep your eyes open
9. You've managed to get home with the right coat
10. Fewer than three friends phone to ask if you're feeling better

10 SIGNS THAT YOUR MAN HAS, AHEM, 'LOST INTEREST'

1. You're the one who buys <u>him</u> Milk Tray
2. He always asks for twin beds when the two of you go to hotels
3. When you say that you want to slip into something more comfortable, he fetches your slippers
4. <u>He's</u> always complaining of headaches
5. He refuses to eat oysters
6. Your favourite Rod Stewart record is *Da Ya Think I'm Sexy?* while his favourite is *I Don't Want To Talk About It*
7. His idea of an ideal evening is one that ends with *Match of the Day*
8. Whenever you suggest drinking champagne in bed he always replies, "Nah, I prefer cocoa"
9. When you ask him to buy you some sexy underwear, he buys you a thermal vest
10. He thinks the *Kama Sutra* is an Indian take-away

10 SIGNS THAT YOU'RE A TECHNOPHOBE

1. You phone the AA to help you fill up with petrol

2. You choose a new hairdryer on the basis that it comes with a plug fitted

3. Even with a 'Video Plus', you can't programme your video

4. You refuse to buy a pocket calculator on the basis that "fingers were invented first"

5. You cook food in the oven as it's quicker than trying to work out how to use the microwave

6. Whenever you take a picture of someone they never say "cheese" they always say, "Oi, you've left the lens cap on"

7. You have to buy a new torch rather than change the batteries in the old one

8. You're always late for work because you spend twenty minutes trying to get marmalade out of the toaster

9. Whenever you go to the laundrette you always ask for a service wash

10. You dread living on your own because then there'd be no-one to set the alarm clock for you

10 SIGNS THAT VALENTINE'S DAY IS NOT FOR YOU

1. The only date you can get comes in a box from the greengrocer's

2. Your mum forgets to send you a card

3. Even the card you sent to yourself gets lost in the post

4. In fact the only card you do get is one from British Gas saying "Sorry you were out when we called"

5. You don't even bother to look in the newspaper personal columns

6. The sexiest look you get all evening is from the newsreader at the end of *News At Ten*

7. You've already made up your mind to take next year's summer holiday early - i.e. the second two weeks in February

8. Not one of the twenty people you sent cards to so much as rings to say "thank you"

9. The only roses you get is the box of Cadbury's chocolates you buy to console yourself

10. You even start to envy people who call each other "bunnykins"

10 THINGS WHICH ARE OVERRATED

1. Health farms
2. Parisian fashion designers
3. The Oxford v. Cambridge Boat Race
4. Australian wines
5. Porsches
6. U2
7. Skiing holidays
8. Picasso's paintings
9. Marks & Spencer's ready meals
10. Doctors

10 THINGS WHICH ARE UNDERRATED

1. The British weather
2. Satellite television
3. Greyhound racing
4. Italian wines
5. Mazdas
6. British chocolate
7. Butlin's
8. Game shows
9. Burger King
10. Dentists

WANT TO BE CLINT EASTWOOD? 10 THINGS YOU'LL HAVE TO DO

1. Invite people to make your day
2. Narrow your eyes as you speak
3. Say "I reckon not" instead of "no"
4. Say "That possibility does exist" instead of "yes"
5. Go to sleep fully dressed
6. Wear sunglasses indoors without tripping up
7. Kill four armed criminals with one Smith & Wesson (Sudden Impact)
8. Kill four evil cowboys whilst smoking a cigar (A Fistful of Dollars)
9. Forget whether you fired six shots or only five (Dirty Harry)
10. Speak with gritted teeth

ON THE 12TH DAY OF CHRISTMAS MY TRUE LOVE GAVE TO ME...

Twelve Lords-a-sleeping

Eleven Ladies lunching

Ten Pipe-smokers pontificating

Nine Drummers getting completely out of their heads

Eight Maids-a-metering

Seven Swan kettles-a-boiling

Six Geese-a-fattening for Foie Gras

Sky Movies Gold

Four Phone-calling Birds of A Feather

Three French battery hens

Two Ninja Turtle Doves

And a partridge in a korma sauce

THE LISTS BOOK

10 WAYS TO KNOW THAT CHRISTMAS IS NEARLY HERE

1. Banks and building societies are covered in tinsel
2. Letters take weeks to arrive
3. Every item in every shop is labelled: "Makes a great Xmas present"
4. The paperboy doesn't just leave your paper on the doorstep
5. The dustmen don't complain about taking away *all* your rubbish
6. The milkman *doesn't* overcharge you
7. Bernard Matthews can't keep the smile off his face
8. Both BBC1 and ITV trail their David Jason specials
9. Women's magazine have articles entitled "101 Things To Do With Turkey Leftovers"
10. There are Old Spice ads on the telly

10 THINGS YOU HEAR EVERY CHRISTMAS DAY

1. "The bang in my cracker didn't go off"
2. "It's the thought that counts"
3. "I've seen that Bond film a hundred times before"
4. "I wonder who thinks up those jokes for the crackers"
5. "Help! I think I've broken my filling on a 20p piece"
6. "I think it's all become too commercial"
7. "Do you think she writes the speech herself?"
8. "This is <u>one</u> day I'm not doing the washing-up"
9. "Who had the nutcracker last?"
10. "We're definitely doing something different next year"

10 CHRISTMAS DAY NIGHTMARES

1. You turn on the TV to find a DJ going round the children's ward of a hospital
2. The car packs up on the motorway
3. Your in-laws decide that they <u>can</u> make it after all
4. Someone insists on reading out every single Christmas cracker joke - and motto
5. The children break all their presents *before* dinner
6. A power-cut during the Queen's Speech
7. The turkey's off
8. The glasses you use for watching TV go missing
9. <u>Everyone</u> buys you socks
10. You run out of Alka-Seltzer

10 UPDATED CHRISTMAS CAROLS

1. Little Drum Machine Programmer
2. Hank The Harlem Angel Raps
3. Away In A Mazda
4. While Shepherds Watched Their Flocks Being Killed To Conform With The EEC Common Agriculture Policy At Night
5. I Saw One Giant Super Tanker Coming In
6. Once In Viscount Linley's Workshop
7. I Arrest You Merry Gentlemen For Driving Whilst Intoxicated.
8. We Wish You A Merry Christmas And Please Don't Force Us To Scatter Litter All Over Your Garden
9. In The Midwinter Mini-Break
10. We Three Kings Singers

THE 10 MOST COMMON CAUSES OF CHRISTMAS ARGUMENTS

1. Which film to watch after the Queen's speech
2. Who gets to keep the Christmas cracker novelty
3. Spending too little on Christmas presents
4. Spending too much on Christmas presents
5. That the sprouts were raw/overcooked
6. Socks
7. Who lost the nutcrackers
8. Someone using the tonic water as a soft drink
9. The washing-up
10. Someone refusing to pull the 'bang' from the cracker which didn't work properly when the cracker was pulled

10 COMMEMORATIVE STAMPS THE ROYAL MAIL HAS YET TO BRING US

1. The arrival of Channel 5
2. The departure of Chris Evans from Radio 1
3. The anniversary of Gazza crying in the 1990 World Cup
4. The engineering miracle of the Sinclair Zike
5. The commemoration of Ronald McDonald's invention of the McChicken Sandwich
6. Fergie's skiing holidays
7. The 'Rear Of The Year' Awards
8. The anniversary of Showaddywaddy reaching No. 1 with *Under The Moon of Love*
9. Magic Eye Special Issue
10. The launch of the new 50p coin

10 WAYS TO KNOW THAT CHRISTMAS IS FINALLY OVER

1. Diet books go to the top of the bestsellers charts
2. Noel Edmonds goes on holiday
3. No-one cares that the nutcrackers are lost
4. Even the neighbourhood cats have lost interest in your turkey carcass
5. There isn't a single blank video tape in your home
6. No-one bothers to replace the faulty fuse on the Christmas tree lights
7. Slade disappear for 11 months
8. Your dustmen disappear for 12 months
9. The Alka Seltzer goes back in the bathroom cabinet
10. The only TV commercials which aren't for the sales are for summer holidays

10 THINGS YOU COULD NEVER HAVE IMAGINED 20 YEARS AGO

1. Alf Garnett's son-in-law would be the father-in-law of the Prime Minister
2. Three of the Queen's children would have been divorced
3. Australian wine would cost more than French wine
4. A double Oscar winner (i.e. Glenda Jackson) would have become an MP
5. Sir Edward Heath would still be an MP
6. Apartheid would end - peacefully - in South Africa
7. An adult comic (i.e. *Viz*) would be one of the country's top-selling magazines
8. It would be 'hip' to like Bob Monkhouse
9. *The Times* would be the cheapest national newspaper - at least on Mondays
10. Buckingham Palace would be open to the public